News

This book is dedicated
to David Jayne, Ken Lucoff,
Terry Koo and Bill Stewart, friends
who lost their lives while covering the news.

watch

How TV Decides the News

AV WESTIN

SIMON AND SCHUSTER   New York

Copyright © 1982 by Av Westin
All rights reserved
including the right of reproduction
in whole or in part in any form
Published by Simon and Schuster
A Division of Gulf & Western Corporation
Simon & Schuster Building
Rockefeller Center
1230 Avenue of the Americas
New York, New York 10020
SIMON AND SCHUSTER and colophon are trademarks of Simon & Schuster
Designed by Karolina Harris
Manufactured in the United States of America

1   2   3   4   5   6   7   8   9   10

Library of Congress Cataloging in Publication Data

Westin, Av, date.
Newswatch.

Includes index.
1. Television broadcasting of news—United States.
I. Title.
PN4888.T4W4   1982   070.1'9'0973   82-10310
ISBN 0-671-42179-4

Acknowledgments

This book became a possibility when Audrey Adler Wolf, a literary agent, came out of a crowd at Duke Zeibert's Restaurant in Washington, D.C., and asked if I had something to say in a book about TV news. This book got published because Dan Green at Simon and Schuster bought it and said I ought to be as opinionated as hell. Catherine Shaw, John Herman and Alice Mayhew edited it down from an overlong and rambling first draft. Most of the research was in my head, drawn from recollections, old memos, experience, opinions and practice that started thirty-five years ago in 1947 when I got my first job as a summer-replacement copy boy at CBS Shortwave News. My grandmother, Rose Radin, was a real estate broker who sold a townhouse to Edward R. Murrow, and he fixed up an interview at CBS News. That's what acknowledgments mean to me. Somewhere along the way, I met or worked with people who taught me something about journalism or about human relationships or budgets or how a camera worked. This book is a product of all those contacts. Later on, as you read, you will understand that TV news is all teamwork. No one does anything alone.

There will be a noticeable lack of names associated with NBC. I regret that. The contributions made by men and women there equaled any made by my colleagues at CBS and ABC. It's just that my paths never crossed theirs, and I am unable to reflect personally on what they did. I'm sure much of the innovative work I think occurred at CBS or ABC was influenced, if not begun, at NBC and copied by us. I apologize for that glaring omission. The people listed here—in alphabetical order—were recalled as I wrote. They were part of my professional life.

Bernie Altman, Bill Anderson, Sam Antar, Roone Arledge, Jules Bergman, Alice Weel Bigart, Frank Binney, Cyril Bliss, Ed Bliss, Mili Lerner Bonsignori, Bob Brandt, Bill Breen, Susan Buksbaum, David Burke, Karen Burnes, Tom Capra, Claudette Caravaggi, Marty Carr, Helen Chamousis, Ted Church, Lou Cioffi, Charles Collingwood, Jim Connors, Lou Cowan, Ken Daglish, Anne Dalton, Vern Diamond, Barry Diller, Sam Donaldson, Barbara Elliot, Mel Ferber, Steve Fleishman, Jim Fleming, Fred Freed, Bob Frye, Gary Gates, Irv Gitlin, Sandra Glick, Stanhope Gould, "B-J" Haidinger, Ted Healy, George Herman, Bettine Herns, Greg Jackson, Peter Kalischer, Esther Kartiganer, Alex Kendrick, Ted Koppel, Ernie Leiser, Shirley Lentz, Marcia Leslie, Phil Lewis, Marge Lipton, Nancy Logerfo, Bill Lord, Elmer Lower, John Lower, George Markman, Maria McLaughlin, Don Meany, John Merriman, Sig Mickelson, Les Midgley, Bill Mildyke, Ron Miller, Jurgen Neumann, Ray Nunn, Stan Opotowsky, George Orick, Lee Otis, Ralph Paskman, Walter Porges, Jan Rifkinson, Ellen Rossen, Bob Roy, Carolyn Russell, Ellen Samrock, John Scali, David Schoenbrun, Carl Schutzman, Gerry Schwartzkopf, Zeke Segal, John Sharnik, Bernard Shaw, Bill Sheehan, Bob Skedgell, Steve Skinner, Bill Small, Lady A. Smedley-Grimes, Joan Snyder, George Strait, Bill Tangney, John Tiffin, Dallas Townsend, Howard Tuckner, Ralph Vignola, Carrie Van Zile, Henry Wefing, Ellen Weinberg, Shirley Lubowitz Wershba, Elliot Westin, Harriet Westin, Kathleen Westin, Mark Westin, Palmer Williams, Bob Wussler, Sharon Young.

There are other people named in the book and their names are not on this page. Some colleagues have requested anonymity, and I am sorry to say I've forgotten the names of others. A few had profound professional and emotional impact and some probably are unaware that they had any effect at all. None of them are responsible for how I distilled their thoughts or actions in this book. The opinions are my own.

AV WESTIN
New York
January 22, 1982

Contents

Stand By for Air

Television news has changed the way America is governed.

Television news has changed the way America votes.

And television news has changed the way America thinks.

The power of television news astonishes even those of us who work for it. Its impact has been extraordinary, the more so because the public, our leaders and even our adversaries around the world have recognized what television news has become and have overwhelmingly accepted it. Indeed, they are making use of it.

Someone has written this story about the first days of the United States: James Madison is seated, working on a draft of the First Amendment. He has just put his quill to paper and scratched out the words "Congress shall make no law . . . abridging the freedom of speech or of the press." The door to his study opens and an aide walks in. "Sir!" he begins. "I have had this vision. Someday there will be a glass box which will sit in our living quarters, and on it will appear moving images: People will be seen and heard laughing, crying, speaking, playing music, cheering. On this box we will watch our government

leaders as they conduct the affairs of state!'' Madison looks up
at his aide, thinks for a moment, and then tears up the paper on
which he had written the text of the First Amendment. "If you
are right,'' Madison says, "then this document is not what I had
in mind.''

Some years ago, I was struck by the increasing number of
critical articles and letters accusing TV news of undermining the
American spirit. It was the period of the Vietnam War, of street
demonstrations and a general uneasiness about our national purpose. Some politicians seized upon this aura of distress, blaming
it on TV news. "Nattering nabobs of negativism" was Spiro
Agnew's description of the tone of television news broadcasts.
A good deal of his attack could be dismissed as political rhetoric,
yet TV news *was* playing a role in intensifying the country's
malaise, though there was and is no conspiracy among broadcasters to bring the nation down in a heap. Still, thoughtful
people in command positions recognized that some of the effects
of our efforts to report the news were, nonetheless, contributing
to the national "down.''

One of the most thoughtful analyses of why and how that
was happening came from Michael J. Robinson, a professor of
political science at Catholic University in Washington, D.C.
Paraphrasing his thoughts, and adding some of my own, Robinson's thesis is that TV news results in a feeling of "dispatriation" among Americans. Things look so complex, so involved
and fraught with contention, argument and even hostility, that
the average American has thrown up his hands and said, in
essence, "It's so much trouble that I do not want to be involved.''

Going back to Madison, he and other founding fathers never
imagined that *every* American would be exposed to the turmoil
that arises normally within every working government. Madison knew that deliberations in the Continental Congress were
not as stately as those grand oil paintings suggested. The artist
had filtered out the disorder and painted a much more serene
picture. Similarly, the anger, insults, shouting and swearing; the
deals, drunkenness, backbiting and conniving were often not
mentioned in the press reports of the day. Reporters, such as

they were, were more likely to deal with the sweeping issues, leaving out descriptions of the nitty-gritty business of legislative action. So, like the artist in oils, the pamphlets and the penny presses of the 1780s acted as a filter. Little of the hurly-burly came through that might tear at the fabric of the new government. When a newspaper from Philadelphia, New York or Washington reached the hinterlands, it was days or weeks late. The contents were often read aloud by some educated gentleman, probably at the village inn or on the town common; that was yet another filter, putting distance between the reality of what was happening in the halls of government and what the citizenry believed was happening there. Madison envisaged a nation governed by aristocrats who needed to communicate with each other. Gentlemen would deal with gentlemen. They would show the way, explaining what was necessary and filtering the rest so that the rough edges would not be too apparent. There was no place for a box in the living room with people seen crying, shouting, swearing or engaged in other head-to-head conflicts.

To be sure, newspapers and particularly the sensationalist "yellow press" exposed or exploited scandals and debauchery at the highest levels of government, but it was television news coverage that provided what Mr. Madison really did not intend: pictures *showing* the reality that our statesmen are not noble gentlemen in a painting but real people who sometimes lose control. As television news broadened its coverage of our political institutions, it began to show irrefutable instances of ineptness, stupidity and scandal. Presidents, congressmen, Supreme Court justices, state legislators, mayors, police chiefs, generals and even clergymen have all been exposed to coverage that provided unfiltered views of them as functioning officials. The result has not necessarily been bad. Corruption or alcoholism, which had previously been covered up by the "old boys' club," was revealed. The rascals were turned out more frequently because their inadequacies or criminality was on display.

In the past, according to a study in 1982 by the ABC News Election Unit, only 40 percent of congressmen involved in scandals were defeated in the next election; the other 60 percent

were reelected despite being tainted. They proclaimed their in-
nocence and many voters gave them the benefit of the doubt.
By contrast, after the Abscam scandal in 1980, four of the five
representatives involved were defeated the next time they ran.
The fifth, who was reelected, was then ousted from his seat by
the House of Representatives itself. The Senate allowed its
tainted member to resign. Why the difference? In Abscam,
voter-viewers actually saw the crimes on TV news programs,
courtesy of FBI videotapes. This time there was no benefit of
the doubt to give because there was no doubt. That was all to
the good. What wasn't necessarily to the good was a growth in
our attitude that "they're all a bunch of crooks" or "no matter
who wins, you lose."

If the public's belief in the worth and integrity of American
institutions was shaken by television news, TV news itself was
being regarded more and more as the most trustworthy institution in the United States. The Roper Organization, one of the
most reliable samplers of public opinion, has been monitoring
the importance of news on television to the American people
since 1959. According to its survey, "Television has led as the
most believable news medium since 1961 and in 1968 . . . it
reached a two to one advantage over newspapers. In subsequent
years, it widened its margin. . . ."

In April 1979, Roper issued a report summarizing its studies.
"Over the span of twenty years," the report began, "we have
seen television move steadily upward in terms of its importance
in people's lives. Television became the dominant medium in
1963 and steadily increased its lead in successive years." The
report concluded that "the public continues to regard television
as the number one source of news." The first question asked of
people who participated in the survey was always, "Where do
you usually get most of your news about what's going on in the
world today?" In the 1979 survey, television led all other media
and was ahead of newspapers, in second place, by 18 points.

The percentage of people relying on TV for all or most of
their news and information has risen from 55 percent in 1963 to
64 percent in 1980.

★   ★   ★

What should television be? An entertainment medium? A cultural medium? Should it educate? Amuse? Inform?

That conflict of identity was with TV from its inception. There were those who saw it as little more than a salesman's tool. In fact, one of the first stations to be licensed belonged to a department store that expected to transmit living catalogues of its merchandise into viewers' homes.

On the other hand, there were those who believed that TV would have its greatest potential as the primary source of information and news. Edward R. Murrow sounded that note in 1958. "This instrument can teach," he said. "It can illuminate; yes, and it can even inspire. But it can do so only to the extent that humans are determined to use it to those ends. Otherwise it is merely lights and wires in a box."

Ed Murrow had symbolically tied America together by coaxial cable and microwave transmission. Sitting in the control room of CBS Studio 41 above Grand Central Terminal in New York, he watched, along with his "See It Now" audience, as engineers slowly merged a picture of the Pacific Ocean with one of the Atlantic. It was the driving of the Golden Spike for television.

With coast-to-coast capability now at hand, CBS began building up its television news staff, and I was assigned from radio to TV as a copy editor. I didn't want to go. To me, television was a sideshow. It was locked into studios, unable to get to the scene of news stories quickly. I was the brash, self-assured kid with a career perking along in radio. Fortunately, my boss told me I didn't know what the hell I was talking about, and I went. I truly became a child of television news, moving from opportunity to opportunity, usually the first "kid" on the block.

I was the first newsman trained by CBS to be a television director; the first CBS Foundation Fellow, which put me into the Russian Institute at Columbia University. The first overseas assignment for a network-news field producer came to me. I worked on the first satellite broadcasts; started the "CBS Morning News with Mike Wallace," worked with Fred Friendly on "CBS Reports" and later joined him to produce the first experimental public television network programming. At ABC, I

created the "Close-Up" documentary series, helped Roone Arledge devise ABC's "World News Tonight" format and later
ran the weekly television newsmagazine show "20/20." Some
sideshow. Once, as I was starting out, someone referred to me
as a "boy wonder." Today, almost thirty years later, I like to
think of myself as a "youthful veteran."

Despite Professor Robinson's concerns about "dispatriation,"
television news has tied America together with a unifying force
unparalleled in American history. It has become our *national*
newspaper.

Television viewers in the United States are presented every
night with a picture of global events displayed so graphically
and with such increasing clarity that they find themselves relating to the world, to the nation, their city or town, and to their
fellow Americans as never before.

There have, of course, been other nationally unifying experiences. The First World War is credited by some historians with
bringing the real end to the Civil War. When farm boys from
Alabama found themselves brigaded together with streetwise
kids from New York in the same divisions in France, they came
away from that experience aware that they were all Americans.
But the troops represented a small segment of the total population, and while they were "over there," the rest of the nation
did not share the experience to the same degree.

Frederick Lewis Allen, writing in *Only Yesterday,* credits the
automobile with forging new links between fellow Americans.
When a man in a small Indiana town could put his family in a
touring car and drive over the next hill to the next town and on
to Chicago, the experience helped unite him and his neighbors
in an unparalleled way. But again, it was happening to just a
few people at different times and in different ways. Railroads
and airplanes, carrying mail-order catalogues and national magazines from their central print shops, enabled housewives and
businessmen all over the country to look at the same ads, join
in the same trends, buy the same products, read the same opinions. Still, there was no simultaneous sharing of the experience.

Radio probably would have accomplished the job for us if television had not supplanted it so quickly and so dramatically. With its use of the three elements—picture, sound and narration —television had no equal.

Americans are now used to the shared experience: mourning a slain President, cheering a victorious hockey team, praying for an astronaut on the moon's surface. Everyone has access the same day to the latest congressional debate; everyone can share the anguish of flood or volcano victims anywhere in the country on the day of the tragedy; politicians can be seen at various places in the country—sometimes tripping over promises in one region at the expense of another. And the nightly news programs are introduced—"anchored"—by the same people.

Television news programs come into our home and catch us where we are most vulnerable: in our living rooms, our bedrooms, maybe even our bathrooms. It is only common sense to understand what it does and how it does it.

How do pictures get from there to here? Is it exciting, dangerous, wonderful, harrowing? Is it honest or is it hype? Do emotions rule or does cold rational logic? Who are the men and women, the correspondents, producers, camera teams, who face wars and riots and Presidents, bathing beauties and racehorses? Technology in television news-gathering is changing so rapidly that equipment that was revolutionary only two years ago is already obsolete; replacement gear is being put into position with easily removed screws so that it can be shoved aside in a few years. Television news remains the most rapidly changing information medium.

1
This Minute's News—Now!
THE EVOLUTION OF NEWS BROADCASTING

The newly appointed vice-president of CBS News had joined us in the mid-sixties from *Newsweek* magazine. It fell to me, as one of the executive producers, to walk him around during his first days on the job, introducing him to the staff but also showing off the technical side of the operation. We passed through the newsroom with its rows of assignment editors, transportation schedule boards and wire service machines. It was impressive but actually not that much different from the kinds of news-gathering paraphernalia that also exist at newspapers or newsmagazines. The new man was obviously not finding anything out of the ordinary yet.

Then we moved into the control room that was the central switching area for the "CBS Evening News." There was the audio board with its multitude of knobs and switches designed to handle sixteen incoming "feeds"—as well as microphones in the studio and sound from film projectors and videotape playback machines. To the front and side of the director's position were banks of monitors. Each camera's output showed up on a separate screen. So did the pictures from each of the film projectors and the videotape machines. To one side, there was a stack of three television screens. On one, labeled WASHINGTON, there were pictures coming in from our operation in the capital showing a congressional hearing. On another monitor labeled CHICAGO, pictures of some news event there were feeding through to be previewed by an editor so that he could select which shots he wanted included in a report for that evening's "CBS Evening News." The third monitor in the stack was labeled LOS ANGELES, and as we passed by, the test pattern on the screen dissolved into pictures as a news story started to feed in to New York. "Look at that!" he said. "Look at those pictures . . . from L.A. . . . from Chicago!" He stood and watched, shaking his head in wonderment. His amazement as a first-time viewer of transcontinental feeds reminded me of how far we had come since Murrow's technicians had joined the Atlantic and Pacific oceans in an electronic superimposition on "See It Now." My reaction by this time was jaded. If there *weren't* pictures on those labeled monitors, that's when we would take notice and start to get worried.

"Today's news today!" was a dream when NBC News created that slogan to introduce its nightly newscast in 1949. Today the dream is reality; in fact, it is taken for granted. The television news industry has spent a considerable amount of time, money and effort devising ways of getting film and videotape back to home base—not in days but in hours and minutes. It is what makes TV news so vital. A newspaperman can pick up the telephone and, like Hildy Johnson in *The Front Page,* cry, "Hello, sweetheart! Give me Rewrite!" "Where are the pictures and when will you feed them to us?" would be our reply to a broadcast journalist. Certainly, television editors pay considerable attention to reporters' scripts, but even when they are read into the home office to be checked by senior producers, the assumption is that pictures will accompany the words when the piece is finally broadcast. Needless to say, it wasn't always that way.

Dan Schorr was the CBS correspondent in Germany in the early 1960s. He and I were in Berlin in August 1961. My job was field producer. His job was to cover the remarkable story of the mass flight of thousands of East Germans out of East Berlin into West Berlin. The story was dramatic, filled with human interest and political overtones. Something important was going on, and Schorr was working feverishly to report every development.

In those days, we shot stories on 16 millimeter film, and we shipped it by plane. I was standing at the Marienfeld refugee camp with Schorr as he recorded his narration and his opening and closing commentary. For some reason, Dan kept fluffing his lines. I kept looking at my watch. The plane from Tempelhof Airport was the last one that day to the West. Miss that one and we were dead on the story for another twenty-four hours. I had visions of being on that site for eternity with Dan still fluffing away. "Oops, sorry—take it again. . . ." Finally Schorr got it right, and there was a race to the airport to ship the film. It was placed in what we call an orange bag—one of those string bags fruit comes packed in. The shipping papers had been pre-arranged at the Tempelhof Airport freight office, but we were so late that permission was granted to drive directly to planeside to toss the bag aboard. We could have been shipping shoes, spare parts or boxes of gladioli for all the airlines cared. It was just another piece of cargo and it got to New York whenever the plane got there.

A few days after that dash to the plane, Schorr and I were having a late dinner at the Cracked Egg, a Berlin cabaret. About two in the morning, we got a call from a stringer that something was going on at the Brandenburg Gate in central Berlin. We raced to Dan's silver-gray diesel Mercedes and were at the gate in about ten minutes. The place was brilliant with white-blue searchlights and alive with East German soldiers. Some of them had submachine guns across their chests, but most were handling jackhammers. Major news events have their own peculiar background sound, and those jackhammers that night still ring for me in a very frightening way. The CBS News film crew showed up and started to work. They were everywhere, photographing the holes being dug for concrete posts, the barbed wire being strung between those posts, and then prefabricated concrete slabs being lowered into position from specially designed trucks. The Berlin Wall was being built right in front of our eyes! Windows in houses on the border were being nailed shut. Barbed wire coils were being dropped off, and at those intersections where barricades were not yet in place, East German armored cars and tanks had parked with their engines idling. U.S. Army Jeeps with recoilless rifles pulled up. GIs appeared in helmets and flak jackets. British and French troops moved up in battle gear. The situation was grim. The pictures and sound were overwhelming.

Early Sunday morning meant it was time to get the story back. Once again, it was off to Tempelhof Airport, packing the film in the orange bags and shipping them by prop plane to London from Berlin. There they were transshipped on a regularly scheduled commercial flight to New York. In 1961, jets were flying, and Pan Am Flight #161 was the flight we all tried to make. Getting film aboard that plane meant that it could get to New York in mid-afternoon in time to be rushed through New York traffic by a motorcycle courier who would take it to a film-processing lab to be developed. Only then, after that cumbersome, time-consuming process, would editors and producers in New York see it for the first time to cut it into a coherent story. As I recall it, though construction of the Berlin Wall began shortly after midnight on Sunday, August 13, 1961, the first film wasn't seen by American television viewers until Tuesday night. Yet the CBS News producers in New York were delighted, and all hands in Germany got congratulatory cables.

If television was ever to provide a same-day news service, it was clear that better transmission technology would be required. The invention of a system called Slow-Scan was an important step in getting a story back quickly. In 1958, NBC News and the BBC joined forces to create an electronic system that would "read" pictures on film and transmit the signal via the transatlantic cable to New York, where it would be reconstituted into pictures again. Based on the system used to transmit wire photos for decades, this device gave NBC News a substantial leg up in the competition. At the time, as CBS News producer in Europe, I was particularly frustrated that our film was still flying across the Atlantic in the "slow" jet plane while NBC's pictures were showing up line by line on some sort of "reader" in New York.

We made all sorts of advances to the BBC to try to gain access to their machine but to no avail. They and NBC News remained allied. Fortunately, in the competitive sense, the Slow-Scan system could not handle too much volume. Each picture had to be read by the scanners very slowly. NBC News personnel would edit the film in London and transmit the "cut" story, but even a minute-long story took hours to send. Eventually, the Slow-Scan editors speeded up the process by literally eliminating every fifth frame from the film. The finished product looked a little jerky on American television screens, but, nonetheless, it was today's pictures, seen today.

The big breakthrough was the communications satellite.

Television signals travel in a straight line. Anything that gets in their way blocks them. Television signals bounce off buildings or tall trees or rocks or any obstruction that is between the transmitter and your set's antenna. City dwellers often experience "ghosts" on their screens—double images or delayed images that trail behind or to the side of the action on the screen. Many of those ghosts occur because some of the electronic signal is slightly late in arriving at your antenna, delayed because some of the signal strength ricocheted off a tall building and lost milliseconds between the time it left the transmitter and the time it was picked up by your set. Television signals also need a considerable amount of power to get them from the transmitter to your set. That's why most television stations can only be seen for little more than fifty miles from the transmitting tower. The signals do not have enough power to travel much farther without an additional boost.

Both problems . . . the straight-line transmission and the need for power . . . blocked the transmission of television signals across the Atlantic Ocean until the Space Age dawned. By putting an electronic relay station into space, engineers solved both problems. First, perched high above the Earth's atmosphere, a relay station could be seen in a straight line by a transmitter in Europe and simultaneously by a receiver in the United States and vice versa. Second, by equipping that relay station with a device to enhance and strengthen a signal, the dying video information coming up from Earth could be revitalized and beamed back down. Though described simplistically, that is what a television satellite is all about.

The first communications satellite was Telstar. It was a nonsynchronous "bird," which meant that it spun around the Earth every hour, changing its position in the sky. Space technology had not yet arrived at the point where a synchronous satellite could be placed in orbit. That was to come a few years later and would mean that the satellite stayed in one place in the heavens, rotating at the same speed "in sync" with the Earth's rotation. The nonsynchronous Telstar satellite spun at its own rate of speed and passed over the mid-Atlantic once an hour. It was visible from the transmitter at Goonhilly Downs in England and from the receiver at Andover, Maine, for eleven to fourteen minutes each hour. It was a very tiny time "window," but in the summer of 1961 it was more than we had ever had before.

Telstar was launched on July 10, 1962. The three American television networks decided to pool resources to produce a fourteen-minute program to beam to Europe. The American networks named Fred Friendly, then the innovative producer of "CBS Reports," as executive producer of their program. Friendly, never short on ideas, decided to show Europeans scenes of America, including Mount Rushmore. Ted Fetter of ABC convinced Friendly that he ought to have some cowboys and cattle in the picture, too. CBS producer David Buksbaum was dispatched to do the job. Friendly gave him his typical send-off: "Don't tell me your problems, just get the job done." He also told him he'd changed his mind—he wanted buffalo instead of cattle as a more American symbol, and he wanted some Indians and some campers in the scene, too.

When Buksbaum and his engineering associate, Al Seigler, got to Mount Rushmore, they quickly discovered that the only way to get a video signal back to civilization was through the CBS affiliate in Rapid City, South Dakota, which received its network feeds via a string of microwave towers carrying the signal north from Denver. To send a picture out, the affiliate's equipment had to be physically turned around—to transmit, rather than to receive. Bill Turner, the station manager, agreed to let the station go off the air for three days to permit the needed engineering adjustments.

Then came a phone call from Friendly. He'd decided to include the Mormon Tabernacle Choir. Buksbaum telephoned United Airlines and asked how many planes would be needed to move the 530 members of the choir company to Mount Rushmore. Four DC-7s would do the job nicely, but where could they land? The Pentagon came to the rescue, opening up a bomber base of the Strategic Air Command within busing distance of the broadcast site. Another problem solved.

Next, Buksbaum rounded up the chief forest ranger at Mount Rushmore. The choir needed a stage. The Forestry Service went to work, building it out of freshly cut wood, doing their part for the American broadcast. As for the campers, they would be positioned a discreet distance away, so that a separate camera could get pictures of them "enjoying" the wonders of a national park.

Friendly had assured Buksbaum that he had made arrangements with the man who was to provide the buffalo. This was Les Price, a tall outdoorsman with a booming voice who was superintendent of the nearby Custer State Park. When Price arrived, Buksbaum explained that he needed six to ten buffalo to run down a path on cue. Price was calmly patronizing. "Look here, sonny, buffalo don't go where they don't want to go." It turned out the buffalo were still sixty-five miles away. "Maybe we better go see them and talk this whole thing over," Price advised. "I think you're right," said Buksbaum.

After a bouncy Jeep ride across the Dakota Badlands, Price and Buksbaum finally found the herd, some of the meanest, smelliest animals Buksbaum had ever encountered. The herd was about fifteen miles from the nearest source of electric power, an abandoned fort built by movie companies for cowboy-and-Indian films. The animals had to be moved. Salt licks were put out along a line toward the camera position. Food was doled out to the animals who conceded to move. The herd made rapid progress, arriving at the fort about a week before the broadcast was scheduled. Now the problem was to prevent them from moving away. For days, cowboys in trucks and Jeeps kept circling the area, forming a live mobile pen for the herd.

The weather on broadcast day turned bad. Heavy rains fell. The rain-drenched faces on Mount Rushmore were reflecting so much light the cameras were unable to transmit usable pictures. By now, only Buksbaum was convinced everything would work; he believed it because he had to. He had flown back to New York to take his position in the central control room where Friendly kept insisting that the sun would shine, the campers' fires would light, the choir would arrive but . . . would the buffalo charge on cue?

The seconds ticked off toward broadcast time. Buksbaum phoned the buffaloes' keeper, Les Price, to ask how long it would take for the herd to get up enough speed to be seen by the camera by the fort. Price had no idea. He had never tried to move a buffalo herd with any precision but figured that thirty seconds would be enough. They also solved another niggling difficulty. The governor of the state of South Dakota wanted to be on the program. The buffalo, after all, were in *his* state park. What could be done? "Does he ride a horse?" Buksbaum asked. "Yes." "Well, make him one of the cowboys driving the herd."

On the air! The honor of America's TV creativity was on the line. Chet Huntley was reading his narration. The sun was out. The Presidents' rocky faces were magnificent against a blue sky. The choir was singing. The secondhand on Buksbaum's stopwatch was running. "Cue the buffalo!" he shouted into his telephone. A barrage of dynamite caps and shotgun blasts went off. The herd, startled, paused for what seemed an interminable moment. Buksbaum thought, "Oh, God, all we're gonna get is a picture of that damned hill." Then, one buffalo snout appeared on the horizon, almost as if asking, "Now?" Up over the rise they came—not the ten or twelve Buksbaum had hoped for but nearly one hundred buffalo—running madly toward the camera in clouds of dust. The Mormon Tabernacle Choir was in full voice! It had worked.

The first synchronous satellite was Earlybird, and because it was fixed in space, it was visible twenty-four hours a day from transmitters and receivers on both sides of the Atlantic. It went up in April 1965, and within weeks, all limitations and restrictions were gone.

It didn't take long for the spectacular use of the satellite to become just another routine. In fact, "feeding the bird" became so regular that the use of the superimposed title "VIA SATEL-LITE" was stopped because it distracted viewers' attention from the content of the picture. Satellite sending stations opened all over the world. The Vietnam War, already the "television war," the "living room war," moved even closer when Hong Kong and Bangkok established satellite links with the U.S.

One of the most ambitious uses of "the bird" was the coverage by the three networks of President Nixon's trip to China. Portable ground stations had been developed by NASA and used by the networks during the American space shots. A transmitting dish was shipped out aboard the recovery aircraft carrier, and the satellite would send back pictures of the orange-and-white parachutes as they drifted down from the sky carrying the capsule of astronauts back from the moon. That technology was put to use again when President Nixon visited China.

The Chinese were determined to be perfect hosts. Nixon's trip was the first opening to the West since the advent of the Cold War, with its bitter exchanges in Korea and across the Straits of Taiwan. The American networks had proposed flying in a television studio aboard a converted Boeing 747. They had also planned to bring in a portable ground station to hook up with the airplane. The Chinese would have none of that.

Taking plans from the Americans, the Chinese constructed an entire broadcast facility at Peking Airport. The satellite ground station was flown in and hooked up to their studio. American technicians brought in the equipment from the States and installed it, always assisted by their Chinese "friends." When all the work was done, a first-class satellite ground station was in operation in China. Every day, we fed stories back for special programs in the United States. Viewers saw President Nixon at the Great Wall, meeting Mao, and they watched live coverage as he moved around the Great Hall of the People toasting the Chinese leaders in the flush of a newly reborn relationship.

Satellites were used for fast-breaking stories as well as planned extravaganzas. In contrast to the two-day delay from the Berlin Wall in 1961, correspondents in Jerusalem in 1978 went on the air live within fifteen minutes of learning that Israeli troops had crossed the Lebanese border in a massive retaliation against Palestinian incursions. American viewers saw the event, heard details from Israeli government spokesmen and listened to U.S. government analyses within minutes.

During the Olympic Games in Munich, viewers were eyewitnesses as masked terrorists held the Olympic Village hostage. Satellites also brought home the intricacies of the Iran hostage crisis, linking Iranian officials directly with hostage families and indirectly with U.S. government officials. The satellite system worked so well that ABC News was able to use it every night to anchor one-third of its regular nightly newscast from Europe.

Flexibility and speed of transmission from overseas were more than matched by developments within the continental United States. News producers quickly realized that it was to their competitive advantage to be able to originate news coverage from points closer to the scene of the stories. They began to rely on affiliated stations as transmission points for stories shot on film or tape by network camera crews working in their areas. Once again, news coverage became wider in its scope and more immediate in its reportage. Before long local-station news directors were thinking in terms of the national impact of stories in their area. Newsrooms at networks benefited because they were being offered important stories by affiliates who now understood how to feed them. However, the millennium had not yet arrived.

Here's what happened, for example, in April 1974, after a tornado in Xenia, Ohio. First, network film crews and correspondents were sent to the scene from their usual base in Chicago. They were flown in on chartered planes. Network news organizations are probably the largest users of chartered aircraft in the United States. Crews are moved at odd hours and frequently there are no commercial planes scheduled to leave when the news demands that coverage teams be en route. Minutes count. On the Xenia story, the crew chartered in to a local airport and began on-the-scene coverage. There were shots of houses flattened by the wind, cars overturned and hurled against buildings. Small dramatic touches were also put on film: a child's doll, a broken bicycle, an unhinged door flapping in the breeze. The survivors recalled their fears and terror as the wind destroyed their town. Rescue workers were interviewed and authorities gave their assessments of damage and estimates of cost and recovery time. Finally, correspondents filmed their "stand up" openings and closes. (Those are the picture elements that place the correspondent on the scene and are a hallmark of most American television news reports.)

There were now four hours until the report had to be ready for broadcast. The network crew and correspondent packed up their gear and flew by chartered airplane to Cleveland, Ohio, the nearest "good" affiliate with the capability to handle the processing, editing and transmission of film to New York for inclusion in the network broadcast. The local telephone company could provide an extra "loop" to connect the station with its switching center, and the station's own operating schedule could be altered so that a film projector could be made available in its telecine room. (*Tele* for television and *cine* for cinematography, or film.)

For those four hours the reporter was, in effect, a messenger. He had to accompany the film to assist in its editing and to provide the narrative script that accompanied the pictures. Although he had a pretty good idea of the contents of the film, he could not be sure of it until it had been processed in Cleveland, a hundred miles away from the scene of the story; only then could he combine his reportage with the pictures. Being away from the scene of a story for hours before reporting it on air was unavoidable in those days. Often, television reporters kept themselves updated on later developments by reading wire service accounts, which they wove into their own scripts. This was one of the areas that news executives found most disturbing, and they kept asking the technicians to solve the problem. We had to find a way, if not to report from the scene, at least to shorten the lag. The answer came with lightweight, portable electronic cameras and portable videotape editing packages.

A dramatic example of the new capability occurred in 1975, when President Ford was visiting Sacramento, California. By then, all presidential trips were covered by videotape cameras.

Film had been phased out as the primary coverage tool on stories that we knew would be wanted for the "Evening News." A presidential trip was almost a certain starter on any evening newscast, so the White House news team was among the first to be equipped with tape. An edit package was sent to Sacramento and set up in a room in the Senator Hotel, which was the site of a scheduled speech by the President. •

Portable edit packages (editpaks) are still pretty heavy. They weigh about eight hundred pounds in their large Fiberglas containers, but they can be carried in airplanes, and they can be prepositioned in anticipation of news events. In Sacramento, the telephone company had installed transmission "loops" directly into the hotel room where the editpak was located. There was no longer a need for an affiliated station's facilities. The portable tape machines could be hooked up directly to the "loop," and the edited tape story could be fed directly into the line back to New York. The need to leave the scene of the story had been virtually eliminated.

With everything in place, coverage of President Ford's day was under way. He was working the crowd across the street from the hotel. Suddenly one of the Secret Service agents accompanying the President shouted, "It's a gun!" and the rehearsed maneuver for the protection of the President commenced. Agents surrounded Ford and swept him away, half pushing him, half dragging him. The agent who had spotted the gun leaped into the crowd and stuck his thumb between the weapon's hammer and the cartridge, and then he shoved, driving the would-be assailant back. Other agents and police swarmed in, wresting the gun down and away from the President.

The recollection of what happened on that Sacramento street remains clear because every bit of it was captured on videotape by ABC News cameraman Carl Larsen. He had been moving just ahead of the President, taping him as he reached into the crowd to shake hands. His camera had caught the frenzied moment—the warning shout, the charging agents. President Ford could be seen, looking startled, being moved out of harm's way. Larsen swung his camera around and got the rest of the action. The would-be assassin turned out to be Squeaky Fromme, a member of the notorious Manson family, and Larsen's pictures showed her pinned to a tree by the police. Larsen unloaded his recorder and tossed the tape to the field producer on the scene, who ran up the stairs to the hotel room across the street, which now was a mini–broadcast studio. The network was notified to expect the feed; the tape was put on the machine and rolled. It fed through the "loop" to the network line, down the network line to ABC News headquarters in New York and then instantly out again to all affiliated stations. The television audience could see the action within thirty minutes of its happening.

The history of the development of TV news is like some unusual game of leapfrog in which one player is editorial content and technology the other. A new piece of equipment lets the editorial side try new approaches to covering the news or conveying information. When the limits of the new machinery are reached, the editors demand more, and the technicians respond with a new generation of equipment to keep the editors satisfied. It's an endless, happy cycle that has been going on since the beginning of TV news.

It was 1953 when I made the trip from CBS Radio News, located at 485 Madison Avenue in New York, to CBS Television News, located in a series of dingy corridors above Grand Central Terminal, and it was like taking a step into Dante's Inferno. The walls of the offices were lined with a pinkish-brown polished marble that seemed to drip with moisture. In the middle of the night, the grimy newsroom glittered with fluorescents, and when dawn broke, the gray daylight that filtered through the absolutely filthy windows was never bright enough to enable us to turn off the overhead lights. There were four of us working alongside Charles Collingwood, who had been selected to read the seven-minute news "packages" that were inserted in the "CBS Morning Show" once every half-hour from 7:00 A.M. to 9:59 A.M. Monday through Friday.

   My title was Editor in Television News. Editors, in those days, were in charge of reading over the scripts that were turned out by news writers for the on-air correspondent. They made certain that the quotations used were accurate and that the stories, rewritten from wire service reports, were correct. There was very little film, and what there was came from the previous night's "Evening News." It was reedited, rescripted and then rebroadcast. Eventually, the title "editor" was changed to "producer," and the responsibilities of the job were broadened. A small budget was provided for additional film coverage. Instead of being limited to shortening scripted stories to make them fit the allotted time on the broadcast, producers were charged with deciding which stories should be included and which should be left out. The "producer" on a television news broadcast was to become the most important figure in its creation. The "editor" remained as part of the team, still responsible for fact checking and for being the conscience of the broadcast's content.

In the fifties, we were learning about television. We were finding out how to use pictures and sounds and narration to report events. We were discovering the impact of television news—an impact geometrically greater than the mere sound of radio or the flat grayness of newsprint. The combination of picture, natural sound and narration was providing us with a brand-new tool.

We were students of one another, shaping the "look" and style and standards of daily television news programming. There were many pioneers, but in my view, one deserves to be singled out. Don Hewitt, who ran the "CBS Evening News," played the significant part in transforming the title "editor" into executive producer, making certain that editorial as well as visual inputs were creatively combined. Hewitt made certain that "innovator" was part of the job description.

The "CBS Evening News" program was about five years old in 1953. It was fifteen minutes long, in black and white, and mainly centered on New York and Washington news. It had originally been edited and directed on the air by a rotating group of people, but sometime in 1950, Don Hewitt emerged as the full-time producer–director of the broadcast. Douglas Edwards took on the job as full-time news correspondent. In his post, Hewitt became the person who invented the wheel. If all of us were learning by watching each other, building upon each other's contributions and ideas, all of us learned most by building upon the foundations established by Hewitt. Many of the procedures he thought up and developed on the air in the early fifties are still in use today.

Hewitt was not a desk man by nature. He often moved into the field, seeking new ideas and testing new concepts. On the day the *Andrea Doria* was struck in mid-Atlantic by the Swedish liner *Stockholm,* Hewitt and Doug Edwards got hold of a plane and flew to the scene. Until that time, the conventional method of coverage on television stemmed from the newsreel days. A cameraman would bring back pictures and they would be edited in a cutting room and then narrated by someone who probably wasn't there. The concept of a broadcast's anchorman doing on-the-scene reporting was something new and daring. How commonplace it seems today, but when Hewitt tried it, it opened our eyes to the possibilities.

In those days, we used single-system sound-on-film. The sound and the narration were recorded on the same piece of film that was capturing pictures of the event. The general practice was for the correspondent to describe what was going on while the cameraman shot the pictures. It proved to be a very limiting convention. Often there were developments in the story that were not apparent directly in front of the camera. Often the narration did not match the pictures. If the reporter "fluffed" lines or ad-libbed a mistake, there was no way to correct the error. Hewitt was dissatisfied with the results. He introduced what we came to call "the double chain" method.

To make the "double chain" method work, Hewitt ordered CBS correspondents on the scene to remain in close touch with their camera crew, but he told them not to narrate the pictures while they were being taken. The cameraman was to film the event and record the natural sound on film. The correspondent would then stand up in front of the camera and record an on-camera opening and closing to the story. Finally he would write and record a narration on film, again standing up so that he could be seen at the scene of the action. The film would be processed and brought to an editing room.

Following Hewitt's plan, film editors would arrange two reels of material. On one, they would put the correspondent's opening, his story narration and his on-camera close. That reel would be locked into a synchronizer, which had space for a second reel of material to be held in place beside it. Using the narration on the "A" reel as a guide, the film editor would cut pictures together illustrating the story being told by the correspondent. The film editors were able to change the scenes to precisely match the narration. Errors could be cut out of the narration track on the "A" reel, and fluffs were eliminated the same way. The "B" reel of pictures would fit like a hand in a glove with the "A" reel of narration. Hewitt reasoned that if the narration reel were put on one projector and the reel of edited pictures were put on another and if both projectors could be made to start simultaneously and run at exactly the same speed, he could sit in a control room and select which video and audio he wanted to punch through to air.

After some fiddling around, the proper projectors were found, simultaneous start-up was achieved and the system worked. Hewitt would put video and audio from the "A" reel narration on the air first in order to begin the piece with the correspondent on camera at the scene. Continuing to feed the narration audio from projector "A," he would switch to projector "B" for pictures. Whenever he felt he wanted to see the correspondent on camera again, he would cut back to projector "A" and then again back to the pictures running on projector "B." Since the projectors were known as "chains" in those days, Hewitt called the technique a "double chain" story. As we used the system more and more, we added "chains." I once directed a broadcast using five "chains" running simultaneously to include narration, two picture reels, sound effects, and music. To this day, producers talk about getting "B-roll pictures" to illustrate "A-roll narration." It all stems from the experimental days when Hewitt was innovating to make conveying news and information more effective.

No one ever decreed in video cement that there had to be a thirty-minute network evening newscast. In fact, the half-hour nightly news came to television rather late. For quite a while, the fifteen-minute broadcast was believed to be sufficient, and there were few in the business who thought that news would ever amount to much in the general scheme of TV programming.

The nightly news first went on the air for fifteen minutes five nights a week in the summer of 1948 on CBS. NBC followed in February 1949 with its version, the "Camel News Caravan." That broadcast, claiming to cover "today's news today," featured a suave announcer, John Cameron Swayze, who wore a flower in his lapel. He would conclude his broadcast with a roundup of secondary news items: "hopscotching the world for headlines." Swayze's broadcast, somewhat livelier than the "CBS Evening News with Douglas Edwards," was the first to recognize the need for its own film crews and a larger staff dedicated solely to TV news. CBS lagged behind, depending on outside news-film suppliers to provide pictures, and splitting writers and other production personnel between its radio and television news operations. Television was a stepchild at CBS; radio was still regarded as paramount. The result was that NBC News took the ratings lead and held it.

At first, NBC scheduled "Camel Caravan" at 7:45 P.M., and "CBS News" went on the air at 7:30, Eastern time. When, in 1954, newly born ABC began to schedule entertainment programs at 7:30, the ratings for both CBS and NBC slumped badly. Before long, CBS moved the network news to 7:15. NBC tried to hang on to the 7:45 time period, but it finally gave up and in 1957 shifted to the same time as CBS.

The time shift was just one change in the NBC presentation. The other, which took place slightly earlier, was the termination of the "Camel Caravan" with John Cameron Swayze and the introduction of Chet Huntley and David Brinkley.

Huntley and Brinkley had been teamed as anchors for NBC's coverage of the 1956 political conventions, an auspicious decision that resulted more from a compromise than from any deliberate plan. Reuven Frank, one of the pioneers of television news, insists that conscious casting played no part in the decision to team the two men. There were some at NBC who backed Huntley, preferring his scholarly style, his good looks and the hint of Edward R. Murrow's authority in his voice. Others pushed for Brinkley, who was known for his wit, his superb writing ability and his dry, offbeat delivery on the air. NBC needed to decide who was going to tie together the convention coverage. After long hours of argument, someone suggested using both men. Everyone at the meeting thought it was a workable solution, and it was adopted.

Huntley and Brinkley's performances at the convention were smooth and professional, and Brinkley's humor caught the eye of many critics, including Jack Gould, TV critic of the *New York Times,* whose comments were carefully read in the executive offices. When Gould praised Brinkley for a "much needed note of humor," the "business" understood that changes in the nightly news were inevitable once the conventions were over. In October 1956, Swayze was out and Huntley and Brinkley were in.

Working out the kinks of a double-anchor operation was one of producer Reuven Frank's many contributions to broadcast journalism. Huntley sat in New York, Brinkley in Washington. The cities were now easily linked by cable, and Frank took advantage of the innovation, switching between the two cities as if the men were seated side by side in the same studio. Brinkley concentrated on national news from the capital; Huntley dealt with the rest of the world. The two frequently divided aspects of the same story, giving the broadcast a sparkling pace. The secondary details of stories, which might have been lost if only one anchor were reporting, were now highlighted by the very act of having the other anchor tell it. The scripts were tightly written, the coordination between the two anchors was well orchestrated, and the broadcast seemed to be in more places where news was being made.

At CBS, I recall, the NBC effort was greeted with derision. The two-man anchor team was referred to as Mutt and Jeff; the switching back and forth was regarded as gimmickry; the field reports were held to be superficial, and Brinkley's staccato style of delivery was thought to be unprofessional compared to the traditional mellifluous tones of an Edward R. Murrow. CBS made no adjustment in its broadcast with Douglas Edwards. Confidence remained high, particularly when the ratings showed Huntley and Brinkley dropping far behind the "CBS News." (This was chiefly due to the fact that many NBC affiliates had dropped the program when it had switched times so "The Huntley–Brinkley Report" was not available in many U.S. cities.)

What was not appreciated at CBS was the growing audience appeal of the NBC effort. More and more people were making jokes about Huntley and Brinkley, but they were not laughing *at* the program, they were laughing *with* it. "Good night, Chet. Good night, David" became part of the American idiom. Something was happening that kept "the team" in the forefront of the television viewer's consciousness. A particularly good instance was a parody of the popular hit song "Love and Marriage." It caught the image of the two men: "Huntley–Brinkley, Huntley–Brinkley. One is solemn, the other is twinkly." For the first time, audience appeal—personality—was playing a major role in judging a news broadcast's performance. The content of the CBS effort was almost identical to the NBC broadcast. The difference was in the faces on the tube each night. It was a glimmer of the "star system" that was to become increasingly important in determining who was watched by more people each night when they tuned in to see the news.

By the fall of 1958, NBC had pulled just about even with CBS in the ratings; the political conventions of 1960 pushed them substantially ahead. CBS went with Walter Cronkite as the sole anchor. NBC had Huntley and Brinkley in the booth. It turned out to be no contest. CBS had a disastrous convention. While Huntley and Brinkley engaged in brisk political repartee with humor and substance, Cronkite carried on alone, reading dull statistics, monopolizing the air time and boring the audience. Attempts to bring in Edward R. Murrow to sit alongside Cronkite to relieve the tedium were failures. Murrow could not ad-lib and Cronkite clearly resented his presence in the booth. At the end of the conventions, the audience stayed with Huntley and Brinkley, and they swept into the ratings lead on the nightly broadcast. CBS had lost its dominance and would be in second place for a long time. NBC rubbed it in each night, ending their broadcast with the announcement: "This program has the largest daily news circulation in the world."

By 1963, William S. Paley, the chairman of the board at CBS, had decided he wanted his news division to move back into the number-one position it had previously enjoyed. Paley was always a man for the bold stroke, and he believed that by expanding the "Evening News" from fifteen minutes to a half-hour, he would achieve audience recognition that CBS News was once again the leader. There was little doubt at CBS News that the expansion would have the desired effect. We firmly believed our demotion to second place was a temporary setback. NBC News was regarded as a flash in the pan, anchored by two admittedly impressive on-the-air performers but not backed up by the substantial corps of correspondents such as roamed the corridors of CBS News.

Still, Paley's decision to drive CBS News back into first place was not without opposition. Affiliated stations were reluctant to yield the extra fifteen minutes to the network. Any time a network program is moved into "station time" (time slots usually reserved for the affiliated stations), it means that the affiliates lose the chance to sell commercials, which costs them money. Since the advertising revenue from commercials running in an expanded network news program would remain with the network, the local stations saw expansion as a direct economic threat. The network overcame that problem by promising to give the stations more money from the commercials sold in the news.

There were some doubters within CBS News itself. They were concerned that audiences would be bored or, in the words of one writer who later left to return to newspapering: "Viewers would be 'newsed out.' "

The dominant question became, What will we put in a half-hour broadcast? More stories? Longer versions of stories already being covered? Discussions among correspondents? Commentary? The universe was wide open.

I was then based in London as CBS News producer for Europe. Watching British television convinced me that their newscasts compared favorably with what we were doing in the States. In fact, in some ways, the BBC was well ahead of us in the business of popularizing information about usually dull subjects. Economics, trade balances, the minutiae of international relations and the intricacies of national politics were presented each night in an understandable and engaging way.

There was one series that particularly caught my eye. It was the BBC's nightly "Tonight" show, hosted by a deft *compère* named Cliff Michelmore. The broadcast naturally included hard news stories developed from that day's breaking headlines. But "Tonight" also had an approach that was different from any I had previously seen. The producers of the program, at least to my eyes, were making a novel assumption: Simply put, they figured that information of a generally topical nature was equally useful to an audience and equally desired by them. Stories were tied to general news trends but they weren't necessarily on the day's headlines. I came away from each evening's broadcast feeling well informed. More important, I found that I was being given information to prepare me in advance for stories that were yet to break. The producers of "Tonight" were assigning and producing material based on their intelligent view of what was yet to develop in the news.

Instead of merely reacting to bulletins, "Tonight" was ready with analyses and background reports. This was all fitted into a loose format that usually ran thirty minutes. It was quite different from the fifteen minutes of carefully structured hard news then common in the United States. It was apparent that the extra fifteen minutes on a nightly news broadcast offered some major opportunities.

In response to the home office's request for ideas, I outlined an approach that was a candid crib from "Tonight." "We should broaden the traditional definition of what is news," I wrote. "We need not tie ourselves totally to politics, economics and international crises. In any broadcast, information need not be tied directly to today's news. Analytical features should anticipate events so that they can be on the air before the headlines." I felt that the half-hour format would enable American television viewers to learn more about the day's events than ever before. I urged that stories be assigned ahead of time and then "banked" to await an appropriate news peg. It seemed to me that, as veteran producers and correspondents, we could figure out what stories were going to break and could fashion useful background presentations. Knowing that a congressional committee was about to investigate hospital costs, for example, would permit us to do a feature on hospital routines; knowing in advance about the FBI's regular report on the incidence of crime in American cities would enable us to prepare a carefully researched and creatively filmed feature on a police precinct in a high-crime district. The mixture of hard news and these background features would bring a different texture to nightly newscasts.

As a result of my memorandum, Richard Salant, the president of CBS News, called me home and I was assigned as the producer of a new half-hour morning news broadcast set for 10:00 A.M. that was to debut in 1963 in tandem with the thirty-minute "CBS Evening News with Walter Cronkite." The "CBS Morning News" was to be anchored by Mike Wallace.

Mike Wallace had done talk shows around the noon hour that had been all froth and flimflam. He had acted on Broadway and run a superhype interview program called "Nightbeat" on a local television station in New York. "Nightbeat" had featured head-to-head confrontations with guests who were pinned in a dark set by a spotlight. It looked like an Edward G. Robinson crime movie of the 1930s with the detective grilling the murder suspects. On "Nightbeat," Wallace's questions poured out in a cloud of cigarette smoke—the extreme close-ups of the guest combined with the harsh lighting gave the program an aura of great drama. Wallace had an instinct for the jugular and he was not afraid of controversy. The newly formed ABC television network picked up the show and called it "The Mike Wallace Interview." Wallace might not have been scared but the commercially fragile ABC network certainly was when his guests began to complain. The show was canceled. Wallace then went commercial as the on-camera spokesman for Parliament cigarettes. There was plenty of back-of-the-hand snickering in the CBS newsroom about hiring this "actor anchorman."

The first time we met was on the way to a luncheon being served at the East Side townhouse of a CBS vice-president, Blair Clark. The lunch was supposed to be a discussion of both the new "Evening News" and the "Morning News," but that's not what happened. The entire conversation was devoted to the "Evening News" and to the glorious ideas that CBS News executives had for that broadcast. Literally no time was spent on our project. Stepchildren? We weren't even in the room as far as the brass at that table were concerned.

Finally, the meal was over. Wallace and I skipped the proffered limousine ride back to the office and walked instead. I had a concept for the "Morning News" that I knew would work. Wallace had an image of himself as a hard-edged newsman with a desire to get back into the mainstream of journalism. We both intended to be different and to make people take notice.

As we walked, we dwelled on the apparent slight we had just endured. As we passed a construction site, with the noise of the rivet guns going full blast, Wallace stopped and virtually shouted: "We'll show them! We'll really show them! Damn it! We will!" We shook hands in a bond of shared determination.

Wallace and the entire crew of the "CBS Morning News" did "show them" in a remarkable way. Innovation then was to become the standard fare on TV newscasts in future years.

We had a fairly rigid format on the "Morning News." It was based, in part, on my belief that television viewers, like newspaper readers, like to know where they can find certain features. Newspaper readers know where the comics are, where the editorial page is, where the pictures will show up and where the TV page and sports news will be printed each day. Carrying that over to the "Morning News," the first segment was the "hard news"—coverage of events that broke overnight. The second segment was the consumer or health material. The third segment initially was either a feature or a Mike Wallace interview and the final segment was the "Daybook," a look ahead at the day's expected developments. Our viewers knew where they could find what interested them most.

We assumed that at 10:00 A.M., the average viewer would be a woman who had just packed the kids off to school and her husband off to work. She might have completed the morning chores and she was ready to sit down with a cup of coffee in order to get caught up on events. Remember, it was 1963. Women's liberation and Betty Friedan's *The Feminine Mystique* had not yet driven their message into our consciousness. Nineteen years later, as this is written, our concept seems intolerably insensitive to women's objectives about their roles. But, in fact, we believed we had a special audience that could be dealt with specially, and it was our determined effort to win women viewers that led us to cover subjects that had not been seen or heard on American television.

Wallace was particularly enthusiastic about communicating with a primarily female audience; he never denigrated women's concerns or patronized their intelligence. We assumed they wanted to learn everything possible about that day's news plus something extra. It was here that the observations I had made of the BBC's "Tonight" show were useful. We anticipated events and consistently broadcast reports that explained what was likely to happen during the rest of the day or tomorrow or in the weeks ahead as stories developed. We imagined our female viewer greeting her husband as he came home from work, primed with some background information about a story that both of them might be watching together on the "CBS Evening News." "Explainers" were a feature of the "Morning News." They were really in-depth analyses of current affairs. We also paid particular and continuing attention to stories about consumer affairs, health, legal developments affecting women and children's rights, religion and education. We were among the first news broadcasts to deal with the Pap test for cancer, pregnancy detection, venereal disease, infidelity, alcoholism, boredom, and psychological "breaks" for women tied to housework with little or no self-motivation. The "Morning News" was described as a broadcast transmitted in a plain brown wrapper.

Looking back to that time, Mike Wallace recalls that there was no area that was forbidden to us. "As long as it was interesting and as long as it was carefully researched, it went on."

The BBC's "Tonight" program had demonstrated the value of "banking" stories that could be used whenever an appropriate news peg came along. The same system gave the "Morning News" more pertinence. Almost every story in the bank found a peg within thirty days. Very few passed into the oblivion of the CBS film library without being aired.

The "CBS Morning News" of 1963 had a small budget and a small staff of correspondents to serve it. Consequently we decided to exploit a form of television news presentation that had, by and large, been frowned upon. This was the "stand-upper" or "sit-downer." A correspondent would "stand up" and recite a script into camera in front of some appropriate location. The "sit-downer" was the same idea but it was done in the studio with the correspondent seated behind a desk. Both forms had been used before, particularly in the days when film crews were limited, before television producers had begun to develop ways to illustrate their stories more effectively. The short rations of the "Morning News" budget led us to dust them off again.

By using both techniques, we could assign a correspondent to do a simple job for the "Morning News," still leaving him free to do a more complex, illustrated report for the Cronkite broadcast at night. The Cronkite show did not need "stand-uppers" because it had a sufficient budget, access to correspondents, and time during the daylight hours to gather appropriate pictures to illustrate most reports.

Many producers believed that "stand-uppers" were "not television." In the early days of television news, we were still defensive about our medium and still learning. There's no doubt that the opinion "if I can't see it move, it's not TV" was widely held. Nonetheless, the "Morning News" needed pieces, often couldn't get the pictures in time for broadcast, and was willing to compromise dogma for content. Somehow, illustrative material would have to come along. It did, in an innovative form.

Bill Stout, a CBS correspondent in the Los Angeles bureau, was in disfavor with the Cronkite staff. Since they wouldn't assign him, he was available for use by the "Morning News." He came up with a story that had universal appeal even though it was strictly a local development in L.A. Taxi fares had rocketed, and one of the cab companies had been accused of tampering with its meters in order to bilk riders. Because of our budgetary restrictions, there was no camera crew available to film a fully illustrated story for the "Morning News." For his "stand-upper," Stout added the missing ingredient that made the difference. He equipped himself with a hand prop: the tiny gear that clicked the meter's numbers into place when the taxi was running. One tooth of the gear had been filed away so that the clicking occurred more rapidly than it should. Stout began with an extreme close-up of the doctored part; as he explained what the missing tooth meant and how it affected the fare, he helped the report along with the tip of his finger, pointing out the file marks. The picture then widened to show him standing in front of a cab as he completed his explanation of the scam. By using a very rudimentary production device, Stout had presented an illustrated, informative and interesting report. Every cab rider in the country who saw the effort would know how a taxi meter worked and how one might better protect oneself from an unscrupulous operator.

Stout's technique impressed me so much that years later, in a memo to ABC News correspondents, I suggested they begin all their stories by concentrating on the smallest entity in them before widening back to the broader aspect. It was, in essence, an extension of Stout's hand prop. "If we are covering a Congressional hearing," I wrote, "begin with pictures of the key witness sitting down, or perhaps with a witness adjusting the microphone or a clerk distributing a text. Then move into the detail of what was said or done." The audience, I believe, gets a greater sense of the impending drama or tension by being able to concentrate on one visual element at the outset instead of having to absorb the overview that wide shots provide. There were other examples, all of which stemmed from Stout's technique. "If we are covering a hurricane, begin by concentrating on some wind-swept birds ('the gulls knew Clara was due. They felt the wind early. . . .'), then move on to the general panorama of impending disaster." It has been my experience that a viewer has to grasp the main points of a story quickly before they are embellished with supporting elements. Starting "small" and then broadening out helps maintain clarity in the short time usually available for a single story on the nightly newscast.

Why all this concern for how stories should be shot or for pacing or the personalities of the anchors? What is television news anyway? Television is show business. Television news, as part of television, is part show business too. As long as show business techniques can be used to transmit information without distorting it, I believe they are perfectly all right.

Yet show business presentation, if taken to an extreme, does distort the very stuff that is supposed to be conveyed. There is a line between the imaginative presentation of facts and its over-production. The electronic equipment that has so dramatically advanced the presentation of graphs and charts has also resulted in the coinage of the word "ka ka" at ABC to describe all the zooms, squeezes, shoves and pushes of pictures on and off the screen. There is no doubt that all the activity on the screen has infused the visual presentation with energy, but too often it has failed to enhance it with information. Whenever possible, less is better. One learns that lesson through a combination of good taste and experience, watching hours of television programs go out on the air.

In the early days of television, when I was learning the director's task, I would sometimes observe directors at work on live drama shows such as "Studio One." Directors moved cameras around and asked for angles and picture composition to achieve dramatic effects. A background was deliberately shown out of focus, for example, to heighten the actor in the foreground. An extreme close-up of a person's eyes would be used to achieve an intimate effect. Directors played with "framing," composing the most satisfying layout of picture elements within the 3 × 4 ratio that makes up a television screen.

The TV director gives the commands to the technical staff, who make everything happen. A director is responsible for the look of his or her broadcast. Sloppy direction of a television news broadcast detracts from the credibility of the entire news operation. The viewer expects the tape to cue in on time; delays break the concentration of the audience. If the wrong film rolls, the embarrassment is even worse; questions begin to arise about the reporting itself. Of course errors and miscues will occur. But if wrong pictures show up night after night behind the anchor, or wrong film or tape inserts roll in, or if there are continual delays in cueing, something is fundamentally wrong.

As directors of news programs, we had a sense of responsibility for making things look right. If the anchorman's tie was crooked, it had to be straightened. If a cable could be seen snaking across the studio floor, it needed to be covered or pushed out of the camera's view. If a guest was to wear a tie-clasp microphone, its cable had to be concealed, either by running it down the back of the jacket or inside the front of a dress.

In setting up a show, we learned how to "block" each shot in sequence, rehearsing in advance which camera would take which shot in which order. Whenever possible, directors looked at all the film segments for news broadcasts, memorizing the audio and video out-cues in advance so that they would end when they were supposed to rather than dribble away with extraneous pictures and sounds. In those days, film stories were cued up on a ten-second roll cue, the time required for the projection equipment to reach its proper speed. We would "ready" the film projector, "roll" the film and, ten seconds later, "take" or "dissolve" or "wipe" the film. On that command, the technical director would punch a button on his control panel and put the output of the projector on the air. It was the director's responsibility to coordinate the anchor's reading speed and the cues to "roll" and "take" the film. Ten seconds is not a very long time, but it seems like an eternity if the anchor is sitting there on camera, looking expectantly at the screen, waiting for the film to begin.

We used to mark our scripts with a series of symbols and slashes: "R" for Ready and "T" for Take. One director, Vern Diamond, used five colored pencils to mark his scripts with the commands he would give. All of us had mental tape recorders playing back the voices and reading tempo of the anchor so that we could mark our scripts precisely on the proper syllable, ensuring that ten seconds later the film would be up to speed and ready to go on the air.

Fred Friendly, in charge of many CBS News Special Broadcasts, was a demanding boss, a stickler for good lighting who insisted that directors who worked for him spend time getting the polished effect that proper lighting can bring to a subject's face. Back lighting, for example, was particularly important to him. Television lighting tends to be "flat"—a great deal of light is focused on the set with even intensity. Friendly had us spend a great deal of time making sure that there was "separation" between the background and the top of the hair of someone being taped or filmed. He wanted the subject to pop out of the picture. Adjusting the "barn doors" on lights put just a "spill" of extra brilliance on a shoulder or even on the tip of an ear and such small touches added elegance to the entire picture.

Another of Friendly's concerns was proper "framing." No extraneous furniture or other distractions were permitted in the background. A subject's head was placed so that it would be seen against a neutral wall or neatly situated between the leaves of a plant and a picture on the wall. The purpose of all that effort was to concentrate the viewer's attention on the face of the person being interviewed.

In those years, CBS News had a broadcast in prime time called "Face the Nation Debates." Secretary of State Dean Rusk, for example, would be closely questioned by CBS correspondents; Senator Everett Dirksen, a conservative Republican, would meet Walter Reuther, the president of the United Auto Workers; an advocate of family planning would debate a member of the Roman Catholic hierarchy. Sometimes the broadcasts would originate at "remote" locations appropriate to the debate's subject. Each one of those events took us more than a day to set up and light. We adjusted the cameras, the podia and the lighting a dozen times to get perfect shots. I was the director for a broadcast originating from the main banquet room of the State Department. No matter how many times we shifted camera positions, chinaware on display in a breakfront across the room glistened in the background light. It was apparent that without a massive rearrangement of the furniture, a large serving platter would be seen "growing" out of both sides of Secretary of State Rusk's head. We were running out of set-up time, so the stage manager was told to open the cabinet and move the dishes out of the way. Horrified State Department officers began to protest. "The dishes had never been moved!" "They were priceless and would be broken!" "The secretary would be upset!" The solution was, however, undeniably the removal of the china. We put it to Mr. Rusk himself, explaining how "Mr. Friendly would want only the best pictures of the secretary on the air." Mr. Rusk replied: "If that's what Mr. Friendly wants, that is what we will do." The dishes went.

That kind of attention to detail began to disappear as videotape became more flexible. As soon as tape could be edited to correct mistakes after the fact, the need to be right the first time

—because it was the *only* time—slipped away. The safety net of videotape eased pressures on the director to pay a great deal of attention to the fine points. Many errors could be fixed up later.

Another development that affected the quality of the director's training was the installation of the Zoomar lens in television studios. Originally cameras had lenses mounted on turrets that were rotated, or "flipped," by the camera operators as they took close-up, medium and wide shots. Directors learned what each lens on the turret could do. If the background was supposed to be sharp, there was a lens that had a great depth of field and could focus on both foreground action as well as the background. If extreme close-ups were needed, there were "long lenses" that could do that job. Getting the proper shot involved the proper lens as well as the proper position for the camera. Directors were used to moving cameras around as well as changing the lenses. When the Zoomar lens came along, that changed. The cameras became fixed. By pressing a button, the camera operator could achieve anything from a wide shot to an extreme close-up without moving—the electrically operated lens system did all the work. Though convenient, the Zoomar spelled the end of an important experience for directors. It has taken its toll in control rooms as television news has become more and more dependent on men and women who are skilled at cueing tape and film but who do not have the developed "eye" for picture composition, lighting and camera movement.

When I started directing news programs, part of the assignment was to select recorded music to be played behind the film clips. We used silent film mostly, and music was used to fill in the spaces in the anchor's narration. "Roaring Storm" was one phonograph record; "Tragic Night" was another. We used to amuse ourselves in the screening room by deliberately playing the wrong music behind the film. "Roaring Storm" would have a singular effect when run behind bathing beauties. We learned that music is one of the most manipulative tools at our command. Richard Salant, as president of CBS News, banned its use because of its potential for distortion. Sound effects also have no place on a hard news piece. Adding crowd noise or explosions is as much a falsification as faking a shot. If any part of a news report is not real, the entire report is suspect.

We've all seen those black-and-white movies from 1938 Hollywood studios. They were literal. Getting the female star from her home to her office in a film meant showing her: leaving front door, entering car, driving through traffic to the office building, leaving car, entering office building, entering elevator, showing the floor-indicator arrow, and then watching the heroine emerge from the elevator to enter her office. Movie producers correctly assumed that their audiences were not educated enough visually to accept shortcuts. But look at the opening sequence of any television situation comedy. The background music's lyrics explain the story line in broad outline; the title picture sequence shows us the characters, where they are located and what the story is all about. Television viewers have been trained to absorb information quickly from a lot of sources. They are now "video educated."

Television news was slow to make use of the "video education" created by TV commercials. It may be that news producers, who deliberately distance themselves from sponsors, were also distancing themselves from certain methods being pioneered by the sponsors—methods that might have been useful tools for transmitting ideas.

When I ran the "ABC Evening News" in 1969, I had a chance to break that mold. Now there was an opportunity to try something different each night, recognizing that all parts of the television screen should be used to reach the viewer. Ben Blank, a creative wizard of television news art, helped devise the "logo" formula. We borrowed liberally from a practice in advertising: Repeat and repeat and repeat the same symbol to reinforce the sales pitch. Think of the black-and-white dog looking at a phonograph and one instantly recalls RCA; a girl in a yellow slicker standing under an umbrella in the rain means Morton Salt. Blank took that idea and created symbols for news stories. A clenched black fist stood for militant civil rights; a clenched red fist for militant students; a helmet meant any military theme; a school bus, half-white and half-black, was used for school-integration stories and a half-white, half-black schoolhouse was a variation on that theme.

Every running story had a "logo" developed for it. "Man and His Environment" showed the silhouette of a man against a blue sky. If the story involved oil pollution, an oil derrick was placed alongside the man. If air pollution was the story, a cloud would show behind the man's figure. Water and sun and tiny cars emitting fumes were displayed in the same way on the "logo" when they were needed. The repeated use of the same symbol reinforced the copy read by the anchor.

The next step, also borrowed from commercials, was to add the "key quote." Commercials often contain a slogan. On TV, the slogan is usually written on the screen at the end of the commercial. "You can be *sure* if it's Westinghouse!" Such slogans help to convey the commercial's message in ten or thirty seconds.

News broadcasts have a similar time problem. The less time it takes to tell a single story, the more stories can be included. The "logos" help speed up absorption and comprehension; the "key quotes" made greater retention possible. If the Pope said "No More War" in the course of a long speech, those three words, displayed over a papal "logo," made the report clearer. When prices of consumer goods went up 2 percent, that number would appear with a dollar sign impaled on an upward-pointing arrow. When the President outlined four points in an announcement of a foreign policy toward China, three or four words from each of the points would appear on the screen, superimposed over a map of China; and if the American Medical Association endorsed more exercise to combat rising heart disease, the words "More Exercise" would pop on above the AMA caduceus, which would dissolve into a picture of the human heart.

The result was to reinforce the conveying of complex information, yet this innovation drew criticism from traditionalists. Richard Wald, then president of NBC News, scoffed at our "cartoons for adults." Maybe they were like cartoons, but within a few years stations all over America were subscribing to graphic services run by the Associated Press, ABC News, and other suppliers. They were cranking out "logos" designed for categories of stories that frequently show up in a news budget: police officers, firefighters, plane crashes, automobile wrecks, the American flag, the Russian flag, pictures of young children, old people, cats and dogs.

A new class of electronic equipment came along in the late seventies, which helped solve some of the nagging production problems faced by Ben Blank as he tried to turn out the forty or fifty "logos" and "key quotes" for each night's broadcast. The time necessary to prepare the artwork was reduced from all day to hours, and from hours to minutes. With the touch of a button, graphs in several colors could be created. "Joy stick" controls enabled bars or arrows to be moved up, down or sideways. Producers could quickly create graphics to make words and pictures match more closely. Errors in design could be corrected instantly. One result: Economic news, which is highly dependent on chart displays and "key quote" reinforcement, is now put on the air in understandable form and has become a regular feature on all network evening newscasts.

In 1976, Dick Wald decided on a bold departure from the conventional format for the "NBC Nightly News." He had been impressed by the need to deal with subjects at a greater length than the current format allowed. He ordered the production staff to reserve enough time each day to present one story in a longer form. In order to "find" time for it, Wald ordered that some other stories on the broadcast be told as little more than one-line headlines. His format for the "NBC Nightly News" began with an extended lead segment dealing with the day's top story. The second segment of the broadcast was to be devoted to a collection of other major reports, produced at the normal running time for a television news story: about one minute forty-five seconds to two minutes long. Then came Segment Three, which ran about four or five minutes. It was followed by the time-saving headline segment; most nights the broadcast concluded with a human interest feature.

Viewers quickly perceived that Segment Three had something special about it. ABC's own research into viewer preferences about NBC showed that Segment Three was a significant factor in gaining and holding ratings. It fitted neatly into the pattern of series first made familiar on many local television news programs.

ABC News took a slightly different approach. Where Segment Three was devoted each night to a single topic, ABC News created a Special Assignment series. Special Assignment devoted two, three or four nights in a row to three- or four-minute reports all dealing with the same subject. One Special Assignment ran in eleven parts and examined America's military capabilities for defense. There were others including coverage of coal as a substitute for oil; illegal immigration; cable television; and sexual harassment of women in the workplace. The more successful Special Assignment series were tied to current hard news topics. (The network evening newscasts have not ventured into the more titillating areas like cosmetic surgery, modeling and sexual perversions. Those subjects have still been left to the local stations, which regularly schedule them during their intensive ratings periods.)

Measured by mail, phone calls and audience research, the Special Assignments resulted in ratings increases. They were heavily advertised and promoted in on-the-air announcements. There were ratings losses when the series did not appear. The Television Research Services Department of ABC discovered that 40 percent of the regular viewers of ABC's "World News Tonight" broadcast missed the series when they did not run. On the basis of questions put to a selection of typical news viewers, it was clear that they preferred subjects that touched their personal lives. Once again, the axiom from the early days of the "CBS Morning News" and the BBC "Tonight" program was confirmed. Audiences respond to information about general topics not necessarily tied to the day's breaking headlines but nonetheless relevant to their lives. And that creates a major contradiction.

The definition of news has been broadened to include more and varied information, and many viewers want to spend more time with a subject. But the time restraints of TV news run absolutely counter to both those impulses. Twenty-four hours of news must somehow be squeezed into twenty-four minutes. There must always be contradictions and compromises. It is accomplished with elaborate electronic gadgetry and a host of people who have been trained for the specific task.

2
Counting Down
to 7:00 P.M.
INSIDE EVENING NEWS

Rhoda Lipton, a producer for ABC News, and a correspondent had been assigned to put together a pictorial review of the months the hostages had been held in Iran. Lipton selected the film and videotape segments; the correspondent had written a script. Lipton had constructed background music from popular songs that were supposed to suggest the mood changes as the months passed. By juxtaposing lyrics and music against pictures, she tried to reflect the feelings of frustration and anger that had grown in the U.S.

Lipton took her assembled film and tape sequences and the narration and music tracks to "postproduction" for their final marriage into a completed piece for broadcast, and as she listened and looked, she realized it didn't work. Sometimes the music could not be heard; other times it was so loud that it drowned out the narration, distracting from, rather than enhancing the mood. The director in charge was harassed and unfamiliar with the concept Lipton had developed and the effect she was trying to achieve. Eventually the "mix" was redone, but when she sat in my office, the dismay was still evident in her face. "It's all teamwork. The producer does a good job. The correspondent does a good job. The tape editor does a good job. All three good jobs add up to a better job." I nodded and she sighed. "Then you hand the piece over to a director who does a bad job; or work with an audio man who doesn't care or who does a poor job and the good work of everyone else drops to the lowest level of performance. It tears it all apart."

Television news coverage, production and broadcasts are the result of close teamwork. Everyone benefits from everyone else's contribution; everyone suffers when any single element is inferior. It is unique to television news and of course it distinguishes it utterly from newspaper reportage. On a newspaper, one person could, if need be, cover a story, write it, edit it and, in these computerized times, even set it in type. Nothing in television news comes even close to such individual action. The correspondent relies on camera and sound crews, producers, tape or film editors, graphic artists, production associates and lighting directors, technical directors, program directors and associate directors. Each person in that group provides at least one essential element in the human chain that puts a report on the air.

At the top of the heap is the executive producer, whose authority has grown immensely since those days in '53 when the job was more or less a broadcast "editor." Anchors, of course, are out in front of the cameras and are, therefore, the most visible element as they read the news copy prepared by or for them. Correspondents and reporters gather the facts, and field producers and in-house "spot" producers help assemble the pictures and edit the scripts, film and videotape into coherent reports. The directors command the technical staffs, bringing together disconnected elements into a smoothly executed collage of camera cuts, tape and film inserts, graphic displays, commercial "pods" and on-air personalities. Yet all that happens because, first, the executive producer has made three initial decisions: what stories will go into the broadcast; how long they will run on the broadcast; and, in what order they will run during the broadcast. Every other action taken by every other person working on a broadcast flows from those three decisions.

Television news is obsessed with time—executive producers spend a considerable amount of their day figuring out how to allocate a broadcast's time to stories. The major factor is the number of stories that have to be included weighed against the amount of time it takes to tell them properly.

The rigid limitation that time imposes on television journalists is not shared by their newspaper colleagues. Even though print journalists talk of the "news hole" in their publications, the space between the advertisements can be varied on any given day. Newspaper publishers can add a few pages if they feel the news warrants it. You cannot add a few television "pages," except in a crisis when all regular TV programming is wiped out to present unlimited coverage. On a day-to-day basis, TV schedules are rigid to the second. Everything must be compressed to fit, a process of elimination rather than inclusion, which forces constant compromise. No opportunity exists to add just one more feature or analysis for "only" thirty seconds more on a regular nightly newscast.

There are two aspects to time that affect content. One is the length of the broadcast. The other is the time the broadcast goes on and gets off the air. This fixation with time is singular to American television. In England or Germany, by contrast, if a program isn't quite ready to roll, one may be treated to minutes of music illustrated with beautiful pictures of scenery or rolling waves.

I guess I've owned ten stopwatches in the course of my career in broadcasting, and other kinds of special timepieces too. My two current favorites include a battery-operated world clock that can tell me at a glance the time in any of twenty-three cities in the world. The other is a small calculator that fits in my shirt pocket. It can tell time of day, date, and it also has a stopwatch capability that can count forward and backward. I'm not unusual in my concern for accurate timing. We deal in seconds within a broadcast and in getting on the air. When the big red sweep secondhand hits the twelve on the studio clocks, we go on the air—not a second before, not a second after. When the red hand hits twenty-eight minutes and twenty-nine seconds, we go off.

I remember standing in the control room at CBS one after-noon when the producer of a special broadcast about one of the Gemini space shots made a mistake and signaled for the broad-cast to go off the air two minutes early. For one hundred twenty seconds, the credits rolled by slowly on the screen, stretched out by very, very slow dissolves from one list of names to another. The theme music, originally expected to last less than a minute, had long since finished and the silence was dreadful. Fred Friendly, then the president of CBS News, came slowly but ominously into the control room. Unbuttoning his jacket, Friendly rolled back his shirt sleeve and undid the clasp on his expensive wristwatch. "Here," he said, handing the watch to the producer. "Take my watch. You need it more than I do."

Because programs have to begin when they are scheduled, editorial decisions are affected. The evening newscasts often go on the air with less than complete information. A newspaper can delay printing its editions by several minutes while waiting for more details on a story. Television cannot delay for even one second, and once something is eliminated or missed on a broadcast, it is gone forever. There is no second edition.

As executive producer, I have often sketched out alternative broadcasts because it was unclear whether key reports would be ready in time for the program. Stories were prepared in script form to be read by the anchors just in case the field reports did not make it. It is not unusual to see reporters and their producers running down corridors with videotape cassettes, trying to get them to video playback machines in time to be inserted in a broadcast which is already on the air. Everything is pointed toward "air," and executive producers share the anxiety of the rest of the senior staff, pushing back that pragmatic decision to give up on a report still being edited in the field, substituting the anchor's summary.

Westin's Rule of Pragmatism states: "Pragmatism increases in inverse proportion to the amount of time left before air." In other words, a producer with an hour left before the broadcast can still fuss with extras and production values. A producer left with fifteen minutes to go has to start dumping the frills. "Brute force" editing is the only method to apply in the last few minutes. Once in a while, if a story is so important that it cannot be passed up, a second attempt will be made to insert it into the broadcast. That's when viewers hear the anchor explain: "We have just received that report via satellite from Iran, and we will bring it to you now." On those occasions, other stories are dropped from the program to accommodate the late-arriving material. That's when senior producers become human adding machines, totaling the time remaining in the broadcast and subtracting news stories to make the broadcast come out on time.

Though there is no question that these time constraints are serious, I get annoyed when I hear the old saw that "all the news contained in a television news broadcast could be put into less than a column of type on the front page of the *New York Times*." The impact of the two media are entirely different, and it is useless to equate them. The sight and sound of passion displayed by a protester, for example, affects a viewer differently than reading the word "anger." The joy of an underprivileged child greeting Santa Claus while receiving a Christmas gift takes time in a TV report. Time is our equivalent of a newspaper's space, and it takes time to allow tears to flow down the cheek of the wife of a man held hostage in Iran, time to allow the President of the United States to say that the economy is a mess. There is no way to compress his speech patterns into column-width quotations. Visual and audible impact is what television is all about, and if we devote the time to it, that outweighs the "sacrifice" of more detailed information that a newspaper can accommodate on its front page.

A more convincing observation is that the network evening news is an illustrated headline service. It is not a broadcast of record. It transmits a summary of life's conditions, good and bad. What ABC or CBS or NBC says is news, is news. What appears on the air partly determines how the viewer looks at the world. What is left out, what is incompletely or improperly reported, distorts.

So an evening news program cannot be a person's sole source of information. There are other television news and current events broadcasts on the air that provide more background or discussion. There are newspapers, news radio broadcasts, newsmagazines, books on current affairs. All must be relied upon if one is to be truly informed. If you rely only on the television newscast, you are woefully ignorant.

From time to time, executive producers have been accused of conspiring to manipulate the nation by using their editorial and creative power in some sort of organized and sinister way. The evidence cited most often is the frequency with which the three networks' newscasts begin their presentations with the same lead stories. What's more, there are many evenings in which one network runs the same stories in virtually the same order as another network. How can that be, the argument goes, unless the people who head both broadcasts have conferred?

The "lead" story is the most important story of the day. It is the news that professional journalists believe must be told first and, usually, at greater length. Sometimes the "lead" is not a single story but a combination of related items that together are the most important element of the day. Herbert Gans wrote in his book *Deciding What's News,* "Leads for the nightly television news . . . virtually choose themselves most of the time." Correct. Leads usually make themselves obvious each day, and though the choice is made by individuals, the executive producers, it is not surprising that they think alike.

Examine the biographies of the men who currently hold the posts of executive producer and you discover there are striking similarities all through their careers. Their education and experience levels are about the same. They are all college or university graduates, some holding advanced degrees. All served overseas, either as producers or reporters. All rotated between the field and the home office at least once on their way up. Many covered presidential or congressional campaigns, riding the press buses and dropping off film or tape to feed edited stories back to New York for inclusion in the nightly newscast. They have all come in direct contact with the news, "touching it," moving out from the simple rewriting of wire stories to gathering material for inclusion in reports on the air. They are well versed in the latest technology, using it to enhance the presentation of information in their broadcasts.

Executive producers have to be concerned with cosmetics, but their responsibilities are primarily editorial. There are five basic categories in the job description, in order of importance:

1. Journalist
2. Timekeeper and logistics expert
3. Financial administrator
4. Innovator, showman and publicist
5. House psychiatrist and sometime "rabbi"

Because almost all of a news department's efforts are pointed toward support of the nightly newscast, which is the department's "flagship show," the executive producer of that broadcast gets involved in decisions made throughout the division. He or she is first a journalist concerned with editorial content and the relative importance of the stories of the moment. There are, however, other demands. Problems of logistics and technology arise as decisions are made about the best way to get material back from the scene of the story. That is the second category. Should it be via satellite or chartered plane? Can the sound portion be fed separately by telephone so that a transcript can be made and studied before the pictures arrive? The clock and the deadline are always there. Spending time on shipping schedules or transmission line availability subtracts from the time for news judgments.

The third category in the executive producer's job description is financial administrator. There is a lot of money to spend. The budget for a nightly newscast is in excess of fifty million dollars a year. The executive producer must spend time each day assessing the relative value of a story in dollars and cents to determine whether it is really worth the effort.

Each network manages its financial controls differently, but usually there are discretionary funds available to the executive producer that supplement the basic news-coverage budget. In a typical case, general-news funds pay for covering a plane crash. That news event may require two correspondents and crews to report on the crash itself, the aftermath and the investigation. The executive producer may decide that the broadcast wants an additional report backgrounding the safety record of the type of plane that went down. He or she might assign a story on the financial impact on the particular airline whose plane was lost, or ask for a correspondent to do an obituary of some prominent person who died as a passenger. If the audience appeal of one broadcast over another rests in those kinds of supplemental reports, the money is well spent. There isn't enough money to do everything (nor is there air time to broadcast everything), so hard decisions are being made all the time. Again, elimination rather than inclusion is the rule. Often, there's not too much time to weigh the cost factor because delay means a missed plane connection for shipping the tape to a transmission point, or it means a satellite blocked by an order from a competing news organization. Decisions like that are frequently made on instinct.

The fourth category in the job description is innovator, showman and publicist. Putting a broadcast together requires some touches of showmanship. If a story is exclusive, because a correspondent has gotten an inside tip or because some film of an imprisoned Russian dissident has been smuggled out of Moscow, it might be played earlier in the broadcast to capture and hold the audience's attention. Pacing a program, putting exciting material together with more conventionally important segments is part of the job. There are times when acting as a publicist for the team effort is vital within the news division itself as well as among one's peer-group competition. A little self-congratulation and crowing is healthy, particularly after the news organization has scored a "beat" by breaking a story before anyone else.

The executive producer has room to innovate. There are, of course, limits on how "far out" the presentation of information can be. Show business techniques, as we've said, cannot be allowed to distort information. Still, within limits, an executive producer can try things. For example, I used to send correspondents back to an Illinois farm community or to a demographically typical neighborhood in Los Angeles to get reaction to breaking stories. The ABC News Precinct became a familiar touchstone for our viewers, who got to know the residents and could thus measure changes in their attitudes. It was a form of instant poll. The evening news has the funds and was the vehicle to try out new approaches. Innovation was built into the job from the beginning, a legacy from Hewitt.

The fifth category on the executive producer's list is house psychiatrist. That assignment can take up more time than any other, and it is time well spent if the organization is to function smoothly. A key correspondent may be in need of special handling because the story of the day has not been assigned in a manner especially pleasing to him. A conflict between two reporters over whose "beat" a story belongs in requires some gentle explanation to the person who is not getting the nod. In a business where egos are heavily involved, psychology is an essential element in making things run smoothly.

There's hardly any way to anticipate when or why or how the shifts between the five categories of the executive producer's job occur. When you are in the seat, subtle signs tell which one of them is operative inside the shop. If the anchor is cranky, it may be because a story was missed or poorly written for him or her. Other categories become operative for reasons that sometimes require a bit of detective work. If the ratings start to slip, it might be due to budgetary restraints which, in turn, lead to reduced coverage of a story. Cutting back satellite bookings to save money might mean that stories are showing up later than they should on your broadcast. Even though the look of the broadcast or the personality of the anchor helps keep audiences tuned in, a noticeable decline in the quality of coverage will send viewers away. There's no doubt that the public does find out through word of mouth, lunchtime conversations and some old-fashioned dial switching that another network is providing better pictures or more complete information. "Click" goes the dial and down go the ratings.

Making decisions on a daily newscast is always a consuming and energy-draining process. Creativity gets pushed aside by practical requirements. Just get the problem solved quickly and move on to the next one because there's yet a third or fourth standing in line to be addressed. There's too little time to think through all the options. If one takes too much time, other questions in other categories come tumbling in.

In order to handle the pressure and the irrevocable fact that television news operates on the basis of elimination rather than inclusion, I developed a series of questions to determine what should go into a broadcast and what should be left out.

- Is my world safe?
- Are my city and home safe?
- If my wife, children and loved ones are safe, then what has happened in the past twenty-four hours to shock them, amuse them or make them better off than they were?

The audience wants these questions answered quickly and with just enough detail to satisfy an attention span that is being interrupted by clattering dishes, dinner conversation or the fatigue of the end of the working day.

Is my world safe? I mean that both literally and figuratively. Does the story deal with the safety of the world? If the nation's vital interests are affected, could it mean war? Does the story have geopolitical or economic implications that concern world safety? The seizure of the U.S. Embassy in Iran, for example, demands to lead the broadcast and requires a large allocation of air time on the program. On occasion, a scientific discovery or an exploration that has an effect on worldwide health or knowledge might fit into this category.

On a routine news day, when no one story has the world-shaking importance to merit consideration under the question *Is my world safe?* the lead slot could go to a story that dominated in one of the other categories. The arrest of Wayne Williams, suspected of being involved in a wave of murders of young blacks in Atlanta, led the "World News Tonight" to displace a report on economic conditions. The world was safe, so the Williams story moved up.

Are my city and home safe? Next to the world and nation, personal concerns center on the home and its immediate environment, the city. People need to know about events that directly affect their lives. Stories about the cost of living, unemployment, strikes, boycotts and shortages demand attention when they are of sufficient magnitude to have an impact. A report about toxic waste pollution at Love Canal in New York, though a local story, has national implications and should get more air time and play higher in the broadcast than harsh diplomatic exchanges between Ethiopia and Somalia. A story about a Supreme Court decision that ended the funding of abortions would move into the lead ahead of almost any other national or international story because the Court's ruling goes to the heart of the health and safety of America's women and children more directly than almost any international threat, short of actual war.

If my wife, children and loved ones are safe, then what has happened in the past twenty-four hours to shock them, amuse them or make them better off than they were? Though a story in this category rarely takes the lead, it certainly belongs on the program. Curriculum battles in schools, potholes in the streets, weather, sports and human interest stories are found here. This is family news. If little has changed in the world, nation, or city and home, then we spare the time to include stories about what has happened to improve the quality of life. Everything we should know doesn't have to start and end with catastrophe, disaster or threat.

There are no right or wrong criteria for selecting or placing stories; however, whether by formalized rules or pure instinct, executive producers have to have some guidelines to help them determine what stories they will put in and what they will leave out.

Even with the guidelines, there is room for debate over news judgment, and such a discussion took place in public in 1978 between Roone Arledge, the president of ABC News, and Richard Salant, then the president of CBS News. At issue was the way Elvis Presley's death should have been treated on the networks' evening newscasts.

The story broke late in the afternoon. At ABC News, the decision to make it the lead story was automatic. Presley's death, under mysterious, perhaps drug-related circumstances, was more interesting than any other single news event that day. Film researchers were assigned to pull footage of Presley performing and to ferret out interviews with him or his entourage. At CBS News, there was also no debate. Guided by standards that mandated precedence to importance over interest, CBS would stay with the lead they had planned—a four-minute packet on the Panama Canal Treaty, including a statement by Ronald Reagan.

It was a decision that conformed to Salant's dictum in the CBS News Standards Book. "We in broadcast journalism cannot, should not and will not base our judgments on what we think the viewers and listeners are 'most interested' in, or hinge our news judgment and our news treatment on our guesses (or somebody else's surveys) as to what news the people want to hear or see, and in what form." In 1976, Salant told Ron Powers, the Pulitzer Prize–winning television critic, "I take a very flat elitist position. Our job is to give people not what they want but what we decide they ought to have. That depends on our accumulated news judgments of what they need." To Arledge now, Salant added: "Our job is not to respond to public taste. Elvis Presley was dead—so he was dead." Any deviation from the choice of "importance" over "interest" was pandering to the audience in a search for ratings.

Arledge replied that people were interested in Presley and that the statement by Reagan opposing the Panama Canal Treaty that CBS had led with had long been expected. Reagan had said many times, "We built it, we own it, and we will not give it away." Arledge contended that such a statement, made by a potential candidate for President, was neither important, because it was so predictable, nor interesting. Presley "dropping dead of a heart attack at the age of forty-two was just a little less predictable than Ronald Reagan coming out against the Panama Canal Treaty." Arledge took issue with the elitist Salant position "I'm going to give them what they should have and not what they want." "Elvis Presley," he said, "affected the lives of millions of Americans who are clearly interested in him, and his death. Unless there is an overwhelming story somewhere else, his death should be dealt with first."

No one "won" that debate and it goes on, but CBS News seemed to shift course slightly in the weeks after. When Bing Crosby died, CBS led its broadcast with the news. Was there a difference between Crosby and Presley? It could hardly have been a question of "importance" as Salant had defined it. Did

CBS News like Crosby's crooning more than it enjoyed Presley's rock-and-roll? Did that affect CBS News's "accumulated news judgment"?

The ABC "World News Tonight" newsroom is dominated by a horseshoe-shaped desk. It is the "rim." News wire machines are sunk into its surface, clattering away behind soundproofing that mutes the noise. Two special television monitors are mounted on swivels so that senior staff can punch up any story from any videotape machine in the building. And there are banks of telephones. The executive producer and the senior producers sit at the outer curve of the horseshoe. The broadcast's editor sits on the inner curve, facing them. That is the heart of the decision-making process.

Television production is a complicated and confusing business. It requires the carefully coordinated efforts of more than 150 editorial and technical people to put a network's evening news on the air. A "clean," or mistake-free, broadcast is a tribute to cooperation. To achieve this goal, everyone working on a program must have a good idea of what everyone else is doing; the "lineup" made by the executive producer is the essential beginning.

A lineup tells the staff what stories are scheduled for broadcast; where stories will originate; what priorities should be set for processing film or editing tape; what graphics need to be prepared and produced; what shipping arrangements should be preserved or canceled or changed; what scripts need to be written and how the narrative should be constructed; what commercials are scheduled for broadcast and, finally, what order and for how long stories are expected to run. Without a lineup, there would be chaos. With a lineup, issued early in the day, scrambling and confusion are held at a controllable level, and the staff sets out with some ordered idea of their individual and collective responsibilities.

Though network television newscasts are thirty minutes long, that half-hour is substantially shorter than thirty minutes. At ABC, six minutes are subtracted for commercials; at CBS, five and at NBC five and a half. In addition, time must be allotted for closing credits and the copyright announcement, the opening announcement, introductions to commercials and the possibility of mechanical delays. The average half-hour network newscast has about twenty-two minutes left for news content. The lineup is the record of the allocation of those minutes.

The staff of the evening newscast assembles at 9:00 A.M. to start preparing the broadcast.

The first order of business for the producers is the "read in." At most newsrooms, "reading in" consists of going through the "situationer" and overnight dispatches, cables filed by the outlying bureaus and correspondents, and reading the overnight files of the Associated Press, the United Press International and the Reuters news service. This takes the better part of two hours, but long before it is completed, there are telephone conversations with the broadcast's own staff producers stationed in the domestic bureaus, particularly the one in Washington, and with the London bureau senior producer, who is coordinating overseas coverage. A pattern begins to emerge for the day's news, a pattern that is fixed in the first lineup.

Stories, including both the anchor's on-camera material and the tape or film pieces from the field, should be combined into a logical progression that threads its way through the day's news. The audience ought to be guided through the news so that it doesn't have to make sharp twists and turns to follow and understand what is going on. My preference is to divide the lineup into segments. In each segment, a narrative of sorts is fashioned, weaving together stories that relate to one another.

Under this system, it is not unusual to find a story in a newscast's lead segment that the Associated Press places way down on *its* list of importance. As you watch the different network news broadcasts, notice how some skip through the headline stories *en bloc,* coming back later to secondary stories that could have been woven in earlier in the program. In my view, for example, developments in the world oil supply ought to be included in segments containing reports from Libya, since they are all related to one another. On other networks' newscasts, the oil story may be split apart from Libyan terrorist threats and placed without reference to related stories. When that happens the viewer has to work too hard and the impact of the story is lost.

The narrative flows from the executive producer's decisions as he or she prepares the lineup, and the success or lack of it, in weaving elements into an interesting, informative and well-paced broadcast, is the real measure of creativity. But the executive producer's prerogative to set the agenda is an attempt to produce a broadcast rather than merely assemble it.

Domestic news dominates the nightly newscasts, and the executive producer has to be the loudest advocate for including more than just the huge headline news from overseas. Overseas bureaus know, for example, that during the national election campaigns their chances for "getting on the air" are seriously diminished. Even during periods when there is no central domestic political drama, there is a tendency to give more air time to Washington minutiae than to medium-weight stories from abroad. There is a crude joke: A producer has to decide whether to order a satellite feed for overseas news. If the story deals with dozens of dead in a South American bus crash, he will pass the story over; if it deals with hundreds killed in a Bangladesh cyclone, he will order the story to be covered and shipped by plane; if the story involves two American hitchhikers who died in a mountain-climbing expedition in Nepal, the producer will shout, "Order the bird!"

The joke exaggerates the situation some. We are an insular nation, and television news coverage does little to break that insulation down. My attempts to do so were hardly more successful than those of my successors who have run the nightly news. We would launch a swing through Eastern Europe by a correspondent who would be told to bring back as many general stories as could be produced in ten days. Some of them would get on the air, but the rest would languish in the "bank," forced out night after night by reports about floods in Kansas or a rise in U.S. postal rates.

It takes a conscious effort to remember that a nightly newscast is not a "program of record" the way the *New York Times* is. The fifteenth day of a strike, with no progress at hand, should

not automatically be reported. The preliminary debate over raising rail fares need not be included. Yet time and again, that kind
of story *is* put in. As a result, better, more interesting and perhaps more important stories from overseas are left out.

Television news broadcasts require pacing and style. The audience has to be allowed to breathe a little between periods of
intense excitement. Whenever possible, a vivid pictorial report
should be followed by an interlude of less exciting material.
That kind of arrangement is not done for cosmetic reasons; it is
designed to give the viewer some room to reflect on the information that has just flashed by.

At ABC, with first a two- and then a three-person anchor
team, pacing could be achieved in a number of ways. The length
of time on the air for each anchor is one way. The frequency of
switches from one to another or from one film or tape report to
another creates a sense of forward movement. The audience
appears to welcome change even if it consists solely of a switch
among anchors. Usually, the logic of the narrative of the news
leads to the switch anyway. A Washington element would naturally be covered from the nation's capital; a foreign segment
would turn up from London; domestic material would logically
come in from Chicago. Wherever possible, lead-ins and tags to
stories are worked out with correspondents in the field, enabling
them to fit their scripts into the narrative, moving the story
forward without duplicating the anchors' material. The result is
that the audience's attention does not wander, and the amount
of substance absorbed and retained is higher.

A typical lineup should be easy to read and contain basic
information. At ABC, using a system I devised, each line is
numbered. The anchor's appearances are indicated by his or her
initials; the copy stories are specified, where possible, with one-
or two-word titles; the reports from the field are marked with
the underlined name of the correspondent, typed in capital letters for easier identification, and the story title. The point of
origination for each story is noted with a code letter. N is for
New York; C stands for Chicago; W means Washington. On

the basis of those letters, the staff knows which transmission lines to order and to check. If the story is being fed from video-tape machines in New York, the symbol NYT—New York Tape—is typed in its proper column: WT stands for Washington Tape. The commercial "pods" that serve as punctuation marks in the pacing of the program are typed in and underlined for easier recognition.

When the broadcast is being formulated, the approximate time of each piece is listed against its line. Those are the "spot times," and as they are totaled, the CUME, or cumulative time, is added up. We all learn to add in "base 60." Forty-five seconds plus fifteen seconds equals one minute. Thirty plus thirty equals one. Seconds add up to minutes—the leftover parts are rounded up to the nearest five seconds. TV news people play a game of "guestimation." How long will it take for the anchor to introduce the report from Iran? Assess the amount of news that has to be told and put down a number of seconds. How long will it take for the correspondent at the Pentagon to report his or her story about plans to evacuate the embassy? Ask, negotiate the time and add it into the mix. The negotiations and compromises go on all day long.

"WORLD NEWS TONIGHT"   Revision #1   Tues., Nov. 6, 1979

#	ORIG	VISUAL	STORY	TIME	CUME
1	N	NT	OPEN	:25	:25
2	W		FR	:25	:50
3	N	NT	DYK/Iran	1:35	2:25
4	W	WT	KOPPEL/St. Dept.	2:20	4:45
5	N	NT	JENNINGS/Explainer & Khomeini	1:15	6:00
6	W		FR	:20	6:20
7	W	WT	DONALDSON/W.H.	1:10	7:30
8	C		MR Ahead (Waldheim & Iran & Braniff)	:15	7:45
9	N		Bumper (Stox)	:10	7:55
10	N	NT	COMMERCIAL #1	1:00	8:55
11	W		FR	:20	9:15
12	W	WT	DUNSMORE/St. Dept. Calls—Iran	1:20	10:35
13	C	NT	MR v/o Phila & v/o Columbus	:25	11:00
14	C	NT	MR v/o Empress & Soundbite	:20	11:20

#ORIG	VISUAL	STORY	TIME	CUME
— "World News Tonight" *(cont.)* Revision #1			Tues., Nov. 6, 1979	
15 N		Bumper (Most Active)	:05	11:25
16 N	NT	COMMERCIAL #2 & #3	2:00	13:25
17 W		FR & Intro	:15	13:40
18 W	WT	KAHN/Soundbite	:20	14:00
19 W		FR Overcharges	:20	14:20
20 C		MR Georges Bank & Intro	:30	14:50
21 N	NT	RODRIGUEZ/Tanker	:45	15:35
22 C		MR	:15	15:50
23 N	NT	MURPHY/Braniff	1:15	17:05
24 W	WT	FR v/o Shuttle & Mrs. Carter	:30	17:35
25 N		Bumper (Football Top 5)	:05	17:40
26 N	NT	COMMERCIAL #4 & #5	2:00	19:40
27 N	NT	PJ Korea & Ohira & Hua	:45	20:25
28 C		MR TMI & Intro	:30	20:55
		SPECIAL ASSIGNMENT		
29 N	NT	*BROWN*/Children of Fear #1	4:55	25:50
30 N		Bumper (Energy Stox)	:05	25:55
31 N	NT	COMMERCIAL #6	1:00	26:55
32 C		MR	:15	27:10
33 N	NT	*RUDD*/Al Capp	1:05	28:15
34 W		FR GN	:10	28:25
35 N		CLOSE	:04	28:29

Rarely does more than one segment change in its running order during the final hours of the production day. With everything else in the lineup standing firm, the entire effort of the news department can be focused on making the changes in the one segment that is affected by late-breaking developments. If a squad of professionals cannot handle five minutes worth of changes, something is radically wrong. With a lineup to define the broadcast's segments, everyone knows how to apportion his or her individual efforts to achieve the required alterations.

When the cry "Change the lineup!" comes from the rim, no one is really surprised. It is a rare day when the first, or white, lineup makes it all the way to air. Each minute brings some new development that could require a change, and between noon, when the white lineup should first be issued, and air time at 6:30

P.M., the pressures for change are continuous. The trigger for change is usually a late-breaking story that is of such importance that it shoulders aside another news item. If a narrative is to be maintained as a principle of good communications with the audience, then the new story has to be fitted in, and sometimes an entirely new narrative has to be constructed.

The staff swings into action quickly. When I was executive producer, I used a felt-tip pen and a long yellow legal pad to write down each new lineup. Computing seconds in "base 60" came easily after years of experience, and when it all added up to the unchangeable twenty-eight minutes and twenty-nine seconds, I would call for Ellen Weinberg, the production secretary, to start typing. Weinberg could type and add while her fingers were punching away at the keyboard. She was my fail-safe mathematical backup. She also managed to decipher my scratching, making editorial sense out of the two or three words I had hastily put down to indicate a story title or a correspondent's name.

In my day, Lawson Fischer was senior desk assistant and at the command "Change the Lineup!" he would load the photocopier with the appropriate colored paper. Our coded system changed colors with each lineup revision so that everyone on the staff scattered throughout the building knew which set of instructions were operative. White was first. It was replaced by pink. Then green paper would be used for Revision #3 and yellow for Revision #4.

Jeff Gralnick, who followed me as executive producer of ABC's "World News Tonight," has a framed collage in his office. It consists of a handwritten lineup on a long sheet of paper pasted on top of the four different-colored typewritten versions. Gralnick had gone through revision after revision, tearing up each one as new developments on three major stories poured in on him at the rim. A Southern Airways DC-9 had lost its engines in flight. That stood firmly as the broadcast lead. The problem was in the second segment of the broadcast. Some Americans held hostage had been released late in the day, but details were sketchy. Then there was a report that a Russian ballet star had defected while on tour of the United States. For a while, so little was known about either story that Gralnick couldn't estimate their importance or what, if anything, correspondents would be able to report. Then, simultaneously, minutes from air time, information started pouring in. "The news wouldn't stop happening," Gralnick recalls. "I thought I had it in order, and there'd be another bulletin!" Finally, at two minutes to six, with the anchors in their seats and the control room crew ready to switch the broadcast onto the network, Gralnick finished scribbling Revision #5, linking the defector story and the hostage story in a narrative. The photocopier couldn't handle long copy paper so his handwritten lineup had to be fed through the machine twice to make a complete copy. So few of them were available that staff members had to read them over one another's shoulders. It really was a crash landing.

In the corner of the collage on his wall, Gralnick has printed "REVISION 86" . . . an ironic reminder of a day in which "Change the Lineup!" never really ended, even while the broadcast was on the air.

At CBS News, Walter Cronkite had "magic time." That's what the producers of the "CBS Evening News" called the total amount of minutes and seconds he appeared on camera each night, telling stories or introducing reports from the field. It was not an accidentally chosen word because to many American viewers, when Cronkite was on the tube, it was a "magic" moment in communications.

The negotiations for "magic time" are a good example of how the executive producer of an evening newscast weighs and balances several factors. Each day, at CBS, the producers would meet with the broadcast's editor and writing staff. The meeting featured a sort of friendly tension between two groups of journalists. The film and tape people wanted their pieces included, the editor and the writers wanted time reserved for Walter to "tell" stories. There was a dialogue—"How much time do you need?" . . . "Is there a lot of news today?"—and they were only wrangling for a minute or so of air time. Walter's "magic time" was always five, but sometimes six, minutes. One of the men who wrote for Cronkite remembers a feeling of disdain on the part of the writers for the "production pieces." "The writers were in charge of the 'pure' news," he recalls. "Walter *told* that news. When it got to a report from the field or a produced analysis piece, the attitude was, it doesn't really count. It didn't matter what the piece was about." The ex-writer remembers "the editors would say 'We have nine minutes of news to tell.' The film producers would say 'We have five pieces we must run.' And the executive producer would say 'You shave here, they shave some there.' "

That sort of negotiation with an anchor also occurred at ABC where Barbara Walters had a "head of state" rule for her interviews. She regularly scored important "beats" by getting the central figure in a story to sit down with her for an exclusive interview. When Walters first began conducting interviews for the "ABC Evening News," their length was frequently determined by what else was on the broadcast that evening. Often, to her chagrin, a prime minister's appearance would be cut to a minute and a half because other correspondents covering breaking news demanded air time for their stories. As a result, news personalities started to turn down Walters' invitation to be interviewed. The solution was to set down a rule that guaranteed in advance four minutes of air time for any interview she conducted with a head of state. Working out that kind of compromise is just one of the many nonjournalistic diplomatic skills that successful executive producers need to call upon in order to keep things humming smoothly each day.

For the executive producer, today begins the night before when he or she makes a midnight telephone call to the Assignment Desk for a pre-bedtime rundown both of latest developments and of crew assignments for news coverage.

The Assignment Desk operates twenty-four hours a day, manned by editors who move crews and correspondents and tape editors and their equipment to the scene of events. Assignment Desk editors are combination logistical experts, journalists and idea people. They have to know plane schedules, satellite timings and whom to contact at local stations and overseas broadcasting systems. They are required to assess stories as they break on the wire services and decide how much effort to make to cover those stories.

Understanding how things operate enables good desk editors to suggest stories for coverage even before they happen. Knowing how the Soviet Union deals with recalcitrant satellite countries in Eastern Europe, for example, enables a news organization to have correspondents, producers and crews at potential flash points even before they burst into flame. When Poland started going through its Solidarity revolution in 1980 and 1981, the numbers of correspondents and crews inside Poland, and positioned in Austria and Sweden in order to reach Poland should the Russians invade, was constantly evaluated. The news-coverage budget would have been broken if a full-scale operation had been put into place and kept there for a long time in anticipation of a Russian military move into Poland. Based on reports from the field and also upon the skilled judgments of desk editors in New York, just the right number of personnel was kept on alert. The rest were allowed to keep working at other bureaus throughout Europe, ready to move but not tied down by false alarms.

Coping with breaking news is the heart of an assignment editor's job. Bill Seamans, the ABC correspondent in Israel, was certain that war was going to break out again in the Middle East in the early seventies. He knew that when hostilities began, Israeli censorship would immediately shut down communications. Working with the Assignment Desk in New York, Seamans devised an elaborate series of coded messages that could be used to transmit information about the scope of the hostilities. In case of all-out invasion by Arab forces into Israel, he was to call to New York, "Grandma has crossed the bridge." When war did break out, on Yom Kippur in 1973, Seamans got through to the Assignment Desk. "It's war!" he shouted into the phone. The assignment editor grabbed for the code book and asked: "You mean grandma has crossed the bridge?" "Who cares about your damned grandmother!" Seamans screamed. "I'm telling you it's war!"

In the early days of television news, there was a tendency to follow the wire service lead or to reproduce on film what the *New York Times* had reported that morning. That is far less so today. Wire services do supply the first tips that a story has broken but the Assignment Desk rapidly mounts a news-gathering effort that frequently surpasses wire information, particularly in television terms: discovering picture possibilities, getting library footage ready, and collecting background information for use by the field team as it heads into action.

It is a far cry from the way things worked at CBS News in 1953. In those days, we played follow the leader with the Associated Press "Budget"—that is, the list of stories that AP editors anticipate and schedule for transmission on their teleprinters shortly after 1:00 A.M. One morning at about 2:30, AP inserted a breaking story that had not been foreseen. A tornado had dipped into Kansas, destroying an entire town. I raced to the Assignment Desk editor with the wire copy in hand, asking urgently how soon crews and correspondents would be on the way to the scene. "If it isn't on the Budget," said the desk man, "it isn't worth covering—and it isn't on the Budget!" We had to wake up a supervisor to get things rolling. Television journalists were so unsure of their own judgment that the reinforcement of seeing something in print was an absolute requirement before anyone moved anywhere.

There are so many stories to cover that one must be cautious about assigning stories that won't make it to broadcast. In Washington, for example, so much goes on each day that many developments must be skipped. Assignments, however, are not haphazard. The White House is always covered. The gallery in the Capitol is always covered on both the Senate and the House sides. Congressmen are quickly interviewed for their reactions to developments on the floor or anywhere else in the world. Key committee hearings are generally open to the press and coverage of the major debates is mandatory. Sometimes, to find out what is going on inside a hearing, a camera crew and correspondent will be assigned inside and another team outside to catch witnesses or committee members on their way to or from the session.

At ABC the Assignment Desk nowadays issues a multipaged summary of "troop movements," giving in detail the prepositioning of crews, producers and correspondents for coverage of anticipated events. The "situationer," as it is called, also lists which other correspondents and production teams are being held in reserve at bureaus throughout the world, ready to move should events require new or strengthened coverage. The situationer is added to or altered as the day proceeds. It is the operational bible of a news organization and is as important in shaping the look of the nightly newscast as the executive producer's lineup.

Setting story assignments is a natural outgrowth of editorial policy. If fresh angles are asked for, correspondents start suggesting them. The best executive producers must keep an open mind. Nothing should be rejected out of hand because of lack of personal interest. Once, I wrote to the staff: "I do not care if the elevator operator or the lowest file clerk makes the suggestion. If he or she is interested in the story, then we should at least examine it in the light of other news developments and available resources." One senior producer at a major network managed to alienate his bureau staffs by hardly listening to suggestions and then commenting "That's a shitty idea." Pretty soon the calls stopped coming in. The result became painfully clear when good feature stories started showing up on the other networks' shows. When the bureaus were asked why certain stories had not been brought to the attention of New York, the replies were sarcastic and graphic: "We decided we didn't like suggesting 'shitty ideas,' so we didn't suggest the good ones either."

Assignment editors and producers cannot possibly come up with every idea. A television news organization must develop ways of funneling ideas into the center, sifting, accepting, rejecting and reshaping. They pay baseball players a lot of money to hit .300. They pay us less but we have to hit at least .800. That means eight out of ten times we have to be right.

Who are the people whose skills and training turn news and information into lineups and lineups into broadcasts?

At the bottom of the ladder is the desk assistant. A good D.A. is sometimes worth as much to the production and editorial team as anyone else in the place. In a well-organized television news operation, D.A.'s can keep right on moving toward the top. But starting at the bottom *means* starting at the bottom.

The desk assistant is responsible for changing the wire service teletype copy paper when it runs out, answering phones intelligently and taking messages carefully. Bulletins and other news wire special notices have to be brought to the attention of senior staff immediately. If D.A.'s learn to recognize the importance of newsbreaks and how to react quickly when they occur, they are acquiring a basic knowledge of what the news business is all about. There is a lot of running attached to the D.A.'s job. Scripts have to be collated and carried quickly to the studio or to the director or to other production centers within the news operation. It does matter if minutes are saved. Most desk assistants serving in a network newsroom will have observed every significant aspect of news-gathering and news production within a year. By then, promotion should be in the offing; if it isn't, it might be time to think about trying something else.

The next rank of support people is the researcher on the editorial side and the production associate, or P.A., on the production side. Researchers on an evening news telecast are combination fact-checkers and junior reporters, but primarily they are fact-checkers. A writer needs to know the date of a particular law in order to comment about its effect over "how many years?" A correspondent isn't sure whether Mr. Jones was Secretary of the Army or on the disarmament talks team under President Nixon. When researchers have demonstrated speed and accuracy and an innovative turn of mind in digging up elusive minutiae, they are given more rewarding and challenging assignments. The job involves much more than looking things up in library books; it is expected that a researcher will get on the telephone or go out to meet contacts.

Television news programs are composed of literally thousands of elements that flash by on the screen. Take a look at the evening news tonight and notice some of the details. The names of all the speakers in news reports are "supered"; that is, they appear superimposed on the lower third of your screen. Someone had to find out those names, get the correct title and spelling and insert that information into the electronic character generator. A picture appears behind or to the side of the anchor in most newscasts. Someone had to find out what picture would be needed or what map should be prepared. Stock prices and the Dow Jones averages are regularly displayed on the screen during most evening newscasts. They are regarded as an important service to viewers interested in the financial news of the day. Someone had to get the correct market closings. That someone is the production associate.

It is up to the production associate to find the right information and have it inserted into the computer's storage memory. P.A.'s must know how equipment works; the good ones learn how to improve the use of that equipment. One P.A. at ABC devised a storage and retrieval system for the computer so that it could recall pictures, in color, of all the news makers who were likely to appear on the broadcast for an entire month. He also worked out a file of city maps so that even the smallest streets could be found quickly and highlighted whenever news coverage required that kind of detail.

When more sophisticated videotape production techniques are called for in longer reports, like the Special Assignments, P.A.'s are involved in the process as soon as the raw tapes come in from the field. Longer reports are shaped over a period of days, if not weeks, by a computerized editing system. The computer "reads" a time code that has been electronically inserted on the videotape. Invisible to the viewer, the time code is seen only on special equipment in the editing room. Each frame of picture on the tape has a number. The P.A. views the raw tape as soon as it arrives and logs the numbers, identifying scene changes when they occur. The producer and the tape editor "instruct" the machine which shots they want to include in their final report. This is accomplished by punching in the time code numbers and waiting while the machine "searches" for the correct picture and ties it electronically into the edited piece where it belongs. It is a perfect example of how a lower member of the team—in this case the P.A.—makes the more difficult jobs simpler by performing the entry-level tasks well. Hours are saved or lost on the basis of the accuracy of the P.A.'s logs. Entire programs are redone because the "supers" are wrong or because the maps are unclear or the statistics on charts are inaccurate. The P.A.'s influence extends all the way to the top.

The team of field producer and correspondent is the core of

the news-gathering operation. Both members are responsible for acquiring information. The field producer straddles the editorial and technical sides involved in getting a story on the air. Though the correspondent writes the story and the field producer supervises the camera crew and edits the pictures, their interchange of ideas and skills must work together.

Most problems in television can be solved by advanced planning. If there is any business in which Murphy's Law applies, it is TV news. Murphy's Law—"Whatever *can* go wrong, *will* go wrong, at the *worst* possible moment"—is drilled into every field producer's brain. It is burned there because everyone has been caught short at least once by some detail that could have been anticipated beforehand. Telephone lines to the office must be located; electric power outlets to run the equipment and lights must be secured; food for meals and bathroom facilities for a long stakeout must be found. In some cases, it becomes the field producer's job to figure out escape routes in case the crowds riot or to decide whether the news team should wear protective helmets and bring gas masks.

In 1960, when I was field producer for CBS, I was stationed with a crew at Haneda Airport in Japan, awaiting President Eisenhower's press secretary, Jim Hagerty, who was to set up plans for the President's expected visit there. Even before Hagerty's plane arrived there were thousands of anti-American demonstrators, some armed with long staves, others with stones, all of them with terrible dispositions. A narrow bridge led from the airport to Tokyo; we knew that if the demonstrators were going to do something spectacular, that would be the place. It was obviously the place where Hagerty's car could be blocked, and that's where we stationed our cameras. The police and the demonstrators clashed violently. On one side, there were hundreds of screaming young men and women, some wearing helmets and all carrying long staves, which they poked toward the police lines. On the other side, there were ranks of police officers, some carrying shields to protect themselves. The screaming and chanting were continuous, and the stuttering of a helicopter's engines overhead added to the din. When the demonstrators tried to reach Hagerty's car, they literally drove a flying wedge into the police, forcing them back toward the bridge. The police lines held. Bodies were everywhere, clawing and pushing and always screaming.

Years later, after I had joined ABC News and Jim Hagerty was corporate vice-president, we reminisced about that day in Tokyo. He told me how rough it had been sitting in that car, waiting for heaven knows what as the mobs swirled around beating and rocking the car and coming dangerously close to turning it over. "Yeah, Jim," I said, "it was rough. But you were inside the car. I was on the outside getting slugged."

Later on that same trip, I was field producer for Walter Cronkite, who had flown to Tokyo to anchor "Eyewitness to History," CBS News's weekly broadcast. The Japanese Parliament —the Diet—is built on the top of a hill, and it was ringed with thousands of snake-dancing young men who were chanting anti-American, pro-Communist slogans. Searching for the proper location where Cronkite could stand, he and I found ourselves at the top of Diet Hill with our camera team at the bottom. We were the only Caucasians, dressed in Western clothes, anywhere in the area. We could not walk down the sidewalk: It was blocked with snake dancers. The center of the roadway was also blocked, so we took the only route possible. We joined the snake dancers. A tub-thumping tomtom kept a rhythm going, and it quickly dominated one's steps like a good dance beat that becomes hard to resist. The demonstrators formed a sort of chorus line that would jog in time to the left, then swing back to the right, advancing down the hill all the time. We tried to avoid their sharp zigzags, choosing instead to push straight down the roadway. We failed. The locked arms of the dancers penned us into their rhythmic protest. Before long our fellow dancers discovered us and recognized that we were different. First there were smiles, then some ripples of applause and, finally, audible cheers. To the demonstrators, we were an obvious display of Western solidarity. Walter remained cool, dispassionate and humorous. There was a sharp stage whisper: "If they see this at home . . . we're finished."

★   ★   ★

The line between field producer and correspondent can be narrow. Most producers are good reporters and writers, with perhaps an extra bit of skill in logistics, organization and the ability to visualize abstract ideas. Many producers have been pressed into service as broadcasters, filling in for vacationing correspondents or staking out a secondary aspect of a breaking story when it gets too big for one correspondent to cover. The "bug" to get on the air oneself does exist and it can be infectious. There are many instances where producers and correspondents begin to compete with one another in the same bureau. The results are inevitably disastrous and—as in a marriage that stops working—the solution is usually divorce.

Ego aside, appearing in front of the camera instead of working behind it can be a frustrating job. Correspondents are ordered on assignments by editors or producers in New York. Their work is assembled by producers, either in London or in New York. The level of interest in the story at home often determines what angles the correspondent must pursue in the field. Correspondents can quickly find themselves reduced to what seem like marionettes, moved about at a moment's notice by people who exercise command thousands of miles away.

The closest producer/correspondent relationship I developed during my overseas tour in the early sixties was with Dan Schorr, then CBS News Bonn correspondent. Once Dan came up with an idea for a half-hour special on Hungary five years after the Russian invasion. His title was "Hungary, the Great Eraser." The Communist government installed after the Hungarian uprising had gone to great lengths to eliminate any traces of the fighting that had raged in the country in 1956. Together we plotted some ways of visualizing that effort; some way to show the before and after. Through the years I have sharpened my facility for visual recall. I can see pictures once and can recall them, almost shot for shot, for a considerable amount of time. At my base in London, I collected much of the film that had been shot during the fighting in Hungary. By the time Schorr and I were ready to go into Hungary to begin shooting his report, the entire revolution was stored in my head in pictures.

Foreign television teams, operating behind the Iron Curtain,

are usually assigned a "guide." It is also customary for the visiting team to pay the guide a salary and to pay for his or her
meals and out-of-town lodgings. In our case, the "guide" was
provided for us by the Foreign Ministry, and his efforts to dissuade us from visiting certain places were relentless.

The best example of the "Great Eraser" existed in a square
facing what had been the headquarters for the AVO, the Hungarian secret police. During the uprising, that square had been
attacked by the rebels. The headquarters building had been
seized, and AVO agents had been marched out and machine-
gunned to death. Some had also been hanged from trees in a
small park across the street. It was one of the scenes that I had
viewed and reviewed in my screenings. Since then the square
had been completely transformed. Instead of a park with trees,
we found a playground with swings and seesaws. The headquarters building was now an apartment house. Traffic had been
rerouted. It looked totally different. Yet there was one familiar
clue: a movie house on a corner opposite a fountain with an art
deco marquee and a circular basin large enough to have once
been a fountain. Our "guide" kept ridiculing our efforts, saying
that there had been no AVO headquarters and no mass killing
there. We filmed anyway and asked for permission to climb to
the roof of the movie theater to take some pictures. We intended
to show the quiet scene, erased of all signs of combat, then
dissolve into scenes showing the battle going on at the exact
spot.

Our "guide's" protestations were effective, and we were
starting to doubt our judgment, questioning whether the climb
was going to be worth the effort. We got onto the roof and set
up the camera for some pan shots from the "apartment house"
to the playground. While the cameraman was making his shots,
I wandered around the roof. There was a copper rain gutter
around the edge of a small structure on top of a water tower.
And there I discovered something that made it all worthwhile.
In the corner of the rain gutter, wedged under a bent piece of
copper, was a spent rifle cartridge case—a small bit of proof the
"Great Eraser" had missed.

Every journalist needs a reservoir of skepticism. It doesn't matter whether one is dealing with a Communist government whose view of journalists is that they are either spies or instruments of government progaganda; with local authorities whose view of journalists is that they are either toadies for officials at City Hall or bastards who are poking into every nook and cranny; with businesses whose view of journalists is that they are either trying to destroy the American way of life or that they are serving a useful purpose by recording our successes. Journalists have to keep probing for the facts. Disbelief, demands for proof and a willingness to trust one's own instincts about a story are necessary attributes.

Field producers and correspondents are the only ones who actually "see" the stories. They write and edit their reports in the field before feeding them back. That means the choices at headquarters are substantially narrowed by decisions made earlier in the field by the field producers and correspondents.

There is much in a television film or videotape report that remains immutable. The pictures taken by the camera crew to illustrate the story are fixed on the tape or film. The questions asked by the correspondent interviewing a personality involved in a story are recorded on the sound track and in every frame of film or tape. The accompanying narration by the correspondent is, for all practical purposes, unchangeably contained on the audio tape or on the sound track. An omitted question cannot be inserted by simply telephoning the subject of the interview and asking for a few more moments of his or her time. Newspaper and newsmagazine reporters can fill in the blanks in their stories by calling back. An omitted sequence of pictures (establishing shots, close-ups, relationship shots or "cutaways") that is essential to illustrate a story cannot be sketched in by an artist or supplied from a film library of similar pictures taken at a different time. Of course, a camera crew could be sent back to reshoot the film or tape, but that takes time and money, and in the highly competitive atmosphere surrounding the three network television news broadcasts, a day's delay in completing a story often means the opposition will have been given the chance to score a "beat."

So much material is received each day from overseas and from bureaus around the country that an entire section of the staff is devoted to "tape operations." Producers and "spot" producers assigned to the videotape rooms can literally construct a complete news report out of dozens of bits and pieces. Furthermore, they can do the job under time pressures that would lead others to nervous breakdowns. An excellent example of their skill occurred the night martial law was declared in Poland in December 1981. Everyone wanted to know what the Russians would do, and Anne Garrels, the ABC correspondent in Moscow, finally found some tidbits of information, which she included in a script she telephoned into the tape room just moments before the broadcast went on the air. Garrels inserted visual references to Soviet tanks, to Soviet President Brezhnev and to decisions made at a recent Communist party congress. Those references became the foundation upon which the spot producers built the piece from file film. Pictures of Russian weapons, of Brezhnev and of the party congress were combined with the Garrels script. The result was a coherent illustrated report that added to the audience's understanding.

The strain of editing a two-minute news report for insertion in a broadcast while the broadcast is *already* on the air is immense, but it is done night after night.

At the next level are the senior producers. These are the people who determine if a story has been adequately covered and whether editorial cuts should be made. The time limits of the broadcast frequently require producers to shorten pieces after they are fed in from the field. In some cases, correspondents deliberately overwrite their scripts, giving senior producers the option of editing them down. This editorial function is crucial. The producer's and senior producer's judgment and recommendation about the worth of a report and its optimum length influence the executive producer when he or she decides whether to include it in the broadcast.

The tier of senior producers composes the next-to-last decision-making cadre of the broadcast. At this level, final script

erage plans are okayed and editorial control concerning fairness
and balance is exercised. It is the editorial heart of a nightly
newscast, and it is marked by a high degree of experience. Most
people at the senior producer level have served in the field, have
been writers, and know a good deal about the FCC regulations
requiring fairness, balance and equal time.

It is a blessing when the senior producers can assume burdens
with the same sureness as the executive producer. No one individual can handle all the phone calls, make all the contacts and
set up all the courses of action. Dick Richter was the senior
producer who sat at my left all through the years I ran the "ABC
Evening News." Somehow we could both be on separate telephones and yet know what the other was saying and deciding.
When people spoke to Dick, they in effect spoke to me. We
could actually finish one another's sentences, and our judgments
about stories were usually identical. The opportunity to be part
of an interchangeable system of editorial decision making made
the stress of running the operation tolerable.

Richter was the house psychiatrist. He would stay on the
phone for long periods of time nursing correspondents through
their difficulties. He knew whose marriages were in trouble,
who was drinking too much and who needed to be brought in
for a rest. That meant not just working ten- or twelve-hour
days, but also walking into the house at night just in time to
receive calls from correspondents almost anywhere in the
world. One correspondent in the Los Angeles bureau timed his
calls so that they came between the Richter family's main course
and dessert. The call would always start, "Hi, Dick. Had your
coffee yet?"

Once his role was extended from psychiatrist to long-distance
referee. Richter picked up the Washington tie line one day to
hear a frantic plea instead of the usual pitch for more time for
one of the Washington spots. It was a writer beseeching him to
do something. It seemed that an enraged correspondent felt he
was being given short shrift and had lost his temper to the point
of seizing a producer's tie in one hand and slapping him with
the other. Do something? Richter was more than two hundred
miles away. Fortunately, the correspondent's temper cooled,

and Richter did not have to jump into a phone booth, strip to his Superman costume and zoom to the rescue.

Richter was a vital lightning rod who defused a lot of personnel problems before they erupted into unresolvable conflicts. It freed me from that duty, which is recognizably important but can get in the way of handling the primary responsibilities of producing the broadcast.

Richter's coequal in the operation was David Buksbaum. To be aided by a combination as strong as Buksbaum and Richter was a miracle. Buksbaum ran the "back of the shop." The film editors and videotape editors all reported to him. He could take absolute oatmeal—poor pictures and a bad script that had arrived from the field—and turn it into an extraordinary piece. His skill with pictures and words became a standard for which the other network newscasts aimed. Correspondents who saw videotaped copies of their work after it had passed through Buksbaum's massage were frequently amazed at how good their work looked. They knew it had been done in the editing process.

Buksbaum also provided the energy spark that lifted the shop to a constantly higher level of achievement each day. One of the film editors said, "Buks can motivate a snail to win a race." Around the office, the word was that if Buksbaum was told in the morning to move the Empire State Building two feet to the left, he would have it done by lunchtime. He put so much of himself into the job each day—cutting, handling the incoming feeds, and editing raw material down to finished pieces even while the broadcast was already on the air. Buksbaum saved the reputation of many less-than-competent correspondents. One correspondent, sent to Chappaquiddick to cover the investigation of Senator Edward Kennedy's accident resulting in the death of a female acquaintance, came back with little film and an on-camera standup that showed Kennedy arriving at the courthouse.

"What did you say in the film?" Buksbaum asked.

"I don't remember," the correspondent replied.

"What happened in the courtroom?"

"I didn't go inside."

Buksbaum shouted to the desk assistant for some Associated Press wire copy and pounded out a script on his beat-up manual typewriter. "Here, you dumb-ass," he said. "Take this into the announcer's booth and record it. We'll try to make something out of the shit you brought back!" The man did what he was told, and, as Buksbaum recalled it, holding up his thumb and forefinger less than an eighth of an inch apart, "We made it on the air by that much."

Pictures are important in television, but words come first. In descending order, the idea, the words, the pictures. Words are the most flexible tool. A good writer can turn almost useless pictures into important information.

Phil Lewis was one of the writers on the "CBS Morning Show" staff in 1953. He transformed the films from the previous night's "Evening News" into suitable material. He couldn't change the pictures, of course, but he certainly could work with the narration. In those early days, we had only a small library of stock footage: scenes taken earlier for other stories but useful to illustrate some newsworthy point. It was during the Korean War, and each morning at about 3:00 A.M. the latest war communiqué would reach us from UN Supreme Headquarters in Seoul. There were always reports on dogfights between American F-86 Sabrejets and the early MIG-15s. We had several filmed sequences of Sabrejets doing aerial acrobatics, peeling off in combat dives and looping around in the sky. Lewis used and reused them day after day to illustrate each day's reported battle action—the same planes doing the same power dives from the same formations. "American Sabrejets *like these,*" he would write, "today fought fierce dogfights over the Yalu River." We did the best we could with what we had.

Unlike a newspaper, a television news report is a continuous ribbon of time, picture, sound and narration. A television viewer has to stay all the way through a report without interruption in order to absorb everything that is in it. If you are reading a newspaper report, you can answer the phone and come back to the paper, even hours later. You can start again at the beginning. If you become confused by poor writing in paragraph twenty-two, you can go back to the top to find out where you lost the thread. Watching a television news report is something else. If the phone rings, the report has been completed by the time you come back. If you lose the thread, it is lost. For a variety of reasons there is an additional burden on television news correspondents to be clear and well organized.

Good television writing comes first from a decent vocabulary. Then one must be able to organize a coherent narrative and make sure that the words do not conflict with the pictures. When the two components of a television report—pictures and narration—are well blended, the transmission of information is geometrically more effective than either of the components alone.

Scripts can be rewritten to take full advantage of relevant pictures. As an example, one memo to the staff explained: "Dan Cordtz recently completed a script explaining inflationary pressures. He wrote (first) that government budget deficits and (second) increasing money supplies were two reasons for the increase in inflation. On examining available video, the producer located film of new dollar bills printed at the mint. Cordtz rewrote his script, changing its order. Now, he cited the money supply first and, against those words, the dollars being printed made sense. Then he cited budget deficits, and the dollars, already established visually, continued on the screen. We were able to make better use of available pictures by the simple expedient of changing the order of presentation. It's a small point, but the result was an effective meshing of script content and picture, and a more cogent explanation of spiraling inflation. Scripts that include brief reference to a picture turn stock footage from 'wallpaper' to illustration."

"Wallpaper" was my term for pictures slapped into a piece with no apparent explanation. Television news cannot demand that its audience work in order to understand content. It all goes by so rapidly that if the content isn't immediately comprehensible the result will be confusion.

Good writing is the starting point. Each line of copy has to be crisp and informative. "Only time will tell" and "tension continues to mount" are two phrases that always receive the editor's blue pencil. We devised a writer's map of Clichéland, which was Xeroxed and distributed to offenders. The geography centered on a body of water called the Sea of Troubles. It was divided in two by almost touching peninsulas: Sword's Point and the Point of No Return. In between flowed Dire Straits. Off in the distance was Tension Mounts complete with its Vale of Tears. My favorite locale was the Cultural Desert, which featured the Last Resort as a vacation spot. Bid's Fair was an amusement park, and most urban residents lived in the Significant Development. There were many more locales on the map that served as a Ready Reminder to writers not to stray off the Straight and Narrow.

And the fewer words, the better. If a picture can do the work, let it. Narration should add to what the picture already tells us. A few years ago there was a gasoline shortage in Los Angeles. For days, lines of automobiles jammed gas stations waiting for four or five gallons of gas. Los Angeles has a notoriously inadequate public transportation system, and when the gas shortage turned into a drought, the buses were unable to cope with the increase in riders. I was on the West Coast at the time, and I was disappointed because the right pictures were not taken by the videotape crew. They had shots of cars waiting on gasoline lines and, separately, pictures of buses. They had no shots of buses and cars together that would indicate their relationship. The producer should have directed the crew to take shots of loaded buses passing stalled cars. That would have captured the essence of the story. And because the pictures did not tell the whole story, the correspondent had to add extra words; time was "wasted."

Occasionally, correspondents called in with "writer's block" —a sudden loss of ability to pull together the strands of a story; the script simply wasn't coming together. The call was a plea for editorial supervision. The senior producers would be told the story elements—what each of the filmed or taped interviews contained—and asked to help construct a narrative line.

One field team had a particularly weak correspondent who was floored by the complexity of reporting how uranium prod-

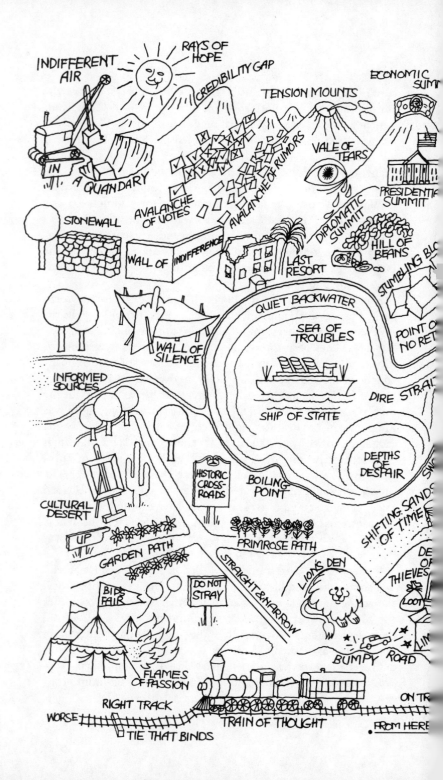

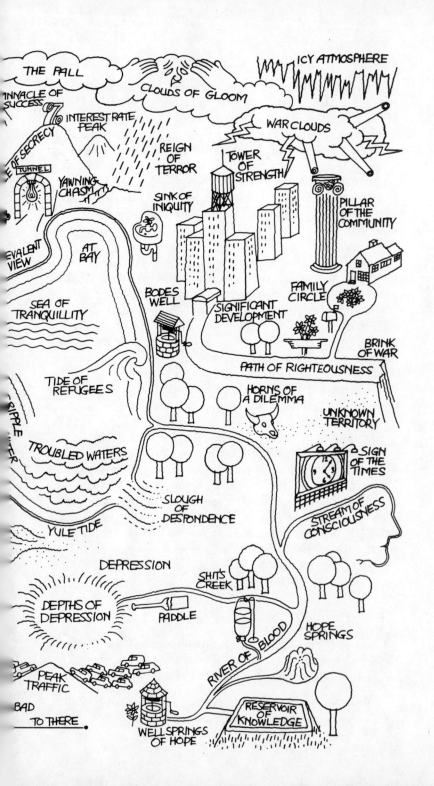

ucts were transported from their point of manufacture in Ohio to O'Hare Airport in Chicago for shipment overseas. The radio-active material was reportedly conveyed by an unguarded truck to an unguarded air terminal for a flight to Europe in a hijackable plane. It was a particularly dangerous situation in light of ter-rorist activities, which were on the increase at the time. The script was a mishmash. The tale wandered around almost as much as the uranium on its unguarded voyage from Ohio to Europe. It was going to take a lot of dictation from the home office to make the story comprehensible. I tried to sketch out a story line for the correspondent. "This morning, sixty-two pounds of uranium left this factory in Ohio," I dictated, "begin-ning a trip to O'Hare Airport in Chicago." I went on, detailing a narrative flow. "Show me how the truck drove through the countryside; how the driver stopped for breakfast at a diner leaving the truck parked in an open parking lot with sixty-two pounds of uranium; then bring us to the gates of the airport, through the gates and into the unguarded freight forwarding shed. Get shots of the uranium being loaded by aircraft handlers and wait around for the plane to take off. Finally, wrap up the piece by telling us how that sixty-two pounds of uranium could be used to make sixty-two A-bombs or whatever."

About an hour later, the correspondent called back with his script. He read it to Mike Stein, the broadcast's editor, who had to fact-check it. "This morning, sixty-two pounds of uranium left this factory in Ohio," the story began. It went on to describe the trip and the dangers and the potentially horrible prospect of sixty-two bombs. The narrative worked. The conversation had helped the reporter organize his thoughts. But Stein was curious about something. "Where did we get the figure about sixty-two pounds of uranium and sixty-two bombs?"

"Av said it."

"Av?"

"Yes, Av."

Stein put the phone aside, looked across at me and asked, "Where did you get the sixty-two bombs and the sixty-two pounds of uranium?"

"Sixty-two pounds of uranium?" I repeated. "I don't know.

I always say that. Sixty-two is the number I use when I don't know the number. It's like "frammis' or 'whatsis' or 'thinga-majig.' "

Stein got back on the phone. "I think," he said coolly, "you'd better do some more investigating to find out how much stuff they are actually shipping. In the future," he added, "if you ever hear the number sixty-two from Westin's mouth, don't believe it."

"Sixty-two pounds" became the office catchword for the un-verified facts and off-the-wall conclusions that occasionally pop up in scripts.

Occasionally, correspondents are at a loss for a way to wrap up their pieces. "Air time is too valuable on ABC," I wrote in a memo, "to waste on what we shall call 'music up and under' or 'time alone will tell' conclusions." The number of reports that had ended with those kind of meaningless phrases was ex-asperating. Sometimes correspondents would introduce com-pletely new thoughts in their summaries. One correspondent presented a report on housing conditions, which had been illus-trated by perfectly acceptable-looking middle-class row houses in a rundown part of Brooklyn. Her on-camera close, however, talked about the decay in the houses and how they were easily the seedbed for urban unrest.

"Where are the decaying buildings?" I asked.

"They were all around," she replied. "You should have seen what was on the next block."

"Too bad you didn't show them in your report," I said. From that experience and from similar ones through the years, it be-came a cardinal rule that "conclusions must be based on infor-mation contained in the body of the report. Do not introduce unexplained ideas or conjectures when signing off," I wrote in a letter to correspondents. "Summing up must tell us, insofar as possible, why it happened, what it means, and, if you know, what will happen next."

"What does it mean?" was a phrase intended to provide a signpost for the audience, inviting it to pay closer attention. It was to become a way to pull together all the information just reported in case the viewer had missed something. To explain how the device would work, I wrote: "Our goal will be to give the viewers all the information about important stories in a form that can be absorbed at the dinner hour with all the distractions that implies. Recent experience . . . has shown that audiences want to understand what the reportage means to them. 'What does it mean?' should become the editorial guideline for all pieces of hard news reporting."

This letter, of the several dozen written over a decade, remains the most important to me. It translated an attention-getting device, a rhetorical question, into an important element in all our reports. A specific example from 1975 dealt with an advance report showing elaborately staged preparations in Saigon for an expected visit of a congressional delegation. It was suggested in the hypothetical example that after showing the flags and bunting and the staged briefings that awaited the American lawmakers, the correspondent should conclude as follows:

> What does this mean? It means that President Thieu has recognized he must impress seven American congressmen with the need to change their colleagues' minds about aid to South Vietnam. It also means that if Thieu fails to do that, the government here will undergo a sharp decline in military strength in the face of strong North Vietnamese and Viet Cong pressure.

Admittedly, the sample script, written as an example, was superficial itself. The expectation was that the correspondent on the scene in Saigon would add more substance. Still, the idea was that the phrase "What does this mean?" would lead to a summary, putting the material that preceded it into perspective. Before too long, as correspondents got the hang of the concept and modified it with their phrases, the level of clarity and pertinence increased dramatically. Viewers wrote to say, "I never knew that." Our goal, getting facts across with increased understanding, was closer.

The limited time on the air for any correspondent's report can unintentionally drive reporting toward what I called "here they come, there they go." If correspondents had done insufficient preparation for those kinds of assignments they were reduced unhappily to describing simply what the pictures showed, that is, delegates coming and going, nothing added. Some method had to be found to let reporters tell what they knew within the time constraints of a half-hour nightly broadcast.

To maintain a fast-paced broadcast and yet improve the quality of reporting, I refined the "whip-around" technique first used during the sixties on the "CBS Morning News." In a "whip-around," one correspondent begins the story and leads to another who picks up the reporting, adding some more details before handing it on to another. The editorial flow moves rapidly and smoothly. At ABC, we would break up a story into its component parts, assigning a different correspondent to each of them. Whereas CBS and NBC might allot three or four minutes to one reporter's effort, we would divide the story among two or three people. The benefit, aside from the pace, was that each individual reporter had to be concerned only with a small part of the total story and could hone and sharpen the script to cover the most important element in that smaller section. The correspondent was encouraged to glean tidbits of information by prowling the corridors of the Capitol, the White House, the Pentagon or some manufacturer's office, and the audience was offered a more informative piece of reportage.

"Whip-around" requires a considerable amount of production coordination. Show producers have to coordinate the editorial flow so that each piece leads directly into the next. In some cases, correspondents have to introduce themselves. "This is Steve Geer in Los Angeles and here, the consumer price index rise is reflected in higher gasoline prices. . . ." In other cases, copy lines are drafted to pick up from the previous report. "If crime is on the upswing in urban centers like Philadelphia, the picture here in the rural areas of Arkansas is not much different. . . ." When the "whip-around" works, it is a first-class television digest of information.

When supplying pieces for a broadcast, the correspondents in the field and the staff all along the transmission belt must know what style of presentation is wanted, what kinds of stories are to be looked for, and how one report is to mesh with another. Having served overseas, I know how it feels to be at the long end of a telephone line or telex circuit. There are so many chances for misunderstanding that extraordinary measures need to be taken to keep everyone informed about home office attitudes. "You guys in the home office don't understand the problems of those of us in the field!" is a common complaint heard throughout the news business. One correspondent used to call the telephone a "barbed wire network" because of the prickly conversations that were held with New York.

I used to send a weekly letter to the correspondents that included some chitchat about ratings or a particular filming technique, but its real purpose was to have them look ahead toward developments in the news. In 1969, just after joining ABC News, I wrote to the correspondents: "I am operating on the theory that a producer should be aggressive and 'produce' a broadcast, not wait for news to happen in order to scramble after it. Anticipating events is most important." If there is any summary of how a news organization ought to operate, that's my view of it. Anticipation means applying one's experience and judgment to trends that are unfolding in front of us. There are patterns in the news that are lying in plain view to be seen and acted upon.

In March of 1969, I wrote to the ABC correspondents in Saigon, setting a tone and direction for our coverage of the Vietnam War. Much of television's coverage of the war had concentrated on "search and destroy" missions, "body counts" and pictures of combat. There was good reason to support that kind of coverage. There were Americans fighting and dying out there. It seemed to me, however, that by 1969 viewers needed something more: interpretation. As Mike Wallace put it, we had been covering the war by "shooting bloody," showing the gore almost to the exclusion of everything else. It was time to "shoot" something else. I wrote, "I think the time has come to shift some of our focus from the battlefield, or more specifically from American military involvement with the enemy, to themes and stories under the general heading 'We are on our way out of Viet Nam.' "

The idea was to develop stories that would show whether the American effort in defending South Vietnam had really been worthwhile. Had we set up and were we defending a democratic government that could stand on its own? Was the infrastructure of the government in Saigon sound or was it likely to fall apart as soon as American strength disappeared? In a follow-up telex to the Saigon bureau staff, I asked for stories about province chiefs and their efficiency or corruption; about "the most representative opposition leader"; about food distribution; the economic strength of South Vietnam; and about the medical care for victims of the war. The responses changed the course of ABC's coverage of the war.

All throughout the war, television was the flash point for the nation's emotions about the United States' involvement in Southeast Asia. We were accused of prolonging the conflict because we had broadcast statements by government leaders who predicted "light at the end of the tunnel," and, alternately, because we destroyed America's will to fight by showing casualties and dealing with body counts.

After the fighting was over, General William Westmoreland, the former commander of American forces in Vietnam, visited us one day in the ABC newsroom. Westmoreland made it clear that he believed that TV news, along with other news media, played a significant role in forcing the collapse of the American efforts to persevere and win. The general, retired by then, had been invited to drop in for a drink by Harry Reasoner. After they chatted for a while, the two men emerged from Reasoner's office, and Reasoner escorted Westmoreland to the elevator. Just as he was leaving the newsroom, the general turned to wave goodbye, saying in a loud voice, "Harry, don't let them make you say anything you don't want to!" Westmoreland was absolutely convinced that the broadcast producers had the power of making Reasoner say whatever they pleased.

My weekly letters were candid requests for frank reactions to the way we behind the executive producer's desk were perceiving the world. "There are a number of general trends that I discern in talking to people around the country and I would like each correspondent, producer, and bureau staff member to think about ways we can cover them." The invitation was spelled out with specifics—about busing and its effects on the 1976 presidential campaign; the use of presidential vetoes to block congressional actions in a head-to-head confrontation between the White House and Capitol Hill; an emerging campaign against the press and against the freedom-of-information "tide" that began with Watergate.

Chief Justice Warren E. Burger's antipathy toward the news media and the rebirth of the "siege mentality" in the government (reminiscent of the Nixon years) were examples of the kinds of stories I expected everyone to be watching for. In one "editorial projection" circulated to the staff, I reflected on a philosophic trend that seemed to be growing. "It's an attitude by many people that there is nothing that can be done to cope with government and the courts as those bodies profoundly alter what is perceived to be the 'American Way of Life.' This takes the form of a feeling of helplessness or ennui or resentment. Stories will show up which will help us illustrate this development. There is a lot of recent social research which documents this phenomenon. It has not yet reached the strength of what Frederick Lewis Allen called 'a national malaise,' but it sure is around." I concluded that "I'd welcome stories that either refute this concern or demonstrate it. I encourage thought about it."

It was important to continue to set standards of reporting and journalism, not because the staff was not already performing at a high level, but because the competition, CBS and NBC, was also stepping up its efforts. In the drive to become the number-one television news organization, the necessity of clear direction remained paramount.

"It is becoming more and more obvious that good reporting is the greatest need on TV news today," I wrote. "Perhaps it is because more and more people are depending on TV for all their news. Perhaps it is because TV news people themselves are becoming more sophisticated in gathering and presenting the news. But whatever the cause, flossy and generalized rhetoric is no longer an acceptable substitute for specific hard facts . . . and casual appearances on the scene are no longer an acceptable substitute for immersing yourself in the story. If you haven't dug beyond the surface for the true meat of the story, you're going to be found out; if only because a competitor will do the job right."

The weekly letter became an integral part of our production as well as our editorial system. Some of the notes were quite short, triggered by a particularly good effort by a correspondent, or by a particularly bad one. "Reporting hard news is serious business," I wrote. "There is a place for light stories, of course, but ABC News correspondents are supposed to clarify complicated issues for our viewers. Making light of intricate subject matter in a hard news broadcast makes you look foolish and serves you, ABC News, and our viewers poorly. It must not occur."

The memoranda and letters dealt with production techniques so that standards of presentation would be consistent. They included admonitions to "avoid using a close-up of the interviewer as set-up material. Watching a man's lips move in a close-up while hearing a correspondent's narration is confusing. Try to use a different shot which avoids the frustration of seeing him speak without being able to hear him."

Television edits its interviews by using "cutaways" or "reverse shots." Those are pictures of the correspondent listening to the speaker. Whenever those pictures appear, it usually means that some of what the person interviewed said has been cut out. Newspapers use a similar technique when they insert the ellipsis (" . . . ") in the middle of a speech or quotation. There is no way three dots can add editorial bias to the story. A cutaway of a smiling correspondent can. Correspondents were told: "We should make it a standard rule for all correspondents to remain impassive during their reverse reaction shots for cutaways. A nod of the head or a smile implies agreement with the thoughts being expressed in the interview. Correspondents neither agree nor disagree, they simply report."

News teams spend a lot of time discussing the use of pictures and the need for imagination and coordination. I paid a lot of attention to them.

"Good television reporting requires concern for good pictures," I wrote. "There has been a tendency to substitute the easy shot for the more difficult one. Too often, correspondents' narrations are keyed to street scenes or other generic or meaningless pictures." That was particularly bothersome to me. Street scenes are the ultimate "wallpaper." They do not specifically illustrate any editorial point; it was a constant theme in my letters to direct field teams away from using them unless they had a definite purpose.

"Minimumly," I wrote, "the correspondent and the cameraman must have a clear understanding of what the opening shot should be and this understanding should often extend to the final shot of the story as well." We were trying to extract from the field team all the creativity and imagination that it contained. Although there is a hierarchy running downward from the correspondent to the producer and then to the camera crew and editor, it was always my view, born from working in the field, that superb crews frequently saved stories with their enterprise. It was important that they keep on doing it.

"Starting immediately," the letter began, "*all* members of the production team must work toward improving the product. We will no longer accept the film editor's excuse that he did not have the pictures. The editor can ask the correspondent to rewrite the narration to make sense out of the available pictures. The cameraman can no longer claim he did not know what we needed. He must ask the producer and the correspondent. And the simplest exchange of ideas between the correspondent and the cameraman will be the only acceptable way to begin work on any story."

Under the deadline pressure of getting a story edited and transmitted, attention to picture detail is always a problem. Too often the competition seemed to have shots that were better framed, closer to the action, or that followed the action more effectively even though our cameras were side-by-side with those of CBS and NBC. On those occasions, outtakes were reviewed after the fact. In almost every case, pictures nearly identical to the competition's *were* available but had not been selected in the editing process.

From time to time, reports were enhanced by electronically

printing the text of messages or documents on the screen. When those words appeared, the correspondent's narration would literally repeat them, reinforcing them in the interest of emphasis and clarity for the viewer. Once the technique was used regularly, it became necessary to set some standards for it. The letter to correspondents one week said, "If the words superimposed on the screen fight the words being spoken by the narrator, the result is distracting and confusing. Producers and correspondents must make every effort to see that the words being spoken are *exactly* the same as the words being supered."

I am constantly distracted when I watch weather reports on local television stations. They super the temperature and other forecast information over a variety of pictures that show people strolling or children skating or traffic moving. There is so much going on behind the letters that I cannot absorb the information I am supposed to concentrate on. "The background pictures used as the base for supering should be more carefully chosen. There should not be bright colors and the shots should be relatively static, free from wild pans and zooms. In fact, where possible, a 'frozen' frame should be selected."

A few years ago, I was a fellow at Duke University in communications theory. Distinguished newspapermen and women —some of them openly critical of TV news—sat down with broadcasters for several weekends to examine each other's craft. I brought along a short excerpt from a report that dealt with a dam break disaster in West Virginia. As part of that program, the engineer in charge of inspecting waste dams in the West Virginia hills had been interviewed. He was supposed to know how safely the illegal dams were constructed. Viewers saw the engineer, confronted on camera by evidence in the form of documents, diagrams or transcripts of testimony by others, literally break out in a sweat. He was asked about his qualifications to judge dam safety. His Adam's apple pumped and he gulped frequently for breath as the questioner bore in on his serious lack of credentials to do the job he had been hired to do. The fact that more than two hundred people had died because one of the dams in his charge had broken was in everyone's mind. The segment demonstrated, even to the severest critic present in the room, the essential strength of television. There wasn't anyone there who disagreed with my contention that at least in that instance, TV was more effective because it combined the three elements of sight, ambient or natural sound, and narration.

Michael J. Arlen, *The New Yorker*'s thoughtful commentator on broadcasting, wrote in his book *View from the Highway:* "Criticisms of television news have multiplied in recent years as network news operations have grown in size and recognized importance. Intellectuals have criticized 'big news' for being too deferential to the administration in power . . . for being too slick in its presentation . . . and, in general, for giving the mass audience what it wants, rather than what it 'ought to have' . . . which, one gathers, is what intellectuals want." Arlen is absolutely correct.

If news has become "popular," then it ought to stay that way, and its executives and producers ought to take reasonable steps to ensure that its popularity and viewership continue to increase. Even one more interested viewer means one more informed citizen. No one's journalism "stripes" will diminish by writing a less convoluted script; by combining pictures well with narration; by using new electronic technology to explain complex issues and to reinforce spoken words. When all that happens, television news—*broadcast journalism*—is at its very best.

In the fall of 1981, a correspondent sent in a report from London about the resurgence of the miniskirt. He concentrated his pictures on the risen hemlines and female legs. His on-camera conclusion had a touch of double-entendre. The New York producers were concerned that his remarks were sexist. They called in a number of women producers and asked them to review the piece. Did they find it offensive? Only after they all had declared that they saw nothing wrong with the words or the pictures in the context of the story was the report cleared for broadcast.

Men still run television news, but more and more women are moving ahead in the business, and their presence affects the way male managers think. They have become sensitive to the concerns of women. They have altered story content because women have been around to advise them, and they have made story assignments because women in the newsroom have pointed out the importance of the developments from their point of view. What has happened to female journalists is very much part of the story of television news. Their emergence in sufficient numbers to have influence has and will continue to affect how news is gathered and presented each night. It wasn't always that way and television news is better for the change.

Harry Reasoner was once something of a male chauvinist. Before he recanted publicly, in a CBS documentary, he told me that though he thought I was a good executive producer, one of my primary shortcomings was that I had put too many women in our newsroom. Not *too* many, I replied, but a good many. I claim responsibility for promoting more women than any other executive in TV news. Others may also claim that honor and if they can prove it, I say more power to them.

There was tokenism in TV news in the sixties. Women could be researchers or news writers and they could be "assistants to" and "associates of." They rarely got the designated slot in the table of organization that carried the full-fledged assistant producer or associate producer title along with the responsibilities. They also didn't get the increased pay that those titles carried. Many quit in frustration; others hung on, hoping for an opening.

Women reporters were too often perceived as sex objects when they first appeared regularly on assignments. Ann Compton, for example, had problems as a TV-station reporter at the annual sessions of the Virginia legislature in Richmond. Men who were straight-laced lawmakers in the morning turned into lecherous stalkers at night. Compton would be invited out for dinner, and she would say, "Why not? I'm a reporter and he's a source." Then it would be made perfectly clear that what was expected was something more than dessert and coffee. Compton got over her naiveté very quickly and extricated herself from after-office-hours meetings. Later, during the Ford administration, she became the first woman correspondent regularly assigned to the White House by a network. Being a woman there was an asset because it gave Ann greater visibility over what she described as "the gray pinstripe suits." Officials were always polite, returned her calls rapidly and gave her extra time to pursue stories with them. It was quite a different atmosphere from the Virginia legislature.

The same difference in attitudes also began showing up in newsrooms by the mid-seventies. Ellen Rossen joined a network news operation in 1978 after working since 1972 at local stations and a news syndication service. She believes women by then had an easier time finding jobs that required editorial and production skills. "They no longer had to start as secretaries," she said. "They were employed at all levels of reporting and production. The level of consciousness had been raised considerably." Affirmative-action programs at the networks and stations had a lot to do with the concerted effort to recruit women. There was a reservoir of bright applicants for every job.

Sharon Young, vigorous, very professional and tough, is one of the veteran field producers for ABC News. She has found that a woman in the field has to establish her credentials more firmly than a man. For the first three or four days on an assignment, "it's all blue jeans and bush jackets; then, when the rest of the press corps starts taking you seriously, you can go back to wearing skirts, blouses or dresses." Although patronizing attitudes continue to diminish, Young says there are still a lot of "There, there, it will be all rights" handed out by male supervisors who feel they have to calm a woman down.

Women in the business are "gutsier" than they used to be. They demand attention for their ideas, respect for their performance, and express opinions openly and professionally. Women know definitively where they want to go in their careers. That's become more apparent as each job category opened to women and as women demonstrated that they were equal to men in the same jobs. Now no category is unattainable, not even the anchor chair.

Barbara Walters was the first regular anchor at the network level, but long before that, women were in key positions at local stations. At first, many were simply news readers, delivering copy prepared by others. Gradually, women were hired to go out and cover stories, returning to the studio at the end of the day to be part of an anchor "team." Since Barbara Walters made the move, she has been followed by others at all the networks. Jessica Savitch and Jane Pauley are on the air at NBC; Diane Sawyer and Leslie Stahl appear on CBS.

For all the progress, there exist some lingering restraints on the willingness to hand out field assignments without regard to sex. Yet it isn't necessarily a matter of home office male chauvinism when there is reluctance to send a woman into a danger zone. And practical considerations in the field must be attended to. The Middle East, for example, presented some of them to Doreen Kays. She covered Cairo and "owned" the story because she knew the language, the customs and the politics of the region. Cairo was a jumping-off point for tougher and more dangerous assignments, and Kays spent a lot of time talking about risky situations with her male camera crew. She told them she expected no special treatment from them. In tight corners, when bullets or rocks or tear gas canisters are flying, each person in the crew looks after every other member of the team.

Kays tried to work out some ground rules, but she believed she failed. Intellectually, the men realized that she did not merit nor want special consideration in the face of danger. Emotionally, "they felt they should protect me if bombs were flying. But if they couldn't cope, a cameraman might miss the pictures and get shot himself. I would be useless on the story, if that were the case." Other women have had the same conversations and have met the same reactions. Marge Lipton, a network field producer in Europe, was told by a cameraman, "The network may want to send you here but *I* won't take the responsibility. I don't want it and I won't take it."

Women, like men, react differently to danger. Hysteria is not the hallmark of either men or women covering life-threatening situations. In Moscow, ABC's Anne Garrels fought off a man who came up behind her and grabbed her by the neck while she was making a telephone call from a phone booth. She let loose with a stream of gutter Russian and managed a well-placed knee to protect herself. Working on the streets of the Soviet Union often brings out self-appointed censors who get fairly physical

when they try to prevent crews and correspondents from filming public events. Sometimes that sort of vigilantism is arranged
by Soviet authorities as warnings to correspondents. They are
particularly anxious to block contacts with dissidents and with
so-called "refuseniks"—Jews who have applied for exit visas to
leave the Soviet Union.

In March 1982, Garrels went to Kiev to visit Jewish friends.
As she was getting off the tram at the railroad station to take the
train back to Moscow, she was attacked by a man who grabbed
her purse. Garrels hung on, finally falling down, but slowing
her assailant enough so that her Russian companion could catch
up to him. The "purse snatcher" was then suddenly joined by
two other men who threw Garrels' friend to the ground and
dashed off to a waiting car with her suitcase and purse. Without
her travel documents, Garrels could not leave Kiev. She returned to her hotel where, strangely enough, everything but her
money was returned a few hours later. It was a clear message
for Garrels, warning her not to be so active in maintaining contacts or pursuing stories involving Jews or dissidents. Bruised
and angry, she protested to authorities, who turned the facts
around, accusing her of slandering the Soviet state. As for being
roughed up, Garrels asserts, "Finally, you forget you are a
woman and simply become a harassed reporter. You shove
back, hard."

Women sometimes have to work damned hard to get their
stories. They have to take risks, and they have to get physical
on occasion. Liz Trotta, then with NBC, once had to shove her
microphone into the face of a political hanger-on at Nelson
Rockefeller's election night headquarters because she did not
have the professional courtesy to let her position the mike to
pick up Rockefeller's remarks. She had been pushed out of the
way by the woman once too often and she shoved back, bruising
her lip in the process.

Interviews with a number of women serving overseas in traveling posts for American television network news organizations
turned up some consistent observations. In professional terms,
there is far less male chauvinism among American news teams
than among European news teams. "Europeans are amazed,"

one NBC correspondent told me, "at how well men and women work together in tough situations for the American TV networks."

Europeans are still reluctant to accord American women their full status as members of the news teams. Sharon Young went to Greece to work on a project and met with Greek television officials. "They listened politely, were most cordial, and then they said they would settle everything when my boss arrived." A cable had to be sent from New York to Athens to assure the Greeks that she was indeed the head of the team with the authority to make all arrangements. Young was also faced with incredulous stares on a trip to Canada with correspondent Lynn Sherr. The Canadians were ready to accept a woman producer with a male correspondent; they were even ready to accept a male producer with a woman correspondent, but when two women showed up as the news team, that blew their minds. They kept asking, "Is this the whole group? Isn't there anyone else?"

All assignments are not in high-risk situations. Women producers, working with male crews, do not generally have to make arrangements to escape from violence. Most stories deal with mundane material. Camera crews are far more sensitive about their female colleagues than they used to be. There's very little "sweetie baby" patronizing and, according to most women network news producers, their commands are listened to without hesitation. Cameramen take direction about the composition of pictures and the lighting of scenes from women or men who have demonstrated they know what they are talking about. Male producers claim to feel the same way about working with female crews. More and more camera operators or sound technicians are women. Men say they give no special consideration to women crew members when it comes to job performance.

Dress codes exist for all correspondents. Men are supposed to look presentable and are to be dressed at least as formally as the people they are interviewing. It doesn't do to show up in a sport shirt to interview the president of a corporation who has turned out in suit and tie. Anything that acts as a distracting element, such as an odd hair style, is bad; it can send the viewer's attention sailing away. It is not a male-female issue. The same things would happen if a male correspondent showed up with a hippie's shoulder-length hair, held in place with a bandana. Nevertheless, Ann Compton believes audiences hold women "to a finer standard and expect a less flawed appearance from them." Women will be more quickly criticized for a sloppy collar or for hair that is unkempt.

There is one strictly female on-camera problem: pregnancy. Ann Compton carried her firstborn while covering debates on Capitol Hill. During sessions of the House and the Senate on the SALT Treaty, she taped a stand-up into-camera report. She told her cameraman that the content of the story involved the entire Congress. He took that to mean that she wanted a very wide shot to show both the House and Senate buildings on Capitol Hill. The picture was wide enough to incorporate both of them, as well as all of Compton's very pregnant figure. The next morning, Jeff Gralnick, the executive producer of the broadcast, instituted what he called "the elbow rule." Compton was never to be photographed below the elbows in order to conceal her blossoming figure from the viewers. Concealment was not due to embarrassment but rather to a desire to eliminate a distracting element from the picture. Compton was in favor of the rule: "I figured that someone in the audience might stop listening to what I said and start wondering how many more months I had to go."

So what is the situation as the eighties begin? Gloria Emerson was assessing that point in a magazine piece she wrote. She had covered Vietnam for the *New York Times* and had been impressed by the fact that Sylvia Chase had gone to Teheran to cover the turmoil there. The fact that a woman had been sent into riots was a measure, Emerson believed, of how far women journalists had come. There are two bench marks of progress: First, women cover every kind of newsbreak from riots to wars to investigations to sporting events. They are on general assignment and aren't even offended to be assigned to fashion shows and homemakers' conferences. They've proved they can do the hard news and, like any such reporter, needn't bridle at doing the fluff.

Second, we can and do fire women who do not measure up. That is the single most important indicator we can offer. The days of tokenism were truly over when that kind of action became possible.

There is, however, one question that remains unanswered. Doreen Kays posed it as she headed back to her hardship post in Cairo. "Having gotten the break," she said to a male colleague, "the real problems start. Do we want to live your life the way you have been living it? Or is there some better way for us to handle our lives as reporters and as women?" Only she and other journalists can answer that one.

Max Robinson is the first black anchor for a network's nightly newscast. Though a symbol of black achievement in TV news, he has not yet matched Barbara Walters' contributions to the image of women in the news business. In time, he could.

Some black correspondents at the networks are making themselves known nationally: Ed Bradley, George Strait, Bernard Shaw, Hal Walker, Lem Tucker. They understand news and journalism and have earned the respect of their peers and the public, but there is still some distance to go before blacks see themselves as sharing equally in the opportunities offered by television news. One said the bottom line right now is that every key position from president of the news department, to executive producer and senior producer, to show director, and right down to the person who pushes the button on the videotape machine in the basement, is filled by a white individual. "The people are here," he said, "but management walks right by them. Why? I don't know. But," he paused and shook his head, "people get tired of waiting. They leave or they give up. We don't have the input. We're not political. Something has got to change for the system to be right."

There are very few blacks operating behind the cameras in command positions in television news. The reason, according to some who are employed as producers, is that blacks who sought employment as broadcast journalists in the seventies decided to try first for the more visible positions on the air as reporters or anchors. Many blacks have come to believe that the push for visibility may have been a mistake. The system upon

which TV news is based puts most of the authority in the hands
of the executive and senior producers and not in the hands of
the reporters, correspondents and anchors. As a result, blacks
found that their input was not really being heard where it could
do the most good in influencing the tone or the extent of coverage. Unlike the situation involving women, who are frequently asked if they find stories offensive or sexist, blacks claim
that they are rarely asked such questions about race.

Perspective on minority viewpoints depends, therefore, on
the sensitivity of the executive producer. Sometimes decisions
are made that, in retrospect, are judged to be uncaring. A case
in point was a series developed for presentation on the "ABC
Evening News" in 1971 when I was executive producer of the
broadcast. We decided to produce four reports as a survey of
"The Mood of America." One story was about a blue-collar
factory worker; one was about a farmer and his family; one was
about a middle-class family whose son had evaded the draft and
the Vietnam War by fleeing to Canada; and one was about an
elderly retired couple living on a fixed income in Florida. It was
a fine series, well produced and probing basic attitudes among
the population as they coped with the war, inflation and the
forthcoming (1972) presidential election. There was one element
that all of us had missed. We had not included an examination
of what was happening in America's minority communities.
Fortunately, Eric Tait, an assignment desk editor, caught the
omission. As a black, he believed that no survey of "The Mood
of America" could claim to be thorough if it did not cover what
he knew to be the substantially different viewpoints among
black citizens. Tait brought the matter to my attention, and we
immediately extended the series for another three parts to fill
the gap. Without Tait to catch us in our insensitivity, we would
not have done our job as broadcast journalists.

"I am where I am because I am black," was the observation
of one man who is on the fast track at a network news department. "It's like having a 'black seat' on the Supreme Court," he
said. "Certain jobs are clearly reserved for a black or a Hispanic,
and the pool of talent is not exactly deep at the moment. So, I'm
the person who will be moved ahead."

Conversations with blacks reveal that they identify three reasons why they have been hired. First, it is because stations need to have them in their newsrooms in order to avoid challenges to their broadcast licenses. That was behind the push in the late sixties when government policy emanating from Washington, D.C., made it useful to count numbers of minorities employed in all job categories, not just in the clerical and maintenance staffs. It caused a problem, however, according to blacks who got jobs at that time. "They [the stations] went out and got any face they could," one newsman recalled. "A good journalist was lumped in with the bad ones. When the poor performer screwed up, it spilled over on the rest of us. 'We told you these minorities can't function' would set us all back."

Second, news organizations discovered they needed "passports" into certain stories. An all-black crew operated better in an urban ghetto. "That wasn't so obvious until the riots in the cities. Then, when they were stoning white crews and the black crews were getting access, the word was passed to hire more blacks." A black producer makes it easier to make arrangements for a black gospel music choir; a black correspondent can get an interview more quickly with a civil rights leader.

Third, they are needed to supply insights into stories from the minority vantage point. All of those interviewed, however, insisted that their own employment was not due to any but the third reason. They all felt that their race enabled them to help with content during the preparation of news reports.

As if to reassure themselves that they are reporters able to handle any story and not mere "passports" for their organizations, some black reporters refuse to cover "black stories" at all. Like women reporters who at first refused to cover fashion and homemaking, it will be a mark of an end to "tokenism" when all blacks feel they can cover all stories no matter what the racial overtones.

Although obviously blacks and women do have special insights because of their sex and race, what television news needs more of, desperately, is specialization: a body of expertise maintained within the correspondent corps in broad areas of geopolitical, socioeconomic, scientific and cultural affairs. That is an opinion born of experience in covering news myself as well as from dealing with reports from correspondents who have been sent hurrying to cover complex stories.

In the summer of 1968, I was in Bucharest, Rumania, working on a documentary about the Communist governments of Eastern Europe when Russian troops invaded Czechoslovakia. To the Rumanians, who had not participated in the invasion because of their own independence from Russian domination, it was a time of nervousness. They wanted their story told to the West, and even though I was there on assignment from public television and not then connected with any American network, it didn't matter to the authorities. To the Rumanians, I represented American broadcasters, and all sorts of transmission facilities were placed at my disposal. I filed a lot of radio reports as a free-lance "stringer." My familiarity with the intricacies of the story was due in large part to the year I had spent as a CBS Foundation Fellow at the Russian Institute of Columbia University, learning a great deal about the inner workings of the Soviet bloc. It was really "touching the news," and much of what I had learned at Columbia came back to find a place in the analyses I was writing as the only American broadcaster in town.

It wasn't to last, of course. By the third day of the crisis, network correspondents and their film crews were on the scene and from then on the reporting was done by them. Still, the experience was not quite over. To steal a phrase from a Broadway musical show, the lesson was simply, "You gotta know the territory!" Many of the correspondents who arrived were clearly ignorant of the special nature of bureaucracy and the structure of government or the role of the Communist party in an Iron Curtain country. Many hours were spent conducting a crash course for my news colleagues on "How a Communist State Is Run."

To be sure, specialization in Rumanian affairs is too much to hope for and would be too expensive to maintain in a news division's table of organization. There ought to be experts, however, on science, economics, the Communist bloc, Asia,

Latin America, Vatican politics, the Mideast and Africa. Those are the minimum and they are practicable to maintain.

Ever since those nights in Bucharest, I have tried to encourage correspondents and producers to study their areas, to attend lectures and to build up reference files. When possible, men and women with particular expertise should be given preference for employment and assignments. Even if they are intended to be "general assignment" staff, it should be a measure for their career advancement. Two of the best foreign correspondents television has sent to the Soviet Union brought that kind of knowledge with them to their posts. Marvin Kalb, former CBS diplomatic correspondent, now with NBC, was fluent in Russian and was a graduate of Harvard's Russian Center before he went overseas. Anne Garrels had an almost identical background before ABC sent her to Moscow. Their competition got a lot of "call-backs" from their own home offices asking why Kalb or Garrels had turned up a superior story. The answer was always the same. They "knew the territory."

The same sort of specialization can apply to local journalists too. On a smaller scale, there is no reason why TV-station reporters should not study local politics, city management and the economics of school board rates. The right questions, asked in an interview, can break a big story. Even if they don't, specialized reporting of the event has to be better and the viewer will be better informed.

Who are the correspondents on television today? Where did they come from? How have they changed over the years?

The first group, the "Class of '45–'50," by and large, had been hired by radio news to report the Second World War. In the first years of the fifties, as television began to develop its own requirements—understanding pictures and paying some attention to nonjournalistic demands, such as shipping film, logistics and lighting, and production values—the men and women of the Class of '45–'50 faded from view. Some, like Charles Collingwood, Edward R. Murrow, and Bill Downs, survived, but most retired or failed to make the transition from

reading a report into a microphone to the television "performance." They simply did not compete on camera with the next
"class" coming up. Larry Leseuer, Ned Calmer and Alex Kendrick of CBS and Joseph C. Harsch of NBC are among those
men who were superb reporters during the Second World War
but who became marginal newsmen on TV as television supplanted radio.

In the next group, the Class of '55–'65, men (and a very few
women) got their hands-on experience in the civil rights demonstrations at home and the Cold War overseas. Although some
members of this group came out of broadcast journalism, particularly radio news, many were graduates of wire services or
newspapers. NBC News insisted on prior newspaper or news
wire experience. Those hired by TV news had only occasionally
worked in radio in contrast to the class they had replaced. Some,
like Walter Cronkite, had been print reporters during World
War II. Harry Reasoner, Bernie Kalb at CBS (now with NBC),
and Jack Chancellor and Sandy Vanocur at NBC were typical
of this group. They were good writers and reporters, and since
television news was in its infancy, there was not much prior
technical knowledge to worry about.

Some of the members of the Class of '55–'65 became documentary narrators later on; some became panelists on the networks' Sunday interview shows; some slipped off to local news
operations, which began to burgeon as the sixties ended, and
some kept climbing toward the anchor chairs.

With the Class of '65, through the end of the seventies, came
the first real wave of men and women who were practitioners
of television arts. They had learned in school what their prede-
cessors had innovated. Because local TV news was rapidly
growing, people were able to get entry-level jobs, often with no
journalistic experience. They learned technique first and applied
it well. They knew how to write and how to shoot pictures and
how to edit them together for maximum impact or sometimes
for pure emotional effect. But sometimes journalism suffered.
This group had done little or no news-gathering before coming
to television. They had begun in small stations, practicing performance and moving onward toward the networks or to larger

stations. Where the Class of '55–'65 had its basis in reporting, the Class of '65–'79 too often had its roots in cosmetics.

By the seventies, news staffs were filled with younger, good-looking go-getters who could cover stories but not necessarily analyze them. Too many of the men and women were "firemen," expected to fall off an airplane and get a story shot, scripted, shipped or satellited in less than six hours. In many cases, producers hoped that the story would be over quickly and that the youngster could move on to some other breaking event before detailed analysis was needed. The young reporter simply would not have the political or economic or social background at his or her fingertips to provide anything more than "here they come, there they go" coverage.

There was one case where a "fireman" went overseas for ABC and was sent off to cover the fighting in Northern Ireland between British troops and the underground Irish Republican Army. On the plane ride to Belfast, he turned to his producer and remarked that he had been doing some reading about the subject. "They keep mentioning Ulster," he observed. "Are we going anywhere near there?" The producer took out her map and began a basic geography lesson.

As the seventies ended and the eighties began, senior news department executives at networks and at the larger local stations made a conscious effort to assemble a blend of talents for the Class of '80. No news staff can afford to be without its "firemen" who can be sent anywhere with full confidence that they will be quick, accurate, fair and balanced, and most important, will deliver a report tonight. On the other hand, no news staff can be without men and women who know how to dig out facts and put them in perspective. Specialty reporters are being hired now: economists, scientists, doctors, lawyers, consumer investigators, art critics. They are being pushed into key positions and given air time to do in-depth examinations of stories and trends.

People are being hired at the networks who have had no experience in television techniques but who, it is assumed, will learn them. Newspaper and magazine writers are turning up on the tube despite their unpolished performances on camera. They are being teamed with producers whose television experience enables them to visualize any story but whose editorial skills need strengthening. The combinations marry good writers with good visualizers. Both learn from one another.

At some point in every journalist's career, the news must be touched. Contact has to be made firsthand with a story, and the elements of that story must be examined, sorted out, catalogued, clarified and distilled into a report and transmitted to an audience. It doesn't matter whether the journalist is working for a newspaper or magazine or for radio or television. Somewhere, sometime, he or she has to confront the reality of the news. Many men and women spend their lives in journalism without ever experiencing that moment of being on a story. Writers may be able to clean up a story after it is dictated into the office; in-house television producers may be able to enhance a story in videotape by adding pictures or subtracting unnecessary words; but unless they have at one time or another been out there, they have missed the essential ingredient. Their judgments will never be as sharp, their understanding will never be as clear, their perspectives will never be as broad unless they too have covered the news themselves at some point in their careers.

Correspondents find details for their stories in a number of ways. Digging out facts from reluctant sources is the most conventional. Sometimes the truth comes in strange ways. ABC's Jim Giggans went along on a heroin raid in the South China Sea. A freighter registered in Taiwan was stopped and boarded by Vietnamese naval authorities. While inspectors searched the ship, there was a lot of apparently angry chatter between one of the Vietnamese officers and the ship's Chinese captain. What the two of them did not know was that Giggans had a Chinese-speaking cameraman on his team who translated the entire conversation.

Was it a confrontation between smugglers and the law? Hardly! The Vietnamese naval officer was politely telling the Chinese captain that this was all being done for the television cameras, that the captain had nothing to fear, and that perhaps the captain ought to show him where to "look." Obviously no heroin was found and the officer left the ship with a carton of cigarettes for his thoughtfulness. Giggans left the ship with a good story on corruption in the navy, which caused quite a stir when it was run on the air.

The work can be dangerous too. In 1979, Tom Schell was covering the seal slaughter in the Arctic. Every year, baby seals are hunted and beaten to death by men using baseball bats, and every time this appears on television, an outraged cry is raised. The seal hunters claim they are dispatching the animals quickly and that seal hunting for fur is their livelihood. They do not look kindly upon television crews and correspondents, believing that their pictures distort what they are really doing. An environmental group, Greenpeace, had taken an extreme step to stop the killing. Their members had entered the seal hunting ground and had sprayed the animals with paint, making their pelts worthless on the fur market and thereby presumably saving the seals' lives.

Schell was in the area to cover the Greenpeace activity. He was captured by the sealers who were convinced that he was a member of the society. They held him captive for a number of days, force-feeding him alcohol and trying to get him to confess to being a member of Greenpeace. Despite becoming drunk, Schell steadfastly maintained his credentials as a newsman. His captors debated whether to kill him by breaking his arms and tossing him into the freezing sea or to let him go. They finally compromised, dumping buckets of green paint over him and then turning him loose to find his own way back to civilization.

Or funny. Sid Lazard was a correspondent for ABC News during the Vietnam War, assigned to cover Air Force activities. Part of his task was to deal with the way trained mechanics maintained the aircraft used in battle. Walking up to a technician who was stripped to the waist and elbow deep in grease, Lazard asked snappily: "Tell me, sergeant. How well do you keep this 'bird' flying on one engine?" The airman looked up, took a very long time to answer and replied, "Pretty well, I guess, sir. It only *has* one engine."

It is safe to say that the decades of the television age have provided too many wars and riots to cover. Every correspondent and producer who has made his or her mark has gone through some kind of war or riot coverage. My riot was anti-Communist demonstrators in Helsinki, where clouds of tear gas and charging mounted police drove us off the streets. My war was the French–Algerian.

In 1962, the French government had decided that fighting to retain control of Algeria was futile. Paris announced it would be pulling the French Army out of action, returning it across the Mediterranean to metropolitan France. Algeria would become a free and independent nation rather than a French colony. The move was not universally popular with the French, and an underground organization of militant terrorists, the OAS, was formed to prevent the French pullout. The OAS plan was to create havoc with unrestricted bombings and assassinations. The scheme apparently was designed to inflame the Arabs with terror, driving them to commit some inhuman outrages. Those, in turn, were supposed to lead the French government to reconsider the withdrawal, and feel pressured to stay in North Africa to protect non-Arabs who were living there. I was sent to cover the withdrawal.

We were in Bab el Oueb one morning, in a small valley in a suburb of Algiers. Our position was well below a series of high-rise apartment houses that served as a center for refugees from the fighting. The French Army, knowing it was soon to be on the way home, was not looking for trouble. The French soldiers, mostly young draftees, were there merely to keep order. The Arabs occupying the houses and the ridge line above our valley also knew the war was winding down and a majority of them wanted no part of any fighting. The OAS had other ideas.

I was watching an infantry lieutenant moving among his men, calming them, telling them not to panic and not to be trigger-happy in the face of provocation, because all the information from the people in the high-rise buildings indicated that no one with any sense of responsibility over there wanted anything to happen.

Suddenly there was a single gunshot. And twenty feet from me, the lieutenant went down cursing, grasping his shattered leg and rolling out of the way of any second bullet. Instantly the sky was filled with helicopters puttering in low and aiming right toward the top of those apartment houses. Flares, tear gas canisters and red dye were dropped to mark observed trouble spots.

Simultaneously we heard a keening sound—the ululation of Arab women sounding their traditional call to battle. In less than five minutes, a tense situation had gone over the edge into one that was out of control. And we were standing in the middle of it.

Newspaper reporters covering stories run the same risk as their television colleagues, but they do not have to get pictures as an essential part of their effort. To be a television journalist, one has to be in the center of the action. The camera crew and the reporters work so closely together that both are likely to be pinned down within feet of one another if gunfire breaks out. There were many examples during the Vietnam War of correspondents and camera crews hit by gunfire or shrapnel and capturing the event on their own film—ABC's Roger Peterson, to name but one. Peterson has a series of pictures that show him bloodstained and rushing back for help after being hit. The sequence also shows him crouched in front of his cameraman, obviously in pain, but completing his report before making his way back for medical treatment.

The effects of being involved in a life-or-death situation never leave one. Years later, with the power to send news teams into dangerous situations, I always stressed that no story was worth getting hurt for. Cables would go out to Vietnam or Angola or Nicaragua or to the Middle East signed with the admonition "Take care, keep your head down." We lost some very fine men covering the news. Each loss causes grief in the newsrooms— grief compounded by the certain knowledge that "there but for the grace of God go I." One producer, Ken Lucoff, died en route to a story because he missed the plane he was supposed to be on, caught the next one and went down with it.

David Jayne, a close friend, was picked to go to Beirut to help Barbara Walters when she was interviewing Yasir Arafat, the head of the Palestine Liberation Organization. Elaborate preparations were made for security in Beirut. That was where the danger existed with gunmen all around, Christian and Moslem factions shooting at one another, guns and bombs available for sale to anyone with enough money to buy them. Barbara and David completed the interview without incident, and he took off in a chartered jet on a "milk run"—to carry the videotape to Amman, Jordan, so that it could be satellited home to the U.S. David never made it. His plane crashed and all aboard died.

During the Vietnam War, a group of correspondents and cameramen were captured in Cambodia by the Khmer Rouge. They were never seen again and are presumed to have been executed. ABC's Terry Koo went back for "just one more picture" of the North Vietnamese advance north of Hue. A mortar shell exploded as he walked across a field. Koo died instantly. His body wasn't recovered for several days. The Nicaraguan revolution in 1979 resulted in the particularly brutal killing of Bill Stewart. His death was seen by millions because his cameraman had been videotaping the scene as Stewart was ordered to walk up to a checkpoint by a National Guardsman. He was then told to kneel. Still holding his press credentials, Stewart was forced to lie down and, without warning, the Guardsman shot him in the head. The international protests that erupted after the incident resulted in the Nicaraguan government's "investigation" of the Guardsman's actions. Coincidentally, it was announced that he had been killed in action a few days later. A special marker has been put in place at the crossroad in Managua where Stewart died. On the anniversary of his death, the government of Nicaragua staged a memorial service for him in the belief that his death played a large part in galvanizing world opinion to oppose the dictatorial regime of ousted President Somoza.

All of us in the business burn with anger when we hear unthinking people accuse television journalists of being irresponsible, or of trying to subvert the American way of life by reporting only "bad news" or by distorting the "true picture" of events. We have sent people to their deaths and have put our own lives at risk as part of our job. We do it because of the dedication to getting the story and bringing it back. The men who were wounded in Vietnam, captured and killed in Cambodia, shot through the head in Nicaragua, and murdered at Jim Jones cult headquarters in Guyana would be well within their rights to tell the complainers to go to hell.

3
Charisma
and Credibility:
The Final Link
ANCHORS AND COMMENTATORS

At precisely ten seconds to 6:30 P.M., Eastern time, Charlie Heinz, sitting in the director's chair in the control room of ABC's Studio 2 in New York, gives the cue "Roll 37!" The command is repeated by the technical director sitting to his left, and down in the basement of ABC's Broadcast Center on 66th Street in Manhattan, a technician punches the "play" button of videotape machine 37. To Heinz's right, the associate director counts down the seconds to air: "Four. Three. Two. One." As the digital clock in the control room clicks to 6:30, Heinz says "Take 37!" The technical director presses a button on the intricate switching panel before him and the output of VTR 37 is cut through to master control and from there is sent across coaxial cables, microwave antennae and satellites. ABC's "World News Tonight" is on the air.

Though the first feed of a network's newscast is at 6:30 and is totally live, the second feed at 7:00 may sometimes be on videotape. The West Coast almost always sees the news on videotape. Live inserts are included in the 7:00 feed only if the first version contained technical erors, or if a late-breaking development requires an update.

The first picture Americans see on "World News Tonight" each evening is of the control room with the ABC News sign displayed high on the wall. Almost immediately this changes to show one of the three anchors sitting at his desk, ready to go on. The announcer's voice, recorded earlier so that the pictures can be "built in" precisely where they are required, begins: "From ABC, this is the 'World News Tonight' with [switch picture] Max Robinson in Chicago, [switch picture] Peter Jennings in London and [switch picture], from our desk in Washington, Frank Reynolds." The anchormen have been introduced before anything else. Anchors are the superstars of TV news. They represent the organization they work for. Sometimes they even compensate for its shortcomings.

At CBS News, the first picture transmitted used to be of Walter Cronkite. Since March 9, 1981, it has been the picture of Dan Rather, sitting at his desk, shuffling papers, ready to begin. The idea is to get the anchor's face on the tube as quickly as possible. Even when he is missing, his absence is explained. "Peter Jennings is on assignment . . ." or ". . . with Roger Mudd, substituting for the vacationing Walter Cronkite." The viewers want to be sure that Old Faithful will be back and that he is alive and well, albeit missing tonight.

"Old Faithful" is not an incorrect image. That natural phenomenon represents a trusted continuity in the recesses of Americans' consciousness. Network anchors represent a similar investment of trust by the audience.

In May 1980, the cover of *Panorama,* a slick new television magazine (it has since folded), featured Walter Cronkite, Frank Reynolds and John Chancellor painted into the side of Mount Rushmore, replacing the Presidents, as symbols of America. It was apt, for anchors are a peculiarly American institution. The British began with an unidentified "news reader," a hangover from the days the Brits call "old-fashioned steam-driven radio," when BBC announcers actually put on black tie to read *radio* newscasts. The Germans used women announcers called

"Speakerines." The French and Italians rotated the assignment when their TV news started out. Eventually, however, they followed the American lead, discovering that viewers preferred to get their news each night from someone they recognized and could trust.

Gordon Manning, once senior vice-president of CBS News, drew a very narrow definition of television news. He refused to allow any reference to a news broadcast as a news "program" or a news "show." "Ed Sullivan produces 'shows,' " Manning would say. "CBS News produces broadcasts!"

"Broadcasts." "Programs." "Shows." There are many show business aspects to television news. For one thing, TV news has "stars." True, most gained that status by developing credibility with the audience through demonstrating reportorial skills rather than by pure cosmetics. Nonetheless, they are "stars" and receive special handling both on the air and off.

In 1979, Frank Magid, the TV news consultant, prepared a tabular breakdown of what viewers found to be "desirable anchor qualities." The list was based on polling Magid had done all over the country and was accurate for network anchors as well as for those who starred on local television news broadcasts.

Although network news executives claim never to have used the Magid chart in choosing an anchor, they are, nonetheless, well aware that personal characteristics and appeal play a part in their choice. Bill Leonard, the president of CBS News, who chose Dan Rather to fill Walter Cronkite's job over Roger Mudd, denies that any surveys were used. Leonard told reporters that choosing Rather was a "news decision." Still, he did admit that some non-news elements played a part. "With twenty-twenty hindsight," he said in one interview, "you might conclude that this man appears 'avuncular' or that man is 'serious,' but in fact an individual just naturally emerges. His performance adds up."

All three network news broadcasts present essentially the same material—so what makes the viewer choose one program over another? Assuming that all three broadcasts are about equal in enterprise, accuracy and breadth of coverage, it comes down

DESIRABLE ANCHOR QUALITIES

	Total Sample	
	Network	Local
Intelligent	69.6%	61.6%
Experienced	64.0%	56.6%
Sincere	39.6%	37.8%
Self-confident	36.6%	34.8%
Mature	33.2%	28.4%
Businesslike	29.3%	26.4%
Positive	27.8%	25.2%
Understanding	27.7%	26.6%
Serious	25.9%	23.1%
Warm	23.8%	27.2%
Enthusiastic	22.8%	25.0%
Bright	15.1%	14.8%
Calm	13.7%	14.4%
Familiar	13.5%	24.2%
Reassuring	11.8%	12.7%
Casual	6.9%	12.3%
Formal	5.3%	3.9%

to familiarity and "rapport" with the presenter. If the anchor is perceived as trustworthy, sincere, serious, warm, enthusiastic, and so on, there's less chance that viewers will switch away to sample someone else. Habits of viewing become fixed and are very hard to break. Few people in the United States have three television sets lined up in their living rooms all tuned simultaneously to the three networks' newscasts. There's not too much opportunity for side-by-side comparisons between one broadcast and another. The result is that once a news team, headed by an anchor, is found satisfactory, there is little motivation for change.

Habit can be broken, of course. If, for example, ABC's entertainment schedule is number one and the family went to bed last night with the channel selector turned to the ABC station, the chances are good that they will begin the next evening's viewing by staying tuned to ABC. Sometimes that results in sampling the ABC newscast; and as familiarity with it grows, new habit replaces old.

Another reason for change could be a sharp alteration in the ratings of the local newscast, which usually precedes the network's evening news. If a local station's effort collapses, many people will have switched to another station. Most will stay tuned there for the network newscast that follows the local program. Again, a chance for sampling a new product occurs. Finally, when the anchor of the network broadcast is changed, new habits can be formed.

When Walter Cronkite retired from the "CBS Evening News" on March 9, 1981, there was a considerable degree of sampling by viewers who had been loyal to Cronkite. They "shopped around," trying the newscasts being presented by ABC and NBC. It wasn't long before viewers found new "homes" for their news viewing. Rather's ratings dropped, and the CBS broadcast fell into a virtual three-way tie with ABC and NBC. The overwhelming ratings dominance of CBS News, which had seemed unassailable, had been ended.

What should an anchor be?

Bob Trout, the veteran broadcast journalist, says he conjures up the last member of a relay team, the "anchor leg" of the race, the person who by dint of personality and effort brings the broadcast to the finish line as a winner. A more conventional image sees the anchor as the individual who ties the broadcast to a home base. Other correspondents may be reporting elements of a story from faraway places, but the anchor keeps the program centrally directed and secure.

In discussions at ABC News, held to select anchors for that network's nightly newscast, Roone Arledge, president of ABC News, would ask, "If the President were assassinated, who would you tune in to watch tell the story?" In another session, he would ask, "When the President grants the three networks a joint interview, who would you want to see up there for ABC News, next to Cronkite and Chancellor?" Those questions probed for two primary qualities anchors must have as broadcast journalists: the ability to cover the big story, and the ability to represent the news organization they work for in direct competition and direct comparison with the opposition.

Personality and star status aside, the anchor ought to be one of those participating in editorial judgments. He or she ought to be in touch with correspondents and broadcast producers, and be the one who structures the copy into a narrative of the day's news. Anchors cannot simply sit back and rely on writers. Regional anchors stationed overseas or outside of Washington must be intelligent advocates of news coverage within their sphere of responsibility. An anchor has to be an all-around journalist and not simply someone who looks good on the tube.

The anchor is the final and most flexible link in the communications chain. Most wear a tiny earpiece connected by a wire that snakes down the back of a jacket or dress and is plugged into a jack box fastened underneath the desk. It's called an IFB, which stands for Interruptible Feed Back. Usually the anchor hears the sound tracks of the reports being played on the broadcast or, in the case of multiple anchors, the IFB carries all audio except one's own voice.

The IFB is connected to a microphone in the control room where the broadcast producer can push a button and relay instructions. It is not unusual, for example, for the producer to use the system to tell the anchor that "the House has passed the Defense Appropriations Bill by a vote of 300 to 135," and then to hear those same words come directly out of the anchor's mouth. That is why the anchor is the most flexible link in the chain. Instructions can be given and taken and acted upon with the least amount of fuss. After all, what is on film or tape reports is immutable. Graphics displayed on a broadcast can be eliminated if the need arises, but only the anchor can turn around on the proverbial dime, instantly changing content.

An anchor has to understand the importance of the news he or she is reading. There is a certain radio anchorman in New York who reads through story after story with no difference in inflection or tone. A small car accident gets the same emphasis as a major clash between Afghan rebels and the Russian Army. He doesn't seem to know what the news stories are all about— all he does is funnel words into a microphone. His credibility is zero; when he comes on the air, I turn the radio off.

If a checklist of anchor qualities is ever made, Walter Cronkite's will provide the base line against which all comers must be measured. Cronkite is a perfect example of a man who really "paid his dues." Combat reporting in World War Two, domestic and foreign assignments for United Press including Moscow during the Cold War, assorted Washington beats for radio news and local television anchoring in Washington, D.C.—Cronkite did them all before taking over the anchor chair. By the time he had arrived at the "CBS Evening News" in 1965, he knew how a story was generated, written, filmed, assembled and produced. In short, a viewer got the distinct feeling that Cronkite knew what was happening all the time.

As an anchor, Cronkite operated somewhere between the ever-involved managing editor and the totally uninvolved script reader. John Armstrong served Cronkite as writer and producer for more than twelve years. He recalls that once Walter got his "team" together and got to be number one in the public's esteem, "he trusted his people." At its height, Cronkite's producing and writing team was unquestionably the strongest in the news business. It would meet with him every morning, and they would tell him what stories were lined up. There'd be opportunities for Cronkite to react or suggest alternatives.

According to Armstrong and others who worked with Cronkite during his final years on the "CBS Evening News," Walter would often suggest story coverage late in the afternoon, at 4:30 or 5:00 P.M., and the CBS Washington bureau would scramble. By then Armstrong had become the senior producer in Washington, and he would get the call from executive producer Sandy Socolow relaying Walter's "requests." "We'd think nothing of sending somebody out to do the quickest possible rehash of the day's wire story on a particular subject," Armstrong recalled. "Or we'd grab an interview with someone and build a story around it."

Visitors always described Cronkite in shirt sleeves, questioning producers and writers, talking on the phone to correspondents or to news sources of his own, checking on story details. He was sometimes called "testy" or "impatient," particularly when efforts to cover a story went astray. He was regarded as "the best broadcast editor" ever seen around CBS News. One staff member who wrote for him described the daily procedure.

"You write as best you can, but he can make it better. He can edit it better. He knows that if he can save two seconds here and five seconds there, that's one more story in the broadcast as a whole."

Cronkite had the final word about what went into the broadcast. He claimed to have veto power over any story. Although he did not watch every piece of film or tape before the broadcast, he made sure to stay well informed about their content, either by talking to the producer or correspondent or by reading the script ahead of time.

Anchors have problems. Their celebrity can get in the way. Cronkite complained that all the fun had gone out of covering political campaigns. "I get off the bus in some small town and the crowd is around me rather than the candidate." In the 1980 presidential primary campaign, Representative John Anderson moved from obscurity to importance by winning some surprising victories. While he was waiting to be interviewed in a live two-way conversation with Cronkite, Anderson's supporters set up a chant. Was it "Anderson! Anderson! Anderson!"? No. "Walter! Walter! Walter!"

If Cronkite ever came on the air with as much as a sore throat or a bad back, people started to ask, "What's wrong?" Cronkite was a story himself wherever he went. He had an effect on the events he was supposed to be covering.

Mike Wallace and I, sitting through a long takeoff delay from Los Angeles Airport, talked about this "star quality" of anchors. "I wince at the word," he said, "but there *is* a quality of 'taking stage.' When you are on the screen, you command the attention of the people who are watching. Some people, first-rate newsmen, first-rate reporters, first-rate writers, simply do not have the capacity to rivet the attention of the viewing audience. If you have it," Wallace smiled, thus acknowledging that he knew *he* had it, ". . . suddenly you become a more valuable part of the news team. Why? Because more people will tune in."

If Wallace "winces" at the words "star quality," he does not object to the word "casting." Part of the great success of "60

Minutes," a CBS newsmagazine, was due to the mix of style and personalities of its four anchors. America tuned in each week in staggering numbers to watch hard-edged Mike Wallace do battle; urbane Morley Safer turn exquisite script and picture into delightful television reportage; clean and earnest Dan Rather; and wry, "old shoe" Harry Reasoner.

According to Wallace, the initial "casting" of "60 Minutes" was accomplished by the broadcast's producer and creator, Don Hewitt, and by Bill Leonard, then the vice-president of CBS News for "soft news." "There was the 'white hat/black hat' business at the beginning between Harry and me," Wallace explained. " '60 Minutes' set out to be a broadcast anchored by Harry Reasoner, but some place along the line, before it got on the air, I think that Leonard and Hewitt decided it probably needed a little more 'grit'; otherwise it might turn out to be a trifle gentle or bland. So they looked to me as a contrast."

Casting was again a consideration when Reasoner left to go to ABC. Morley Safer was picked to replace Harry. Safer began to produce harder pieces, becoming less like Reasoner and more like the hard-driving correspondent he had been in Vietnam, where he had made his reputation as a brave and probing reporter, unafraid of authorities who were trying to conceal a considerable amount of ineptitude.

Physical exhaustion caused by the "60 Minutes" production schedule led Wallace to take the lead in urging that a third anchor be added to the team. The question was "who?" Dan Rather emerged as the leading candidate. He had a national reputation, earned, in large measure, from his challenging coverage of the Nixon administration as CBS News's White House correspondent. Again, casting played a part. Wallace remembers that the question was, "Is the Rather style going to be too close to the Wallace style?" After consideration, it was decided that Rather was "more of a gentleman. He is unfailingly courteous, unfailingly quiet but nonetheless insistent." Wallace describes Rather's quality as "more of a sheathed sword but one that is still carried."

Some critics of the "60 Minutes" staff viewed Rather's style and qualities far more harshly. One of them thought Rather represented a "new breed of television journalist—the reporter-as-performer-and-participant, the good-looking guy who gets personally involved in his stories, playing basketball with one interview subject and skin-diving with another." It appears that even within "60 Minutes" itself, there was a debate over where to draw the line between the traditional view of the anchor's role, which insists that the journalist be detached from the story, and the "new breed," which finds nothing wrong with becoming involved, as long as it does not distort the story. Participation can make telling a story more understandable and more enjoyable to watch. With anchors moving out from behind their studio desks to cover the news, the trend will probably continue toward participation.

I had known Mike Wallace to be a great anchorman since his days on the "CBS Morning News." He was professional, pleasant and demanding. He was flexible when things went wrong and could handle on-the-air situations with calmness and confidence. He went on the air each morning knowing as much about each story as he possibly could. He was never thrown by a failure of the teleprompter device from which he read his script. If it broke down, and it often did, Wallace was able to ad-lib the story without error.

Asked what makes an anchor, Wallace responds by saying it is a combination of qualities that gives him or her that special aura of integrity and credibility. Wallace built up his news credentials principally by working in local news, covering civil rights and politics. He had worked mostly in New York and Chicago, where much of his experience was gained by conducting thousands of interviews. "So much of reporting on radio and television is in the interview," Wallace explained. "When you talk to political figures and sports figures and entertainment figures over a period of almost twenty years, little by little, you 'fill your vessel' of experience." Wallace believes that to be a good anchor you have to "pay your dues."

Mike was not a facile writer, but he was a very careful editor. Some of the scripts that the "CBS Morning News" staff gave him were tossed back to be rewritten. He got testy some mornings, sometimes without much reason, but he was not afraid to admit mistakes or to apologize to a staff member if he had been too harsh. Working on the overnight, it was easy to develop a habit of being "too harsh." If, as Wallace said, an anchor helps to shape the character of the broadcast, then, in the early morning, the broadcast was also shaping the character of the anchor. He and I were reminiscing about that and I started to ask a question: "Being an anchorman on an early morning news show . . ." He interrupted me, finishing my preamble: ". . . is not good for your health!" He went on: "When we first went on the air at ten o'clock, I would have to get into the office around five-thirty or six, which meant getting out of bed at four or four-thirty. I have never recovered from that experience. It did something to my metabolism. I have never slept properly since the beginning of the 'Morning News.' "

After two years of broadcasting at 10:00 A.M., the "CBS Morning News" was moved to the 7:00 A.M. slot. Wallace found his health seriously affected. "I still can't believe it," he said. "I would get out of bed at three in the morning, day after day. You're not on the lobster shift. You're not on the regular shift. You are no place. You go to bed at nine. You get five and a half or six hours of sleep. It's the first time in my life I began to take a sleeping pill."

When Mike Wallace came to CBS News in 1963 to start the "CBS Morning News," he replaced Harry Reasoner's "Calendar" show in the 10:00 A.M. time slot. As a result, for years, Reasoner and Wallace were coolly distant around the office. It was inevitable, however, that they would run across each other on joint assignments and discover how genuinely likable they both are. They became good friends, particularly after teaming up as cohosts of "60 Minutes." Reasoner also anchored the 11:00 P.M. "CBS Sunday News," and he would fill in for Walter Cronkite when Walter was away on vacation or assignment. Reasoner wanted his own evening news anchor chair and Cronkite was clearly not moving on, so in December 1970, Harry left CBS and "60 Minutes" to join ABC's "Evening News" as coanchor with Howard K. Smith. His arrival imparted a note of instant credibility. It was a prime example of the stature an anchor carries.

Until Harry's arrival, many affiliated stations did not broadcast the "ABC Evening News," preferring to run their own local programs. At a meeting of the ABC affiliates, he called them a disgrace to the industry, and although some bridled at the harsh words, all came on board within a year. The "ABC Evening News" ratings rose dramatically as more people in the country got the opportunity to sample the product. Reasoner's presence was the catalyst.

Reasoner began his career in journalism in 1942 as a newspaper reporter in Minneapolis. After the Second World War, he was a drama critic and then a radio news writer. He tried the United States Information Agency in the Philippines and then came back to broadcast journalism. In 1956, he joined CBS News as a reporter and drew assignments ranging from politics to civil rights to natural disasters. He then hosted "Calendar," took over the "Sunday News" and joined "60 Minutes."

As anchor, Reasoner would read pages of script as they were finished by the staff news writers. He'd edit the copy, changing words, eliminating unnecessary adjectives and adding the "Reasoner touch" wherever he found it was needed. Occasionally, a page of copy would come back with "D.T.S.T.L." printed on the top. Translated, that meant "Droppable to Say the Least"; if the broadcast were running out of time, pages so marked were easily cut. Another code was "O.M.D.B." That meant "Over My Dead Body"—a story Harry would not read under any circumstances. In those cases, we could either try to edit the piece into acceptable form or drop it entirely. No one kept a box score but my recollection is that we dropped many more than we rewrote. Reasoner's judgments, based on his experience as a reporter, generally prevailed.

No workaholic, Reasoner enjoyed lingering over an elegant lunch and chatting with a group of "chums" in his office. He always managed to find a way to take a break from the day's workload, and the hospitality he offered from a bottle he kept in his office added to the conviviality. His habit of coasting with pals at the Des Artistes bar was in marked contrast to Barbara

Walters' intensity of purpose when she came to ABC in 1976 to coanchor the "Evening News" alongside him.

I have known Barbara Walters since 1954. She was a "guest booker" and writer on a CBS morning broadcast for which I was the director. One morning Barbara was in charge of organizing a fashion show. We were to rehearse at 5:30 A.M., but just before going "on camera" for a preliminary check, she came rushing onto the set distraught. One of the models had failed to show up. At the time it hardly seemed like one of the turning points in television, but I told her to model the dress herself. That's what Barbara Walters did, and it has enabled me to claim that "I'm the guy who put Barbara Walters on the air for the first time in her career."

Barbara Walters was hired by ABC executives in 1976, because they believed she would attract a vast audience to the "Evening News." As host of the NBC "Today" show, she was an established "star," and she was among the best interviewers on television. Although she had never covered the news as a street reporter, her on-the-air performance inspired credibility, and in 1976, with the women's movement showing strength across the nation, the first female anchor for an evening newscast was also expected to bring in viewers. Perennially in third place behind the CBS and NBC newscasts, ABC believed that a spectacular personality appearing as a principal presenter of a news broadcast would conceal the underfunded and undermanned news operation the network was running. There were some excellent correspondents and producers at ABC, but they were too few in number, and they always were playing "catch up" with CBS and NBC, whose news departments put more manpower and equipment into the field for news coverage. If Harry Reasoner's arrival at ABC in 1970 had brought credibility and an enhanced news image to the network, the attempt to do the same thing all over again with Walters backfired. People tuned in but only to discover that ABC News was poverty-stricken. Its news image was hurt rather than helped in the long run.

For a few days, during the first week of her new coanchoring duties, Barbara Walters brought a spectacular amount of "sampling." ABC News enjoyed the highest ratings it had ever achieved for its "Evening News" up to that time as people tuned in to see what all the hoopla was about. The audience decided, however, that the Reasoner–Walters team was not what it wanted, and the regular patterns of viewing were quickly resumed.

People who tuned in to see the news wanted to see the *news,* not a nightly version of *Who's Afraid of Virginia Woolf?* Reasoner's demeanor on the air made it perfectly clear that he regarded Walters as an interloper. The broadcast's format had reserved time for "chitchat" between the two anchors, presumably to allow for their reaction to stories being reported from the field. What passed for conversation had overtones of sarcasm, and Reasoner's facial expressions conveyed a patronizing tolerance of Barbara. Roone Arledge, by then president of ABC News and the man with the mission to fix the problem, described his impression while watching Walters and Reasoner: "It was like coming into a married couple's home after there had been a big fight."

Barbara Walters' experience as Reasoner's coanchor revealed that sitting behind a desk and reading news copy is not her strongest suit. When she reads copy she has written herself, her performance is fine. Anchoring the "Evening News," however, required her to read copy written for her by others. Under time pressure, which almost every night results in anchors getting a "speed up" signal while on the air, Walters' voice tended to rise in pitch and become strident. What Barbara needed was a more relaxed situation on the air. The "Evening News" was not that kind of broadcast.

Walters was not without humor about her difficulties. She has a slight speech difficulty with the letter R. One night there was a story about Mount Ararat. She came out of her office and handed the edited copy back to George Orick, the writer. "Why couldn't it have happened in Mount Kisco?" she sighed.

Barbara Walters was a pioneer and consequently a target. Much has been made of Walters' million-dollar-a-year contract.

She had already been earning a high salary as the major figure on the NBC "Today" broadcast. Getting her to move to another network required the offer of an anchor chair, which she coveted, but it also required financial security. After all, she was leaving an established base at NBC to venture into an unknown and potentially risky situation at ABC. If the ratings were to climb because of Barbara Walters' presence on the "Evening News," the revenues from that program would have gone up, and for ABC it would have been an investment well worth the money. It didn't happen that way, and the million-dollar paycheck became a millstone. If she did something well, the performance was dismissed by her critics as merely to be expected of someone being paid a million dollars. If she made a mistake, the "I told you so's" chorused loudly.

The unkindest actions were those that were taken by news executives at other networks. Privately they paid tribute to her talent all the time. She has a number of letters from correspondents and news department presidents, vice-presidents, and executive producers at NBC and CBS praising her enterprise on one story or another; lauding her for her sharp questioning of Presidents Ford and Carter; marveling at her ability to get exclusive interviews with the Shah of Iran or Fidel Castro or other inaccessible public figures. But she also has clippings from newspaper and magazine pieces in which the same gentlemen wrote about her work with sarcasm. The fact is that if Barbara Walters were a man with a high salary, they would have treated the matter very differently.

Barbara is an extremely shy person, and that trait made her seem distant and aloof to the staff. When she arrived, the stagehands at ABC's Studio 7 did not help ease her adjustment to the new surroundings. They had known Reasoner for many years and would ostentatiously engage Harry in preshow banter about sports and baseball scores when Walters entered. She was left out entirely. The studio crew played to Harry; Barbara generally got their backs. The newsroom divided into factions; Reasoner had his supporters, Walters hers. On one occasion, miffed at a Walters interview that had lasted almost seven minutes one night, Reasoner went out with one of "his" producers and turned in a report on the Dallas Cowboys lasting just as long. Supporters of each of the two stars kept a count of how many minutes the other had appeared on the air. I would be asked why one or the other had been given the advantage. They both had identically sized offices at either ends of the newsroom, separated by the executive producer's office, which I occupied.

My first assignment from Arledge in June 1978 was to separate Reasoner and Walters on the air. We never showed them together on the screen again. We also sharply reduced the total amount of time they were on the air in their anchor roles. By increasing the number of reports from correspondents in the field, and by having one correspondent "throw" to another in a revival of the "whip-around," we actually cut the Reasoner–Walters combined air time to less than three minutes a night. (By contrast, Cronkite's on-camera time averaged six minutes.)

In fact, Walters and Reasoner were not hostile to one another, but after a while, it was apparent they could not communicate. The miscues that normally happen under the pressure of a live broadcast were exaggerated; before long, they simply could not work together.

There should have been a way to make the Reasoner–Walters combination work. If I had been able to motivate Harry, perhaps he and Barbara could have overcome their differences. Reasoner and I talked about it one afternoon in his office. "It's not you or anything you can do," he told me. "I came here to anchor my own broadcast. If I can't do that, I've got to leave." In 1978, he returned to CBS.

Anchors have become like champion knights of medieval times. They represent their organizations in the field just as knights did when they rode into the lists at a tournament. Anchors have the prestige to get heads of state or high government officials to sit down and talk. Anchors are dispatched to summit meetings to uphold the honor of their news departments and corner the biggest names first.

A historic case in point occurred in a running competition between Walter Cronkite, John Chancellor and Barbara Walters, which began in November 1974 and ended in April of 1979. The "playing fields" were the Egyptian–Israeli summit meetings, the Camp David Accords and President Anwar el-Sadat's dramatic visit to Israel to meet Prime Minister Menachem Begin. Cronkite, Chancellor and Walters were seeking any advantage in covering the story. Some claimed they were also competing by arranging the story. It was "television diplomacy," seeing history made by TV on TV.

Round one went to Cronkite on a carom shot. Egypt's President Sadat had told his Parliament that he would go anywhere, even to the Israeli Knesset in Jerusalem, if it would enhance chances for peace. Israeli Prime Minister Begin had said Sadat would be welcome, but Sadat was waiting for a formal invitation, as he told ABC's Peter Jennings in an off-camera interview. Jennings passed the word about Sadat's position to ABC's Bill Seamans in Tel Aviv, who got to Begin in the hallway of the Tel Aviv Hilton and asked him about it: "Would there be a formal invitation?" Begin replied that he would consider it and then went in to tell a banquet audience that he would use American ambassadorial channels to extend one to Sadat. ABC News felt pretty good about apparently being the carrier for Sadat's message and Begin's reply.

What ABC did not know, however, was that CBS was also in the field. Time worked in their favor, enabling Walter Cronkite to make a spectacular television showing on the same day.

Even though Jennings had gotten to Sadat first, it had been off camera. Cronkite, on the other hand, had a later, on-camera interview via satellite between New York and Cairo. "I'm just waiting for the proper invitation," Sadat told Walter. Asked how such an invitation could be arranged, Sadat replied, "Why not through our mutual friends, the Americans?" That was at approximately 9:00 A.M., Monday, November 14, 1977. For the next several hours, CBS News personnel in Israel tried to set up an interview with Prime Minister Begin. They found him at the dinner in Tel Aviv.

Begin agreed to go to a nearby hotel room, which CBS had set up as a mini–broadcasting studio and, via satellite, he too was interviewed by Cronkite. Begin said he would send Sadat the formal invitation he wanted in a letter to be transmitted the next day through the American ambassador in Israel. Cronkite's producers took the Sadat interview and the Begin interview and, even though they had been conducted separately and hours apart, edited them together. Answers were intercut with Cronkite questions, making it appear that both men had been interviewed simultaneously. Since CBS explained in advance what was being done, it was an acceptable journalistic technique. The effect was stunning. "Cronkite Diplomacy" was the *New York Times* comment. Through adroit editing, Walter Cronkite had apparently accomplished a diplomatic breakthrough for Mideast peace.

If round one went to Cronkite, rounds two and three went to Walters. She had always been highly regarded by Israeli officials and had met and gotten to know Begin even before he became Prime Minister. She sent Begin flowers when he was hospitalized for heart attacks. He had let it be known to his aides that he thought Barbara was among the smartest women he had ever met.

Sadat, too, was a friend. When Walters began as coanchor of the "ABC Evening News," Sadat agreed to appear on the premiere broadcast. It was not an auspicious event. He kept harping on Barbara's million-dollar-a-year salary. It was a subject that would better have been left unmentioned.

When Sadat went to Jerusalem in late November 1977, Barbara had arranged for *separate* interviews with him and with Begin. She had asked for a joint interview but Sadat was adamantly opposed. Despite having been edited together in the Cronkite effort, Sadat would not willingly appear on the same program with an Israeli. Yet as the two men met in Jerusalem, Barbara recalls, Begin "impulsively asked Sadat to 'do the interview together for the sake of our good friend Barbara.' " Sadat agreed. The interview was brimming with affability; the two heads of state joked, joshed, answered some questions and sidestepped some others.

Justin Friedland was the ABC News producer for the interview. It was his job to set the cameras in place, be sure the microphones were working, but most important, to edit the videotapes down to a length to be satellited to New York. He grabbed the tapes and sped by limousine to the Israeli Broadcasting Center in Herzliyya. Working away in one of the editing rooms there, Friedland realized that he was surrounded by Israeli technicians who had gathered to marvel at the incredible scene before them. There were Sadat and Begin sitting down and talking together.

One of those technicians was also a part-time employee of CBS News and he urgently called the CBS News office in Jerusalem to inform them of the ABC coup. CBS started to scramble to catch up. They found Walter Cronkite and, with him in tow, began to arrange for a similar joint interview with Sadat and Begin. It took them some time to get things set up, but at last it was done. By now it was late at night. The two leaders were no longer as exhilarated as they had been with Barbara. Their answers were shorter and delivered almost as if by rote. It was not as good a performance by either Begin or Sadat. Cronkite apparently sensed it. He thought the CBS cameras had been shut down. They were still recording, and what they caught was a revealing bit of the competitive pressure. Cronkite's final question, on tape, was directed to one of his aides: "Did Barbara get anything I didn't?"

Walters scored again in April 1979 during President Carter's visit to Cairo and Jerusalem. The peace process that had started as a result of Sadat's visit in 1977 was coming unstuck, and Carter had flown to confer separately with both leaders. Carter had left Israel for one last stop in Cairo on the way back to Washington. Cronkite and John Chancellor had tried to get interviews with Begin to discover what had gone wrong. Begin put them off but agreed to see Walters at 4:00 P.M. The ABC News team set up in Begin's apartment to await his arrival. Four o'clock came and went with no Begin, and as the clock moved toward 5:00 P.M., it began to look as though the interview would be off. Meanwhile, in Cairo, President Carter was still conferring with President Sadat.

At 5:00 P.M., Begin showed up, sat down, and was ready to begin talking. He had scarcely begun when the telephone rang in the kitchen. Begin took the call. Minutes later, he came back, all smiles. It had been President Carter from Cairo, telling him that President Sadat had accepted the American proposals to get the peace talks moving again.

"What has happened?" Barbara asked.

"I can tell you that the President gave me good news," he replied. He went on to explain. By the time Cronkite and Chancellor finally got in to see Begin (who only permitted them to question him in a joint interview), the Walters interview was already on the air in the United States, transmitted by satellite. His "good friend Barbara" was way out in front.

There is no harder worker in the field than Barbara Walters. She will work long into the night to edit a story to meet a broadcast deadline. Ellen Rossen, an ABC field producer, was with Walters in Cuba for the Conference of Non-Aligned Nations in Havana. "Barbara could have said 'Good night, I'm going to bed,' but she didn't want me to sit by myself," Rossen recalls, "so she walked me over to the TV station and fed the piece with me. She didn't have to do that. She's a star, but she works."

At the Havana conference, Barbara Walters had to get in touch with King Hussein of Jordan; Yasir Arafat, the head of the Palestine Liberation Organization; and Fidel Castro. She wanted to interview all of them, but in the tightly guarded conference hall there was hardly any way to establish contact. She solved the problem in a unique and strongly feminine way. She showed up in the press gallery carrying a box of her personal stationery. Since her handwriting is, by her own admission, unreadable, Walters dictated a series of notes to the world leaders who were seated in the conference hall below her. Rossen took down the letters in her finishing-school script. Hussein got the first note:

Dear Your Majesty,
     Can we confirm our interview? I'm sitting in the Press Gallery in a pink blouse. Wave if you can see me.
                                                      Barbara Walters

The notes were sent out to the floor by runner and, as Rossen recalls it, "Pretty soon, there's King Hussein looking up at her.

I said, 'Barbara, wave.' So she waved. There she was, telling heads of state to wave at her in a pink blouse. It was marvelous!" She got the interviews without a hitch.

Throughout 1977, it remained clear that the Reasoner/Walters coanchorship format had to be changed. Meetings were held constantly in Roone Arledge's office to develop a new look and style of presentation for the ABC evening newscast. Since there was no Cronkite at ABC, planning revolved around making *news content* the star of the broadcast. If the stories we presented were more interesting or more incisive, we believed we could counter the superstar status that Cronkite brought to his CBS program. The question remained, How?

There has always been criticism of network newscasts' dependence on Washington news or New York's view of the world. My experiences while visiting local stations repeatedly demonstrated that the networks are believed to be editing their newscasts with geographic blinders on. We wanted to break the New York–Washington axis, which concentrates editorial input in the hands of women and men who live and work in the northeast corridor.

The "subanchor" or "floating anchor" concept was set up to accomplish that. It was Roone Arledge's idea that anchormen and women should move out from studios to the scene of the news. It proved successful.

During the threatened strike by coal miners in West Virginia in the winter/spring of '78–'79, Frank Reynolds led a team of ABC correspondents to the coal fields. Like the other networks, one correspondent in the team did a report on the miners' preparations for the strike; another correspondent covered the mine owners' position; a third correspondent handled the government's role and the efforts to mediate.

What made ABC's coverage different was Reynolds' role as the on-the-scene anchor. Viewers saw him standing in the coal fields with pickets all around. He linked each of the separate pieces from there, not from a studio. Frank found and reported profound distress among miners who, though determined to strike, also realized they were doing it in defiance of the law and a court injunction. The conflict between economic needs and deeply held convictions was the human equation. Reynolds discovered it in the West Virginia coal fields and used it to put the individual correspondents' pieces into a clearer perspective. Viewers of ABC News came away with a little better understanding of the situation than viewers of the other networks' newscasts had received. Someone described it as "a fingernail's worth of difference." True, but in a competition between three essentially equal news-gathering organizations, that "fingernail's worth of difference" delivered night after night will eventually earn the viewers' respect and trust. They'll keep tuning in.

Our experience with the Reynolds "subanchor" led logically to the concept of permanently positioning anchors outside of the traditional New York studios. In a sense, we devised a dance of the seven veils that we called "World News Tonight," concealing our lack of a single superstar with a fast-paced mix of three people who would be presenting a wider range of more interesting stories, reported from the scene whenever possible. Anchors were to be based in Washington, London and Chicago.

It was obvious from the beginning that the Washington anchor would be the most important. Washington is the news center of the United States. What happens there affects us all directly and quickly. Whoever was going to anchor from there had the responsibility to judge which stories in Washington deserved to be pushed on to the air against similar pressures from London and Chicago.

Anchors have extra clout, which enables them to get stories inserted into the broadcast. From that fact grew the advocacy system. For example, the regional anchor in London, who watches all the news in Europe and the Mideast, can decide more effectively from there what stories should be included. When an anchor advocates the inclusion of a story to the producers in New York, they are more likely to listen and to keep the story in. Once their decision making was based on strongly advocated positions outside of the normal New York–Washington circuit, the breadth of coverage increased immediately. The "advocacy system" proved itself time and again, resulting in ABC News's coverage of stories weeks or days ahead of NBC and CBS. Again, if competition for audience respect and credibility depends on providing a "fingernail's difference," the advocacy system can provide that advantage.

Frank Reynolds was the prime candidate for the slot as Washington anchor on "World News Tonight." His credentials to be an anchorman and advocate were impressive. He started as a newsman at a radio station in Indiana. In 1949, he moved to Chicago, and, in 1963, he joined ABC, covering presidential politics and other major domestic stories. In 1967, he became anchor of the "ABC Evening News," and when I joined the network in 1969, I teamed him as a coanchor with Howard K. Smith, who had been virtually unassigned in the ABC Washington bureau.

Reynolds' demeanor on the air can be somewhat stiff. He has a radiant smile when he flashes it but his "burden on my shoulders" attitude sometimes comes across if the news is particularly weighty.

There are certain stories that Reynolds does not like to read. He recognizes their news value, but he is uncomfortable because of their nature. On the "ABC Evening News," he would frequently reappear on camera with a pained look after a report from the field that he found offensive. He had a habit of tapping his fingers on the desk if reports by correspondents were too risque for his tastes. "This is going to be a finger-tapper," I'd say to him as a piece began. "It will be worth at least four taps when you come back." Jollying Reynolds proved more effective than ordering him to stop his facial or digital editorializing.

John Armstrong, as ABC News senior producer in Washington, knows there are classifications of stories that Reynolds will not read without some gentle nudging. A case in point was a news report about a police show winning more Emmy nominations than any show had ever won before. Reynolds balked. "C'mon, Frank," the Senior Producer said, "it's not the end of the world." Reluctantly, Reynolds delivered the story on the air but his facial expression conveyed disdain for his producers' news judgment.

Frank's emotions were very much on view on the day John

W. Hinckley, Jr., tried to assassinate President Reagan in Washington. His performance was the subject of much criticism and comment by his colleagues, the press and the audience. He seemed personally affronted and outraged by the act. When word came that the President had been hit by one of Hinckley's bullets, Reynolds burst out "Oh my God!" The twists and turns in the breaking story's coverage seemed to heighten the tension he displayed. A note was handed to him by an aide with the name of the alleged assassin on it. He did not believe the source, refused to read it until confirmation was secured, and brusquely tossed the paper aside.

It was, as an observer described it, "a roller coaster day," and one of the lows came after the false report of the death of Press Secretary James Brady. Reynolds, like his competing anchors, Rather on CBS and Kalb, Mudd and Newman on NBC, had been told that many sources confirmed that Brady had succumbed to a gunshot wound in the head. There had already been several reports that Reynolds had refused to broadcast, doubting their authenticity. Finally confirmation seemed to come from the White House itself, and Reynolds realized he could no longer wait. Even as he was pronouncing the words, he was wondering what impact they would have on Brady's mother if she were in front of a TV set.

Reynolds and his competitors on the other networks began eulogizing Brady. They were in the middle of their recollections when word came from George Washington University Hospital that Brady was, in fact, still alive though in very critical condition. Rather's reaction was contained. "Your confusion is matched by our own," he said. Reynolds, by contrast, slipped into tight-lipped fury. "Let's get it straight!" he snapped, clenching his fists. "Let's get it nailed down. Let's end the confusion so we can report this accurately!"

Reynolds makes no excuses for his emotionalism. He believes he was reacting as any human being might when confronted by a deluge of conflicting information pouring in from every direction. "The viewer had to understand all the difficulties all of us were experiencing as we tried to get the news out to them," he said. "We are not Olympian gods, and I don't think I flew off the handle under those circumstances."

Some newspapers savaged Reynolds for bordering on the hysterical, but the letters and phone calls of viewers were mostly supportive, indicating that his personal involvement struck an empathetic chord on the other side of the TV tube.

Despite his present emergence as ABC's principal anchorman, Reynolds' career in the anchor chair has been a troubled one. The ABC Affiliates Board wielded considerable influence with corporate executives in 1969, making it clear that Reynolds was not their kind of performer for the long haul on the "Evening News." The board members believed he was too stiff, not "warm" enough to attract and hold a larger audience. There were regular calls for his replacement or at least for some indication that someone else would be brought in. Part of the pressure was relieved when we teamed him with Howard K. Smith and when, as a result of a better-produced broadcast, the ratings began to climb. Reynolds was kept on the air because he was authoritative and because he was one of the few performers with anchor status on the staff.

A great deal of that progress came unstuck for Reynolds, however, as a result of Vice-President Agnew's "unelected elite" speech in November 1969. Many who heard the Vice-President's references to commentators and anchors, and their use of "raised eyebrows" to express opinions, believed they were aimed in particular at Reynolds. Agnew quoted Reynolds' reply to an interviewer for a television documentary about television news in 1968. Reynolds had said that TV news anchors did include their own feelings in the process of deciding what would ultimately go into the newscast.

The Vice-President cited that as evidence of how the "unelected elite" colored the news each night. (Ironically, I was the interviewer, and the documentary, "The Whole World Is Watching," was presented on the Public Broadcast Laboratory.) It was not an unexpected assault on Reynolds. During his commentaries on the "Evening News," which ABC permitted each night, he had frequently dealt with the Nixon administration in a highly critical way.

As a result of Agnew's speech, ABC News examined its policies. An outside study was conducted concerning the organization's fairness and balance. The conclusion was that policies and practices at ABC News did not warrant Agnew's criticism nor did they result in any procedural changes that I knew of. Years later, Reynolds recalled a telephone call from a vice-president of the news division. Though he was not asked to refrain from criticizing Nixon, it was suggested that some comments could also be aimed at Hubert Humphrey as a liberal Democrat.

Reynolds recalled that he felt constrained to remind his caller that Humphrey, a former Vice-President and a recently defeated candidate for the presidency, was teaching political science at the University of Minnesota. There seemed to be hardly any way for Reynolds to comment negatively about the quality of Humphrey's teaching abilities. Reynolds continued to do verbal battle with the Nixon White House, winning the Peabody Award for his efforts. Nonetheless, some executives of the ABC Affiliates Board let it be known again that they believed Reynolds' day had come and that he should go.

An accident of contractual timing then took place at CBS News, which precipitated that departure. Harry Reasoner's negotiations for a renewed deal at CBS were flagging. Somewhere along the way, a phone call that would have kept the talks moving toward their expected successful conclusion was not made. Reasoner was suddenly a free agent. A deal was struck. Harry would be coming to ABC News in December to coanchor the "Evening News" broadcast with Howard K. Smith.

Ironically, the November 1970 election coverage at ABC had been coanchored brilliantly by Reynolds and Smith. The morning after, Frank was basking in well-deserved praise when he learned he was out of his anchorman's job. It was a badly handled affair and it almost destroyed his career. After a while, he emerged again as ABC News national correspondent, covering presidential politics and handling ABC's Watergate coverage. Although he was not the anchor, he often got assignments usually reserved for anchors. He was named to represent television as one of the three questioners during the Carter–Ford debates in the 1976 presidential campaign and remained well respected and liked by his colleagues and peers. When Roone Arledge arrived as president at ABC News, Reynolds was the prime candidate to resume the key role of presenting the news each night, this time on "World News Tonight," from Washington.

Peter Jennings, already based in Lond
foreign desk anchor for the broadcast.
ering the news overseas were extensiv
Vietnam, and because he had worked
the hottest fighting of the Lebanese
Arab story. He had also anchored th
1967. Jennings' Canadian accent, slightly mou...
living overseas, gave his delivery a pleasant distinction. ...
nings' early days in the field, he often dropped into English rather than American idioms. "*Sh*edule" rather than "*sk*edule" would turn up in his narrations. He would introduce Senator Kennedy as "the American Senator Kennedy" as if there were some Pakistani Senator Kennedy who required special identification by comparison. One year I sent him a copy of a dictionary of American English usage to help him remember the idiom of his home audience.

The "advocacy system" from overseas proved especially useful to him. His interests in Middle Eastern developments led him to significant beats. His insistence led us to assign him to interview an obscure Iranian cleric living in exile outside Paris. As a result, Jennings presented the Ayatollah Khomeini to American news viewers several months before he was propelled into prominence by the fall of the Shah. With his trenchcoat well belted, his credentials well established, and his area well advocated, Peter Jennings flourished as the foreign anchorman.

Chicago was selected as the best place to put a national anchor in order to soften the New York–Washington editorial dominance. Eventually it came down to Max Robinson, who had been established as a well-known personality in Washington, D.C. He anchored the most-watched news broadcast in the capital area. He was hired as one of the three anchors strictly on the basis of his reputation in Washington, which stemmed from the way he handled himself on the air during the Hanafi Muslim hostage incident in Washington, and from the respect that many journalists in Washington had frequently expressed for him.

Robinson did not make the leap from local to network news without difficulty. He had covered local politics but had little

ence with national election coverage. A team of research-
an an "election school" for Robinson when he was assigned
participate in ABC News's election coverage in 1978. He was
intensively drilled in facts about many of the races he would be
called upon to analyze from his anchor position in Chicago. He
did the best he could, but under the pressure of returns pouring
in, he was reduced to little more than reading numbers with no
analysis. He had been unable to absorb all the information he
had been given in his "crash course," and his previous experience with national politics was too limited to provide a basis for
instant recall. As that distressing night proceeded, the producers
bypassed Robinson and relied instead on Barbara Walters and
Frank Reynolds in New York for returns, analysis and interviews.

Robinson's experience underscores a central requirement in
an anchor: "credibility." This derives from what Professor
Edwin Diamond, who conducts studies of TV news at MIT,
describes as "broad experience at home and abroad, running
foreign news bureaus, covering both politics and wars." Without some experience of being directly involved with news coverage to call upon, an anchor can quickly be perceived as a sham,
unable to handle critical information quickly and believably.

In the network television ratings sweepstakes, and in the image
and credibility standings as well, the importance of the anchor
was never made clearer than when, in 1980, ABC News began
to bid for the services of Dan Rather at CBS. As a result of that
exercise, the face of CBS News changed dramatically and more
quickly than expected.

No one at CBS News wanted Walter Cronkite to retire. He
had talked about it in countless interviews, particularly as he
moved toward his sixty-fifth birthday. He was a man who fully
expected to be around, if not every night, then at least often
enough to anchor elections, conventions and other major stories. Although he had indicated that he wanted to make 1980
election coverage and the inauguration of the President in 1981
his ultimate assignment, very few in the hierarchy at CBS had

really faced the issue. If anyone seemed to have the inside track to succeed Cronkite it was Roger Mudd. He substituted for Cronkite almost every time Walter was on vacation or ill or on assignment out of New York or Washington. Richard Salant, when he was president of CBS News, clearly favored Mudd, whose low-key style and slightly Southern accent were in striking contrast to Dan Rather's more clipped staccato delivery.

Mudd had made his reputation on Capitol Hill covering the Senate after joining CBS News. Fred Friendly was then president of CBS News and decided in a stroke of television production genius to focus national attention on the Senate's debate of the Civil Rights Bill in 1964. Friendly told Mudd that he was to appear on every CBS News broadcast with some kind of a report on the debate's progress. For sixty-seven days, Mudd met that commitment. From 7:00 A.M. until 11:00 P.M., in rain, heat and darkness, Mudd showed up on news broadcasts. When the debate was over and the bill had passed, Mudd was no longer a regular correspondent. He was a "star." He was assigned to anchor the "CBS Weekend News" on Saturdays, and, logically, he shifted over to sit in whenever Cronkite was out of town during the week.

Those who worked with Mudd began to understand his point of view about what was worthy of inclusion in broadcasts that he anchored. He clearly demonstrated a bias in favor of Washington-oriented stories. What happened on Capitol Hill was deemed to be more important than most other news. A House of Representatives subcommittee would get air time; a labor dispute in the Midwest would not. On the "Weekend News" it was understood that Roger could have almost free rein at the top of the broadcast, where the hard news would appear, if Paul Greenberg, the executive producer, could have equal latitude at the bottom of the program. The result was straight-laced reporting dominated by Capitol Hill news as the broadcast opened, followed by innovative segments covering music, health and sports, which were reported by the sartorially splendid and highly articulate Woody Broun.

Yet Mudd rarely ventured outside politics and government operations on assignment. He turned down "suggestions" from news management that he report from Vietnam. He reportedly refused an assignment to go to Saudi Arabia for a special report, saying he "didn't know anything about the subject." When he was passed over as designated successor to Cronkite, Mudd went off the air at CBS and reemerged months later in a key "subanchor" role at NBC News, reporting each night from Washington. In April 1982, he became coanchor with Tom Brokaw, replacing John Chancellor, who has continued on the broadcast as "commentator." At CBS, when Mudd left, the word around the corridors was "regret," but the comment heard most often was "Rather simply worked harder to get the job."

Cronkite's departure scarcely diminished the level of expertise residing in the anchor chair. Rather's credentials were broad, perhaps even broader than Cronkite's had been when he took over the "Evening News" in 1963. Rather graduated from college in 1955 and then held jobs with UPI and the Houston *Chronicle*. He switched to radio news, and four years later he swung over to television. He was the local TV reporter that CBS News relied on to provide coverage of hurricane Carla. The network, impressed by that effort, hired Rather and sent him to run its newly created Dallas bureau. He participated in most of the civil rights coverage of the early sixties and was in Dallas to cover President Kennedy's trip there on November 22, 1963. He managed to find out seventeen minutes ahead of everyone else that Kennedy had died. For four days, almost without sleep, Rather was on top of the Dallas story, including the subsequent capture and later murder of Lee Harvey Oswald. That stint got him promoted to covering the White House; a move prompted, in part, by the mistaken belief that a reporter from Texas would be able to perform well in a White House run by a Texan, Lyndon Johnson. The word around CBS News in those days was that the relatively inexperienced Rather was not working out. It was simply a case of too much too soon. He was replaced and sent to London as bureau chief.

Dan Rather learned how to be a political reporter in London. Rather's assignments had not really required investigative reporting when he was covering civil rights demonstrations or hurricanes or even Kennedy's assassination. A reporter need only show up, keep his or her eyes open, see that the cameras were in the right place and rolling and, by and large, let the stories tell themselves. In the sixties, civil rights leaders, eager to get their message on national TV news broadcasts, gave reporters tips and stories. In the White House, daily news briefings and official news handouts were interspersed with carefully contrived "leaks" and an occasional invitation to visit the President for a nice chat. What Rather needed was firsthand experience in digging out news stories from reluctant sources.

Television was just starting in Britain, and it had no clout at all. In the sixties, when Rather was there, handouts and press releases were rarely delivered to the American news organizations' offices. Putting bits and pieces together into a good story took legwork, imagination and doggedness. Rather met the challenge and his air work improved visibly. When he returned after his London stint and a tour in Vietnam to cover the war during the Nixon administration, Rather really was a reporter.

He proved it during the Watergate investigations when, as CBS White House correspondent, he relentlessly pursued the Nixon conspiracy with sharp and challenging questions. In fact, his demeanor was regarded as too hostile by some of the CBS-affiliated stations, and pressure was brought on CBS to remove him from his White House assignment. CBS News didn't buckle, and Rather kept up his pursuit.

Most of the details of the story of Dan Rather's appointment to succeed Walter Cronkite have been told publicly. His contract at CBS was expiring and Dan and his agent decided to see what opportunities might be available at ABC and NBC. Having an agent or business representative is a mark of the degree to which broadcast journalism has accepted the "star system" of television. Contracts for performers are lucrative and have so many tax implications and personal "perks" like automobiles or special researchers or requirements granting prior approval of producers that agents are needed to work out all the details.

In the Rather negotiations, NBC dropped out first, so it came down to ABC, where discussions were held for a long period of time about what role Rather might play. When the negotiations reached a serious point, CBS News awoke to the fact that they were likely to lose a very important star. It was under the pressure of that potential loss that Bill Leonard, president of CBS News, went to Walter Cronkite and began to talk about a "date certain" for his retirement. Until ABC's negotiations with him seemed to be heading toward a conclusion, Rather had not been the front-runner for the Cronkite job. In fact, though there had been some consideration given to a Rather–Mudd anchor at CBS, it was the conventional wisdom that Mudd would get the job alone.

One Sunday, Dan came across Central Park in New York to my apartment to talk about ABC News. He had held long conversations with the other executives. Roone Arledge had spent many hours with him, philosophizing about broadcast journalism. Dan said he just wanted to talk over old times and compare notes on how things worked at ABC against the background of our common experiences at CBS. Over coffee, we reminisced. Rather explained how he really enjoyed being on the road. "I thrive on it," he told me, "and my idea of an anchor job fits into what ABC has been doing with its three-anchor system." Sitting behind a desk was not his idea of what an anchor should do. "I like to go. I like to do. I like to see. If I can't do that, then I can't do reporting and I'd quit."

As we talked, it seemed to me that he was torn between the opportunity offered at our newly strengthened operation and the chance to be the one man named to succeed Walter Cronkite. He would always be compared to Cronkite. That wouldn't necessarily be bad, but the change from Cronkite to anyone else would probably result in comparisons and some of them would undoubtedly be unflattering. Whoever took over from Walter might suffer a ratings loss because some viewers would shop around. Important guests who normally contacted Cronkite would now seek out Barbara Walters or John Chancellor first. Rather would be blamed for any diminution in CBS News performance, whether he was responsible for it or not. As we talked, however, I realized that the pull of Cronkite's anchor chair was irresistible and was overcoming all the arguments about chances and opportunities that ABC could offer.

We broke up after four hours of coffee and conversation. Rather's personal style is polite, almost courtly. He profusely apologized to my wife for intruding on our Sunday as he left. The next morning, I told Roone Arledge that, in my view, the chances of Dan Rather joining ABC News had "gone south." Four days later, Bill Leonard held a news conference at CBS headquarters in New York. He announced the appointment of Dan Rather as the sole successor to Walter Cronkite.

On Friday night, March 6, 1981, an era ended. Walter Cronkite stepped down as the anchor of the "CBS Evening News," turning over the mike to Dan Rather, who began on the air the following Monday. For weeks before the final broadcast, Cronkite had been receiving honors from the White House, from city governments and from prestigious societies. Many television stations presented minidocumentaries of his life, showing him as a young reporter during the Second World War and filled with snippets from many of his anchoring duties at CBS.

ABC News took out full-page newspaper advertisements thanking Cronkite for his "extraordinary contributions" to the broadcast news profession. In anticipation of his departure and the possibility that viewers would be sampling other newscasts, both NBC and ABC prepared special reports and extra advertising to lure them away from CBS and Dan Rather. It was certainly evidence that network news executives recognized the power of the anchor to retain viewers. With the star gone, it was expected to become a new universe.

Cronkite's final broadcast was a professional one, as usual, featuring, among other stories, a long report on secret nuclear-weapons tests conducted by South Africa. After the final commercial, Cronkite came on and said: "For almost two decades, we've been meeting like this in the evening, and I'll miss that. But those who have made anything of this departure, I'm afraid have made too much." Cronkite recalled that he had succeeded Douglas Edwards eighteen years earlier in 1963, and that he would be followed by Dan Rather on the following Monday.

"This is but a transition," he said, "a passing of the baton." He outlined some of the projects he intended to pursue as a CBS correspondent rather than as anchorman, and then he concluded: "Old anchormen, you see, don't fade away. They just keep coming back for more. And that's the way it is, Friday, March 6, 1981." After giving that familiar tag line, Cronkite paused, and with a smile he added, "I'll be away on assignment, and Dan Rather will be sitting in for the next few years. Good night."

If ABC had failed to woo Dan Rather from the lure of the power and prestige of sitting in Cronkite's anchor seat, it had not failed in its attempt to shake up the competition. After all, Cronkite was now gone.

Not long after, ABC was to make a similar move against NBC, trying to win the "Today" show anchor, Tom Brokaw. Brokaw's career in broadcast news began in 1962 when he worked in Omaha. He moved to Atlanta in 1965 to report on the civil rights movement and switched to NBC in Los Angeles as a reporter and anchorman in 1966. From the West Coast, Brokaw moved to Washington, eventually becoming NBC's White House correspondent during the Watergate period. NBC liked his style as a reporter and gave him more assignments as anchor on documentaries, election night and, finally, on the "Today" show. When ABC News tried to lure Brokaw away, NBC countered by assigning him to coanchor its "Nightly News" with Roger Mudd. Once again, the arrival of the Brokaw–Mudd team meant that another familiar anchor face would be leaving the scene. John Chancellor was to retire as anchorman, become a commentator, and make room for Brokaw and Mudd. Within a year's time ABC's efforts, though thwarted, had changed the face of TV news.

Even before he relinquished the anchor chair, John Chancellor had thought he would like to move on to the role of commentator. "There's a considerable amount of information in my head," he remarked. "I'm anxious to share it thoughtfully." Cronkite also looked forward to supplying commentary because he did not believe he was free to express his own opinions while anchoring. "I'd like to be hard hitting without impinging on the independence and integrity of the 'Evening News.' " On a few occasions he stepped out of his role as anchor, most notably in 1968, after a second visit to Vietnam. His thirty-minute comment on the war, presented, not on the "Evening News," but as a TV news special, had an unmistakable message. Cronkite was against the war—he was in favor of getting out as quickly and cleanly as possible. In his book *The Powers That Be,* David Halberstam reports that after Cronkite's broadcast, President Johnson turned to his press secretary, George Christian, and said that it was a turning point: If he had lost Walter Cronkite, he had lost Mr. Average Citizen. "It was the first time in American history that a war had been declared over by an anchorman."

For almost any reporter, the prospect of becoming a commentator is seductive. It may even seem easy, but in fact, it is a formidable task. Most of the commentators with network news departments started their careers in World War II. They had broadcast from the most dangerous places in the world. Bill Downs landed at Omaha Beach in France; Richard C. Hottelet was arrested by the Nazis; Charles Collingwood got to Paris minutes behind the Free French. David Schoenbrun was in North Africa and France; Howard K. Smith escaped to Switzerland on the last train from Berlin; Eric Sevareid reported the Blitz in England; and Edward R. Murrow flew bomber missions over Germany and reported from the burning streets of London. These men and others had earned the respect of millions who listened to their radio reports to find out what they had to say about what was happening *behind* the headlines.

With the decline of radio and the emergence of television, some commentators dropped out because they could not make the transition. Others returned to "beat" reporting. Most disappeared from the public eye and, as a result, lost the public's interest. Murrow had died; Collingwood appeared only occasionally; Schoenbrun was forced out by office politics; Hottelet went to the United Nations as a reporter. The giants had passed from the scene, and few others came along to replace them. While David Brinkley was still at NBC (he switched to ABC in

1981), his comments were a now-and-then thing, which the network's management would try, then drop, then revive again. For a time, ABC tried "guest commentators." The trouble was that too many of the guests merely read from pieces they had already prepared for publication elsewhere. One woman delivered a commentary she had once presented on public TV.

CBS Radio kept a form of commentary going with its "Spectrum" series. Advocates of a particular point of view were given fairly free rein. An announcer read a disclaimer at the end: "This has been 'Spectrum' . . . different points of view which do not necessarily represent the opinions of this station or of the CBS Radio Network." The broadcast's approach was one of "preaching to the choir." Those who agreed with the points being expressed applauded the advocates; those who opposed what was being said simply ignored them.

By the end of the seventies, commentaries disappeared from the nightly network newscasts, not to be revived for several years. What happened? One explanation has to do with the disappearance of the single anchor on local news programs. For almost the entire decade of the seventies, the lone anchor was replaced virtually everywhere by increasingly popular and effective *teams* of men and women. Anchors also came out from behind their desks and started getting involved in story coverage themselves. More and more, the all-knowing "father" or "uncle" disappeared from the television screen.

The field of recognized commentators to whom audiences would turn for their opinion dwindled until, by the end of the seventies, there were really only two who appeared full-time on the networks: Howard K. Smith at ABC and Eric Sevareid at CBS. Though Brinkley, Reasoner, Reynolds, Rod MacLeish and some others did commentary from time to time, Smith and Sevareid stood above the rest.

For a while, Frank Reynolds worked in New York as anchor–commentator for ABC. But in spite of his best efforts to get material worthy of analysis, he came up dry on many nights. Sound commentary demands that the speaker have access to information on a "background," or off-the-record, basis. Some sources can be tapped in New York, and people are willing to

ANCHORS AND COMMENTATORS   157

chat on the telephone, but the main business of gathering information on behind-the-scenes developments occurs across a lunch table or on the cocktail circuit in Washington. Without that kind of ever-fresh material, the commentator's subjects became bland and predictable. The same thing happened to Harry Reasoner when he anchored from New York and tried to do commentary twice a week. Reasoner's efforts were generally wry, designed to counterpoint Howard K. Smith's sterner contributions from Washington the other three days a week. Still, there were days when Harry drew a blank. The commentaries that began, ". . . a man I know told me . . ." usually meant that Reasoner had nothing much to say that day.

Eric Sevareid and Howard K. Smith worked hard writing their comments. They attended briefings in Washington and traveled among the heavyweights of government, politics, and international affairs. They managed to retain the aura of "expert," which they had earned during the Second World War and in the intervening years.

John Armstrong was senior producer for the "CBS Evening News" from 1969 until Sevareid retired in 1979, and it was his job to find out what he was going to talk about each night. "Eric operated almost independently of the show," he recalled. "The executive producer would call and ask, 'What's he talking about?' I'd ask Sevareid, and he'd give me one sentence and that was the last we saw of him until he finished writing it." Sevareid would always turn in copy after lunch, sometimes as late as 4:00 P.M. Then it would go to New York where, Armstrong insists, "[They] never, never tampered with it."

When Sevareid was on the money, it was recognized that he had no equal. A case in point was the Monday evening after the "Saturday Night Massacre." Over the weekend President Nixon had moved to block the special prosecutor's investigation of Watergate. The Nixon White House had fired the prosecutor, the attorney general and his assistant. The FBI was guarding the records of the special prosecutor, and there was genuine fear that the investigation would be halted and the files destroyed.

At CBS News throughout the weekend, everyone was anticipating Sevareid's Monday comments. They were not to be disappointed. As Rick Kaplan, who was there, remembers it, "Eric lit into the administration. It was brilliant. Everyone read what he had to say. We telexed it to all the overseas bureaus and there were smiles on everyone's faces."

But those who were keeping score felt that the quality of Sevareid's commentaries was deteriorating from one good one in three to one in twelve. There was a certain lack of clarity. Once two producers, after reading Sevareid's comment about busing in Louisville, had opposite views of what he was recommending. "He was incredibly subtle," one remembers.

Sevareid feared live television. When he started doing his commentaries, they were always videotaped, so the fluffs, bobbles and gulps could be eliminated. He often took ten tries to get one perfect. At the end of his career at CBS, he did only one take, leaving the fluffs in.

Sevareid stopped doing lighter pieces. He used to venture a thought about spring; now he concentrated on polemics. "He was affected greatly by Nixon," John Armstrong says. "He didn't exactly burn himself out but what better time was there than the Nixon period for a commentator to write?" Yet Armstrong discovered that people he knew still waited for Eric to come on each night. He used to talk about it with his mother-in-law. "She thought Eric was like a preacher for her. He brought 'the revealed news word.' "

Many meetings ensued among producers and news department executives to discuss "The Sevareid Problem." Finally a compromise was worked out. Sevareid's commentary would run only four days a week and the broadcast's producers would choose which day to pass him by. But there was concern about the appearance of censorship. Leaving out a commentary that might be controversial could be construed as muzzling.

No CBS News executive wanted to be the man who took Eric Sevareid off the air. There was that oft-mentioned sense of "History" about him. Murrow was gone but Sevareid was still around; a tangible link with the past. Nevertheless, his work was slowing down. When his time came to retire, there was no joy around CBS News. There was a feeling that an era of broad-

cast history and "class" was slipping away. Would he or someone like him ever come back? At CBS News, the standard reply
to the question "Who will replace Eric Sevareid?" was "No one
could replace him."

Howard K. Smith would spend most of his morning research-
ing and writing. His script would be sent to New York so that
the "Evening News" producers and ABC management could
read it in advance. Occasionally they would call Smith to suggest word changes for clarity. Smith usually decided on the
subject of the day, though at the suggestion of the broadcast's
producers he might switch, especially if a breaking story required his perspective.

When Smith began regular commentaries on the "ABC Evening News," it was regarded as a significant contribution to the
broadcast. ABC's underfinanced operation frequently left it
without on-the-spot coverage of major events. A Smith commentary helped fill that gap. Howard had been a hawk on Vietnam, so when he began to advocate that the Nixon
administration end American involvement, it had considerable
effect. His greatest influence was demonstrated when he called
for Nixon's resignation. The wire services and many newspapers picked it up as evidence that the nation had turned against
the President. It was a level of influence to which all commentaries aspired.

Nonetheless, public accolades did little to blunt the impression among many CBS and ABC News producers that the two
or more minutes allotted for commentary could be spent more
usefully. Younger producers, those raised as children of TV
rather than of print, began to turn out concise, *pictorial* analyses.
Economics, defense spending, the tangled interrelationships of
government and business and other intricate subjects became
matters for their attention and creativity. Those kinds of pieces
became standard, and because they were part of the mainstream
of visual news, they were included within the main body of the
nightly newscasts. Commentaries remained *outside,* often after
the last commercial, like an afterthought.

The commentator, a man sitting at a desk and talking directly

into camera, a "talking head," seemed an anachronism, a throw-
back to the era when getting pictures was a formidable task.
Given limitations of staff and equipment, there had not been the
time nor energy spent to absorb commentary into the mainstream of production. That rigidity was its undoing.

Will there be another era of commentators? Perhaps. John
Chancellor is expected to attempt to restore it as a valued part
of the nightly news. Not everyone thinks it will work.

David Brinkley isn't sure that commentary will regain its
status on the nightly newscasts. "Commentary gets to be a sort
of high-wire act," he told one interviewer. "You're saying,
'Look, folks, how brave I am in taking an unpopular position in
full view of fifteen million people.'" Nonetheless Brinkley
began to present a weekly commentary each Sunday after leaving NBC to join ABC News. As the host of a weekly news and
interview program, Brinkley uses some of his air time to sum
up the week's top story, adding a personal observation along
the way. Still a Sunday talk show is not the evening news.

The question remains—who, if anyone, will be the next commentators? There are few individuals with the right credentials:
Cronkite, Chancellor, Brinkley. Bill Moyers, who made a reputation as a thoughtful observer on public television, has joined
CBS and begun regular appearances as an analyst and commentator alongside Dan Rather. Robert MacNeil, the coanchor of
the MacNeil–Lehrer report on public television, who has already been tapped for election-night analysis on ABC, might be
chosen. George Will, a conservative columnist, has started to
make regular TV appearances, and Hodding Carter, the State
Department's spokesman during the Iran hostage crisis, has
emerged as a reporter and an analyst.

As Smith and Sevareid left, there were no clear replacements
at the networks, but as planning for lengthened formats of forty-
five minutes and one hour continued into 1982, all the plans
included time for commentators. The thought was that "we'll
need them again if we go to an hour." Both men set standards
that will be hard to match. As it was said when Sevareid left
CBS: No one could really replace him. That meant nobody
really would.

4
"My God, the Pope May Have Been Shot!"
IMMEDIACY AND ACCURACY IN CRISIS COVERAGE

Bill Blakemore, the ABC News correspondent in Rome, was on the telephone to Bob Frye, the senior producer in London. It was routine, one of the daily sweeps of all the bureaus that Frye made. Across the room from Blakemore in the Rome office, Aldo Bisci, the bureau editorial assistant, sat listening to Vatican Radio's regular description of the usual Wednesday afternoon papal audience in St. Peter's Square. Suddenly, Bisci heard the Vatican Radio announcer shouting, and from what could be heard out of the confusion, he realized something terrible had happened. Bisci cried out to Blakemore and Bill said to Frye, "My God, the Pope may have been shot!" The line went dead. It was 11:21 A.M. Eastern time.

Frye crossed quickly to the central news desk area in the ABC London bureau and punched the PL—a private line to New York that doesn't need to be dialed and rings through instantly twenty-four hours a day. It is attached to a small loudspeaker so that anyone around the newsroom in New York is able to listen. "We have an unconfirmed report that the Pope has been shot," Frye said. "We're moving people to Rome now!"

Howard Schoenholtz was acting foreign editor that day. He began the job of news-gathering and of getting ABC News on the air. It's routine now, a routine born of a lot of experience. "Order a Rome-to-New York 'bird' and let it go forever," he said, and the ABC Traffic Department started making the necessary calls for the satellite.

Jeff Gralnick, ABC's man in charge of special events, in addition to his role as executive producer of "World News Tonight," was waiting for a meeting of news executives to begin when he heard Frye's call from London. Gralnick spun forward in his orange swivel chair and snapped a switch on the tie line— a special phone to Washington. "Find a broadcaster and sit him down in the chair," he said. "We're going on the air!"

The domestic editor that afternoon was Wes Downs. When he heard Gralnick's command, he "hit the Flash phone" attached to the wall by his desk. The Flash phone ties together all the technical staffs of the network for emergency conference calls. In a well-rehearsed response, Downs rang the phone's bell three times and then announced:

> "This is Wes Downs at the Central Assignment Desk. It is Wednesday, May 13, 1981, at 11:28 A.M. We are going with a live special report from Washington studios on the possible shooting of the Pope. We will feed the full network immediately."

Then Downs called the roll:
"Network Operations?" "Net ops. O.K."
"Central Switching?" "O.K."
"Traffic?" "Traffic understands."
"TV-5?" "TV-5 O.K."
"Videotape?" "Videotape ready."
"Projection?" "Projection O.K."

Each of the technical staffs was alerted and ready to supply its facilities to handle a major effort for an extended period of time.

Here I am in 1949, a junior writer and radio reporter at CBS News, getting on the air occasionally and thinking that television was just a "sideshow" with no real future. My boss told me I didn't know what the hell I was talking about and transferred me to TV.

Edward R. Murrow *(above)* watched as technicians merged pictures of the Atlantic and Pacific oceans on monitors during his "See It Now" broadcast in 1952. It was television's equivalent of the driving of the Golden Spike, tying America together from coast to coast.

Technology always meets the demands of the editorial side for faster transmission of the news. In 1961 *(left)*, we covered the building of the Berlin Wall and watched East German troops on patrol. The film was shipped and took two days to get to New York. In 1972 *(below left)*, during President Nixon's visit to China, films we took in snowy Peking were satellited back for same-day viewing. By 1982 *(below right)*, lighter videotape cameras made it possible to move in closer for better coverage, like this, for a special program on Pope John Paul II.

Douglas Edwards, left, was the first anchorman for the "CBS Evening News." Don Hewitt, right, became the broadcast's regular producer in the early fifties. He "invented the wheel" for TV news presentation, developing so many techniques that those who followed him still use the ones he originated. After leaving the "Evening News," Hewitt created and became executive producer of "60 Minutes."

CBS

In the Control Room of CBS Studio 41 during the 1966 three-network-pool inaugural broadcast of the synchronous Earlybird satellite. Left to right: Robert Hammer, CBS Operations; Dick Knox, program assistant; Joel Banow, associate director; Fred Friendly, president of CBS News; Vern Diamond, director; me; Hal Classon, technical director. Earlybird, positioned above the equator and visible from sending and receiving "dishes," truly began the era of satellite transmission of breaking news stories.

CBS

TV news production depends on teamwork. Dick Richter *(above left, with Harry Reasoner)* sat to my left when we produced the "ABC Evening News" in the early seventies. Editorially we were so compatible that we finished each other's sentences while making news judgments. David Buksbaum *(above)*, here shown with aides at the 1972 Democratic National Convention, was the energetic editorial/technical genius of the team. He would take a terrible script and turn a correspondent's "oatmeal" and "wallpaper" into polished reporting.

At the "rim" of the "Evening News" in 1977: phones, newswires, scripts make it the heart of the operation. Right to left: Jeff Gralnick, who succeeded me as executive producer; me; Rob Patulo, a program associate who could recall pictures of every news maker and maps of every city; and David Jayne, senior producer, who was to die in a plane crash in Jordan while carrying videotapes to a satellite transmission point.

Roone Arledge, president of ABC News, brought leadership and corporate financial support to the news department. An active executive, he frequently dropped in to review the day's coverage in the "World News Tonight" production offices.

Gathering and delivering the news is dangerous business. Roger Peterson *(top)* continued recording his story after being hit by shrapnel in Vietnam. Then he went to receive medical treatment. Terry Koo *(center)* was killed on the last day of his tour of duty as a news cameraman. He tried for one last sequence of pictures of the North Vietnamese army advancing near Hue. A mortar shell exploded and Koo died instantly. Bill Stewart (bottom), in Managua, covered the revolution in Nicaragua. Shortly after videotaping a group of National Guardsmen at ease with their guitars, Stewart and his camera team were stopped on a road outside of town by another guard unit.

Stewart walked forward to find out what the trouble was. As his crew videotaped from a distance, he held out his press pass but was forced to kneel and then to lie down. The guardsman came up and kicked him in the side. Then, without pause, he coldly shot him in the head.

ABC

ABC

Ken Lucoff *(below left)* was part of the ABC News team with Stewart in Nicaragua, and he delivered the formal demand for an investigation of the killing to Nicaraguan President Anastasio Somoza. Ironically, Lucoff himself was to die a few months later in a plane crash en route to another story in Latin America.

ABC

ABC

Anne Garrels *(above)* monitoring Soviet TV news in her Moscow apartment. Well schooled in Soviet affairs and the Russian language, she frequently scored "beats" as ABC Moscow correspondent. The KGB had her mugged in a Kiev street as a warning to stay away from Jewish friends. Ann Compton *(right)* at the Democratic National Convention. Compton discovered that many politicians who were lambs during the day could become wolves at night. Doreen Kays *(below)*, in Cairo, had a pact with her male camera crew when they went into riot situations. They were not to give her special care because she was a woman alongside them in danger. Knowing Arabic and the politics of Egypt enabled her to "own" the story in Egypt while Anwar el-Sadat was alive.

Barbara Walters *(above)* with President Anwar el-Sadat and Prime Minister Mena-chem Begin. Sadat did not want to be seen sitting side by side with Begin on TV, but when Begin said "Let's do the interview together for the sake of our good friend Barbara," Sadat agreed and TV history was made. Ellen Rossen *(right),* "20/20" producer, checking a cameraman's shot, believes women are now treated as equals by news crews, with no more patronizing "sweetie baby" in the field. Marge Lipton *(below),* ABC News bureau producer in Poland when martial law censorship was in effect, arranged to have videotapes taken out of Warsaw wrapped around the waist of a tourist.

E. ROSSEN

M. LIPTON

With Mike Wallace in the studio for the "CBS Morning News" in 1963. Covering women's health and social problems on a regular basis for the first time, the broadcast innovated many techniques that became standards for news presentation in the years ahead.

CBS

Walter Cronkite being "fitted" in the 1966 election night anchor position. Left to right: Vern Diamond, director; Al Thaler, production supervisor Hugh Raisky, set designer; Cronkite; and me. Walter would sit in the chair and tell us where he wanted his telephones, TV monitors, and anchor assistant to be.

CBS

On the "20/20" set in 1981 with Barbara Walters just before her live interview with former President Nixon. One of TV's best interviewers, Barbara kept reviewing her planned questions, discarding some and sharpening others right up to air.

ABC

It was now a little more than seven minutes since Frye's call. By now, Barry Serafin, a Washington-based correspondent with some anchoring experience, had been hustled into the anchor chair. He was ready to go on the air with the first bulletin. The ABC Special Reports slide went up on the network's transmission line, signaling all the affiliated stations that a major news story had broken and was about to be reported. Central Switching shifted control of the network's lines to Washington, and at 11:36 A.M., Serafin was on the air. A picture of the Pope had been found and electronically inserted into the screen behind him. "Good afternoon," he began. "There is a report from Rome that Pope John Paul the Second has been shot. . . ."

Now that we were on the air, the next problem was how to sustain the coverage, to continue to uncover new information and to present it in an interesting way. Phone communications with Bill Blakemore in Rome had been reestablished, and they were hooked, or "patched," directly into Washington. Blakemore could speak directly to Serafin, and the conversation could be fed directly onto the air. Blakemore elected to stay at the ABC Rome bureau, monitoring Italian television. Whatever they reported, Blakemore repeated and American viewers learned at once.

In New York and Washington, material was gathered to support the broadcast. Medical experts were found and one showed up in the studio with a full-sized breakaway model of the human abdomen. He used it to explain how a bullet might have damaged the Pope's liver, spleen, intestines and stomach. Translators were brought in to monitor Italian radio. A Roman Catholic priest was found to explain how the Church would function when the Pope was incapacitated.

When pictures of the immediate aftermath of the shooting and of the alleged assassin came in from Rome on the satellite, they were played and replayed, sometimes in slow motion, to trace the smallest details of the event for the viewers.

And help came from an unexpected quarter. Wes Downs, still on the Domestic Assignment Desk, got a phone call from an Iranian student at college in Kansas City. He had recognized the picture of the man the Italians said was the would-be assassin.

The student said the man's name was Ali Agca, a well-known Turkish terrorist in the Middle East. Downs passed the tentative identification to London, and researchers there began to hunt through files. Sure enough, Agca turned up in several stories about terrorism in Turkey, and the information was quickly added to the flow of facts pouring out on the air.

Normally, the network's number-one anchor would sit in the chair for extended coverage of such an event, but that day Frank Reynolds was heading toward New York to attend a function at Columbia University. He was in a limousine from LaGuardia Airport to his hotel when Bob Frye's call reached New York. By the time Reynolds arrived at the hotel, the news had been on the air for at least an hour. As he stepped out of his car at the hotel entrance a passerby recognized him: "You'd better get to your office, Mr. Reynolds. The Pope's been shot. . . ." Frank turned around, got back in the limousine, sped to the studio and, after a quick briefing, replaced Serafin and went on the air.

Bob Seigenthalter, who oversees production of continuous coverage of major events, was riding in a subway en route to a speech he was to make on Wall Street when Frye's news came in on the speaker. Seigenthalter, like all of us, carries an electronic paging device, activated by the Assignment Desk editor, who calls a special telephone number. When that call is made, the pocket device starts to beep frantically, which means "Call the desk immediately!" As Seigenthalter emerged from his subway ride, his pocket was shrieking with beeps.

Seigenthalter heads a quick response team of men and women. He assembled two producers and two transmission engineers to arrange for live camera originations in Rome, another camera team to supplement the people already in Rome and another correspondent to handle the extra work that live and continuous coverage from Rome would entail. The group piled into a limousine and headed for JFK Airport to make the next scheduled plane for Rome. "The next plane to any major event is like old home week," Seigenthalter commented. "Every network's 'swat team' is aboard, and it's like a college reunion." All of them arrived in Rome at 7:00 A.M. the next morning, and from then on it was nonstop until the Pope was declared out of danger.

★   ★   ★

The immediacy of television is unparalleled. That same immediacy makes TV news dangerously vulnerable to the commission of mistakes on the air. Newspaper editors and reporters can put some time and distance between themselves and the event they are reporting. Print journalists have much more opportunity for clarification, reflection, detail and perspective. There is time for fact checking, calling back to verify one's notes, mulling over some potentially misleading phrase. There is, as *New York Times* associate editor Tom Wicker explained, a chance to "follow plenty of false leads in private" while running down a story. This is the editing process of journalism.

In its live and continuous coverage of a breaking story of such significant proportions, TV news compresses that process. The coverage takes on a life of its own, developing momentum and drive, which forces correspondents to race rather than walk from one story element to another. The anchors become, in effect, editors and reporters. Reporters on the scene of the breaking story may add important details; still it is the anchor who summarizes, repeats, amplifies and ultimately evaluates the material coming in from the field. All those judgments are taking place under time pressures and in the midst of near chaos. Dozens of facts, rumors, conjectures and ideas are surging about every minute. The system does not provide for a detailed review of material. Much of what pours in is raw data, edited in the head of the correspondent as he or she reads from notes hastily scribbled at the scene. Interviews are done with eyewitnesses whose own credibility is unchallenged and unchecked. The system provides for only two alternatives: Accept the material or reject it.

Frank Reynolds' view provides an anchor's firsthand summary of what is happening every second. "In a breaking story," he explained, "editing is being done as you go along. If we had some time—even thirty seconds or a minute—to think about what we are saying, it would give us a chance to be reflective. But we don't have the time, not even five seconds, let alone a minute."

Critics argue that the scramble to get on the air first is merely a result of the competition for ratings and undermines the credibility of TV news. Why not take more time or even forgo live coverage in favor of bulletins and special reports that could go on the air when facts are verified and clear? On-the-air editing would thus be substantially eliminated, and misinformation would be sharply reduced. That sounds like a proposal by those who are more comfortable with print than with television. The public, which demands "the latest" from TV, would probably not stand for it.

Even with their longer editing processes, newspapers make serious errors. A newspaper carried the headline "Dewey Defeats Truman" in 1948, and a newspaper announced that former President Ford would become Ronald Reagan's vice-presidential running mate in 1980.

Might there be a better way for network news to handle crisis situations? Perhaps an editorial "filtration" team should get all incoming information first before passing it on to the anchor to report. Such a system would slow down the information flow slightly, but if it caught even one error or freed the anchor from the burden of making even one critical judgment under pressure, it would be worth it. Still, that is a pretty big "if."

In the case of the reporting of the attempted assassination of President Reagan, even if there had been an editorial "filter," it would have been only as good as the information coming through it. First, there were official denials that the President had been hit. White House spokesmen initially reported that Reagan got away from the scene unhurt. When witnesses phoned in that the President had gone to George Washington University Hospital, the word "gone" to the hospital was carefully and repeatedly stated, lest anyone believe that the President had been "taken" to the hospital. In light of the White House spokesman's statement that Reagan was unharmed, the concern was to avoid even the slightest impression that the President had been wounded. In fact, all networks speculated that Mr. Reagan had "gone" to the hospital in order to visit his wounded press secretary and Secret Service guard.

It was forty-five minutes before a White House spokesman announced that the President was indeed wounded. The "filtration" system mounted by the anchors themselves had held the line against exaggeration by insisting on confirmation of each detail. Marvin Kalb, anchoring for NBC in Washington, had closely questioned a correspondent on the air when he had (incorrectly) reported that Reagan had undergone "open heart" surgery when "open chest" surgery was meant. Kalb also remained skeptical of reports that had the President out of the operating room, then back in again and then out. He cautioned NBC correspondents reporting from the field to take their time.

Again, even if an editorial "filter" had existed, including a review panel and a procedure of coverage based upon special bulletins rather than live and continuous broadcasting, the erroneous reports of the death of Press Secretary James Brady would most likely have gotten on the air. Good reporting always requires confirmation of a story from more than one source. In the case of the report of Brady's death, there were at least five separate sources apparently confirming the story.

One report came from a Secret Service contact who said that organization's own internal communications system had confirmed the death; a second came from someone inside the FBI's hierarchy and stated that the director of the FBI had been told that Brady was dead; there was a report from the hospital itself from someone who had just come from the floor where Brady was being attended. Senator Howard Baker's aide on Capitol Hill reported the death. Finally, a White House spokesman apparently confirmed the report when asked about it by a correspondent. Later, the spokesman was to insist that he had been misunderstood and that he was, in fact, actually answering another reporter's question on another subject when he said "yes."

Five independent sources, all apparently confirming the news, left little doubt that James Brady had succumbed. Even the network that had waited for the fifth confirmation was presenting a Brady obituary when a different White House spokesman at the hospital came out to deny the report. No manner of "filtration" process would have prevented that error from being broadcast.

In covering the assassination story, the networks had tried to be as comprehensive as possible without damaging their credibility. The public's level of trust of television as its primary and fastest news source has also, paradoxically, made it less tolerant of errors on the air. The assignment is almost impossible. Instant coverage and total accuracy will never be achieved. If any lesson is to be learned from the failure in the Brady case, it is that television must realize that an extra effort will always be required to separate confirmed fact from conjecture, and hearsay from responsible speculation. The solution is not to withhold information but to qualify it. Reports withheld from the public may do as much disservice to the viewers as the reporting of unsubstantiated but identified conjecture and rumor. The proper approach is a middle course. Sources should be identified and explained so that their credibility can be judged by the audience. A casual passerby in the lobby of a hospital who saw the President is an eyewitness only to the fact that the President walked in assisted by two men. He is not a judge of whether the President looked pale (he had presumably never seen Mr. Reagan before) or whether the doctors on duty looked harassed or nervous.

The strength of television is its ability to go to many places quickly, to gather information about many aspects of a breaking story. Speed and a high degree of accuracy is what viewers expect to receive when they turn on their TV sets. These need not be sacrificed as long as responsible judgments are exercised *first*. Three sources for each story element ought to be the minimum requirement unless the information is delivered first person by a recognized spokesman. If that individual gets the story wrong, it can no longer be the fault of the broadcaster, who ought to remain cautious no matter what the source. Finally, the public ought to realize that they are also part of the communication process. They are receiving what the TV news people are sending. Viewers must realize that the process of editing on the air has built-in risks, which must be accepted in exchange for getting information quickly. Prudence in viewing must match prudence in broadcasting.

When an extraordinary event breaks suddenly, anchors and correspondents are thrust onto the air for continuous live coverage with no warning and only their own instincts and experience to guide them. Most of the time, however, special-events coverage is planned. An inauguration, a royal wedding, a papal coronation or a funeral all start with extensive preparations. Usually, every move in a procession is rehearsed, every speech has been listened to and timed, every marching band has been heard. There is a running order for each of the events. By examining it in advance, a producer can create an editorial lineup that encompasses all the points that must be covered. One can depart from it at will but there is an agenda.

Along with the lineup, the "book" becomes essential. The "book" includes prescripted items of information that can be dropped into the correspondents' commentary. That is where the real content is stored. It is not in the broadcaster's head; he or she is bound to forget important facts if they are not written down in the "book." The book also contains prescripted lead-ins for film "packages," prepared in advance to illustrate aspects of the story being covered. Those packages make up the "bank."

At CBS, during a space shot, for example, there would be "book" items about astronaut safety. There would also be a lead-in to a "bank" piece of film showing the escape mechanism that astronauts could use if something went wrong while the rocket was on the pad. The lineup would reflect the possible use of a safety sequence during an early part of the launch coverage. If there was a "hold" or delay in the launch schedule—and there frequently was—the control room would tell Cronkite to find "number 7 in the book." He would flip to that page and there would be the prescripted lead-in to "number 7 in the bank." He would know it was cued up, ready to roll on an exact word in the lead-in. It all looked smooth on the air because of hours of preparation beforehand.

The "book and bank" system has been refined through the years. Producers have their own particular method of keeping track of all the editorial points that need to be included if the broadcast is to be at all thorough. Jeff Gralnick, as executive producer of ABC's election night coverage in 1980, had a twelve-page color-coded lineup before he went on the air. It was based on the expected times for "calls" of election races in each state. Gralnick could estimate fairly closely when enough votes would be counted in order to "project" a winner. Against that time line, he had ordered the preparation of what he calls his "insurance policies," short videotaped vignettes, which were designed to profile the winning candidate in each race.

The ABC anchormen, Frank Reynolds and Ted Koppel, had a book of lead-in copy at their side and were prepared to read the appropriate scripts immediately after an election race was decided. Bob Roy, the senior producer assigned to turn out those "packages," decided that they should run no longer than one minute and forty seconds because he knew that Gralnick would simply "dump out" of a longer piece, cutting it off the air, in order to get back to Reynolds and Koppel for their reports of later results of other races.

On election nights, for example, there is a degree of over-preparation. Pieces have to be produced in anticipation of victory by any of the candidates in the race even though odds give some virtually no chance. Upsets may surprise the viewers; they cannot surprise the producer of bank material. In the race for Maine senator, for example, Roy had produced a "Cohen wins" and a "Cohen loses" package. The race remained too close to call all night, and all night both prepared reports about the candidate were kept sitting side by side, waiting for the voters to decide which one would see the light of a television screen.

Every four years in the United States, the longest running *planned* special event in broadcasting occurs. It is the reporting of the presidential political campaign, which begins with the first caucuses in January and runs through the political conventions of summer, the election in November and the inauguration of the new President the following January.

What a job it is and what impact it has. There can be no doubt that television news reporting shapes the voting patterns and concerns of Americans. There is no doubt that what television journalists concentrate on as major issues affects the way voters vote. And television's own invention of computerized election "calls" and "projections" has changed the way votes are counted and how the results are explained.

Most political campaigns provide more pictures and hoopla than any other recurring event. There are crowds, bands and balloons. Political campaigns can overwhelm the senses with all the video "opportunities." Smart press secretaries know how to "use" television. They will do everything possible to schedule a candidate's appearances or significant speeches early in the day so that the pictures can be edited into a report for TV and fed into the network news. Candidates alter their travel schedules so they can be interviewed not only by network correspondents but by local television personalities as well. Two minutes on any TV tube is worth infinitely more than one more meeting off of it, more than any formal position paper handed out.

Initially, when television newsmen and women were learning how to cover politics, the pictures and the excitement of the campaign dominated their coverage. Crowd counting became a measure of a candidate's success. In the 1968 campaign between Nixon and Humphrey, the war in Vietnam had evoked riots in the streets; Bobby Kennedy and Martin Luther King, Jr., had been killed; faith in our national purpose was shaken. Humphrey's attempts to shake off his image as a member of a war administration failed. Richard Nixon was elected President, though holding on to a dwindling popular lead by the end. Still, with so much going on, a typical evening news report during the campaign consisted of pictures of crowds, a snippet of natural sound like a band, more crowds, perhaps a cut from a news conference or speech, and then the stand-up close, wrapping up the piece. There had been so much going on that caught the camera's eye that hardly any attempt was made to analyze the speeches or to put the campaign strategy into perspective. When it was all over, political scientists, politicians, newspaper reviewers and television journalists themselves, savaged television's effort as "all flash and no substance." Commentators wrote that "TV concentrates on the crowds and not the issues" and "Mickey Mouse could be elected if he were packaged right." We were, in fact, failing in our job and we knew it. The criticisms were not ignored.

In the 1972 campaign between President Nixon and Senator George McGovern, all three networks demonstrated that they were revamping their efforts in response to criticism. "Overview" reports became a feature of the evening news broadcasts. Senior correspondents were assigned to produce stories that would put issues, strategy, policy and substance on the air. There would still be daily coverage of the "here they come, there they go" aspect, showing candidates getting on and off planes, but all programs regularly carried more probing reports.

The networks increasingly relied on polling to find out what Americans thought about the issues. CBS and the *New York Times* created a joint effort. Later, NBC joined forces with the Associated Press and ABC with the Louis Harris organization. Their information helped provide some guidance to the questions raised during the campaign.

The 1972 campaign also saw an attempt to find a political Middletown, U.S.A. After checking demographics and population size and income levels and racial mix, we selected Columbus, Ohio, as the "ABC City" for the election. The idea was to send a crew, correspondent and producer into Columbus for the entire campaign. By checking the pulse of Ohio as it watched the campaign proceeding, we believed we could discover what issues were important, how the candidates' positions were being interpreted and even who would win.

In Columbus, in 1972, week after week, people continued to be more concerned with local matters such as whether Ohio State's football team would win. They paid little attention to what Richard Nixon or George McGovern were saying. Almost everyone interviewed at work or at home or in the grandstands on Saturday had already made up their minds before the campaign had begun. Our conclusion was either that Nixon was going to win in a landslide or that the whole basis of our coverage scheme was faulty. In the end, our first conclusion was proven correct. Nixon won with the largest margin of electoral votes since FDR had swept back into office in 1936.

It used to be that candidates had standard speeches they delivered over and over again on the stump; just the beginning changed: "I'm pleased to be back in Peoria"; "It's good to see Seattle again"; "My father was born here in Oklahoma so I consider myself a Sooner." All that had to go when television crews came aboard the campaign planes and whistle-stopping disappeared. "The Speech," as it quickly became known to the regular press corps traveling with the candidate, lost its newsworthiness, and with its loss reporters began to badger the candidate for snippets of news. The coverage became focused on possible "slips" by the candidate or on reactions to polls showing one man ahead, or on real or imagined tensions within the candidate's campaign apparatus.

An incorrect answer to a question just thrown in at a news conference by a local reporter could seriouly damage a campaign. One single item could skew the entire process as the candidate labored to climb back from a gaffe that TV exposure blew out of proportion. Candidates have become supercautious, fearing that stridency on the tube will alienate voters. Too often, the result is the bland, plastic smile and no substance. It's possible that voter–viewers discern that shallowness, and that they dismiss both the candidate's message and the daily coverage as anything meaningful.

Since the first television campaigns, more preplanning of coverage takes place. Editorial meetings devote a considerable amount of energy each week to scheduling reports for broadcast on subjects other than the daily campaign color. The razzmatazz, in fact, has become secondary. The greatest amount of time is now expended on analysis of issues. Scenes of the candidate moving through crowds have been largely replaced by "overviews," candidate profiles, strategy discussions and the results of polls.

If TV news was once criticized for spending too much time on the appearances of a campaign rather than its substance, it might now be argued that it spends too much time conjuring up angles to cover and analyze. During every presidential campaign, complaints are heard from correspondents and bureaus not directly involved in covering the political process. Overseas bureaus, in particular, go virtually on a standby status because they have learned that air time each evening will be dominated by campaign reportage. "There are other things going on!" is the constant call from the field. The cry generally does no good and the broadcasts on all networks are saturated with national politics. There is reason to suspect that the viewer dislikes a news diet overstuffed with politics too. Some studies indicate that news viewing levels fall off during those periods in which the network newscasts are dominated by political campaigns.

Certainly television coverage of the national nominating conventions has been less popular since it began in 1948. Gavel-to-gavel coverage sold a lot of television sets in 1956, and it came to be regarded as the true test of a news division's prowess by 1960. But by 1972, local baseball games, movies and even reruns of ancient detective shows outdrew the conventions in audience ratings on many nights during the proceedings. ABC started providing selective instead of gavel-to-gavel coverage, and CBS plans to do the same thing in 1984.

When the campaigning is over for the candidates, there is still a race left for the networks: election night. A network's performance on election night is considered one of the bench marks of its professional quality. The ratings are studied, and, in recent years, the number of "calls" made first have been trumpeted as a mark of journalistic competence. It wasn't always that way.

Douglas Edwards was the anchorman for CBS News election night coverage in November 1950. A large radio studio had been taken over, cameras moved in, blackboards erected, and all night uniformed pages chalked vote tallies in appropriate spaces. The totals came into CBS News from the wire services whose reporters went to the state-wide or city-wide Boards of Election throughout the United States. There they waited for the counting to be concluded, and then they transmitted the results. It was slow and haphazard. Results would trail way behind in states requiring hand counting or come in strange spurts from more efficient precincts. Occasionally, when a candidate conceded, a national summary board would be shown, totaling how many Republicans or Democrats had won seats in the Senate or House or in the governors' mansions.

Edwards kept up a lively monologue, helped along by copy written for him by those of us who digested features from the wires. There were stories about a candidate who had been elected even though he had been in jail, about a candidate who had driven his opponent to the polling place in a gesture of good will, only to lose by one vote, about voters in the Midwest who had braved blizzards and voters in California who had stood in the rain. That was the extent of the analysis that Edwards provided. It was very simple and very much like watching a baseball game. No one knew how it would come out until all the votes were counted.

The chalkboards and the uniformed pages were replaced by DDUs: digital display units. Political experts were invited to the studio to provide analysis. Though a semblance of expertise was projected through the long election nights, no one really knew anything definite. It was a question of waiting until the precincts had counted the ballots and reported them to state-wide collection points.

All that changed in 1961. In that year New York City held a mayoralty election; and though CBS News relied, as usual, on the wire services for vote tallies, NBC News tried a different approach. They sent reporters to each police precinct to wait for the counting to get under way. NBC had the figures long before the police had sent them to the borough or city-wide collection point. NBC posted election results hours ahead of CBS.

As a result, Bill Leonard was put in charge of the CBS election unit. He and the political pollster Louis Harris worked with officials at IBM to devise a system based on statistical probability—the theory that a small sample of voters, if correctly selected, could accurately represent the entire electorate. If a way could be devised to find out how that small sample voted, and if those votes could be counted more quickly than others, then projections could be made of how the entire electorate was voting. It was a stroke of ingenuity that profoundly affected the way elections have been reported and analyzed ever since.

What emerged was a system called Vote Profile Analysis, or VPA. It was based on "model precincts" selected to represent the demographic and political composition of the electorate. A study was made of each state and a "model" was constructed based on many "cuts" representing the essential makeup of the electorate. "Key precincts" were then chosen along urban/sub-urban/rural lines; ethnic lines; racial lines; along income and previous voting patterns.

It took a lot of research to find the perfect components which, when combined, resulted in a statistically valid picture of a state. Sometimes, for example, an all-black precinct would be put into the state-wide "model" so that it would represent the racial composition of the electorate as a whole. Care had to be taken, however, so that the all-black precinct did not skew the geographic representation within the state model. A downstate or rural precinct had to be balanced in the "mix" by the inclusion of a sufficient number of urban, big-city precincts if the model was to be accurate. VPA was not based on just a few precincts. There were hundreds in each state; thousands across the nation. By 1964, for example, in the presidential race, the 172,500 precincts in the United States were represented in the computers of NBC by 6,000 "keys"; 2,000 were in the CBS system, and a few more than 1,000 were in the ABC operation.

When the proper mix was found, the framework for the state-wide "model" would be inserted into the computer. On election night, reporters are sent out to the "key precincts" to await the vote counting. They have only one result to ascertain and phone in to the network computer center. The machines add in the data, filling up the outlines of the statistical model, which has been created in advance. Since the number of key precincts in any state rarely exceeds two hundred locations, the VPA precinct counts are usually completed and phoned in just minutes after the polls close in a state. Now anchors can go on the air and say that "according to VPA," candidate X looks like a winner in the race. Language is carefully tailored so that no network anchor ever declares someone a winner. Phrases such as "projected winner" are used. Sometimes the races are "too close to call" on the basis of results from the 100 or 150 voting precincts in the statistical model. Statisticians refer to a margin of error of "plus or minus factors which could range from two to five percent." The networks make sure that when they "project" a winner, he or she has achieved a lead well beyond any margin of error. Strict guidelines were established prohibiting any "calls" from being made if the guidelines were not clearly met.

Once again an outcry went up as people discovered that the baseball game no longer had to be played to the finish for the winner to be known. Some claimed that the systems were subverting the American way of life. Some demanded laws to prevent the networks from calling races. The networks themselves adopted a variety of regulations by which they barred calls until all polls in a state were closed. Still, television viewers were learning how other states were voting, often before their own polling places had shut down. If voters in the West learned that voters in the East had already given one candidate enough support to elect him, would the Western voter not bother to vote and thus be practically disenfranchised? When it was realized that the networks could not legally be barred from using their newly developed technology, proposals were advanced that would require a universal poll closing time across the nation.

One scheme envisages a twelve-hour block of time beginning at 9:00 A.M. in the East (6:00 A.M. in the Pacific time zone) and ending at 9:00 P.M. (6:00 P.M. PST). All voters would cast their ballots solely during those hours and then the networks could start reporting the tallies and adding their projections without fear of affecting the outcome. So far, Congress has not acted upon the proposals. In fact, candidates have already embraced the networks' computer "projections" as part of the political process, claiming victory or conceding defeat long before the final vote tabulations have come in from official channels.

By 1964, CBS had realized that a lot of information was available in the computers after the data for the model precincts was supplied. After all, if a state "model" had been built to include a Roman Catholic bloc, the computer printout could tell how they were casting their ballots and consequently to what extent a religious issue had weight. The same sort of material was available on blacks or farmers or city dwellers. Information about the whys and hows of the voting in key precincts was now broadcast even before the votes in the rest of the state were tallied and posted in the slower-counting voting districts.

"Exit polls" were devised in the early seventies when the

networks recognized that they could get an early handle on trends and issues by asking people how they voted as they exited from the polling places. Despite Americans' veneration of the secret ballot, people are surprisingly candid after they have voted. Initially the questions put to the emerging voters were designed to get explanations of the effect of issues. No serious attempt was made to count noses. As the seventies moved toward the eighties, however, news departments found themselves relying more and more on "exit polling" to guide them on the likely outcome of races. Despite a potentially high margin of error, "exit polling" was particularly useful for coverage of the primaries. Issues are likely to be major considerations in races held among members of the same party seeking a nomination or convention delegates. "Exit polling" provided the basis for many interpretive reports that appeared on nightly newscasts on primary day. Since they did not deal with who was winning but with why people voted, there was no violation of the network's own rigid rules concerning "calls." "Exit polling" continues throughout election day, so it is possible to "call" a race without waiting for an official poll closing.

On election day, 1980, NBC decided to do just that. They put aside their prior criteria for "projecting" winners with computer "models" and used the results of exit polls instead. NBC began its election night coverage by saying that Ronald Reagan had won. The network consistently called state races within seconds of poll-closing time, clearly basing their statements on information collected before any votes could have been dumped from ballot boxes to be officially counted.

The danger in "exit polling" calls is obvious. Voters who emerge may not be telling the truth. Despite precautions, there is no way to check the fact that they did vote the way they said they did or, indeed, that they voted at all. In a landslide election, it probably doesn't make much difference, since the margin of error built into the system protects against a small swing in "truthfulness." In a close election, it remains to be seen how much risk exists. It also remains to be seen if the three networks' competition in future elections will be based on the original carefully constructed and rigidly guided statistically based models or if they start down another course based on "exit polling." If the credibility of a news organization depends on the accuracy of its reportage, "exit polling" could be its nemesis. A wrong choice, made in the interest of maintaining the "fast call" race, might go a long way toward embarrassing all of us.

Special events departments and election units are necessary luxuries for network news divisions. Like fire departments, they remain in place, ready to react to the unexpected. On the one hand, they have to be able to move quickly and thoroughly on a breaking story; on the other hand, they have to prepare with meticulous precision for scheduled events like space shots or election night. The prestige of a network's news department rests on a triad of programs. First, there is the evening news, coverage of special events, politics, and elections is the second, and the third leg is documentaries and the magazine programs. Like any three-legged stool, a weak leg can send the entire structure toppling. These days, the combined performance of all three must be the criterion by which a news division should be judged.

5
The Extended Form
DOCUMENTARIES AND MAGAZINES

Understand this about documentaries on television: They are troublesome to advertisers and special interest groups. Despite poll after poll that shows the public wants more of them on the air, the fact is that the public turns them off when they appear. A documentary can average about 30 percent less in the ratings than the program it replaces, and because documentaries cost more to produce than other forms of informational programming—in the eighties, a one-hour documentary was budgeted at $235,000 in production money, plus another $200,000 in administrative overhead costs—they seldom earn back their expense in sponsor revenues. Why do the networks take the heat? For the prestige, which is substantial; for the awards, which are meaningful, and occasionally to get out of trouble with vociferous public interest groups or the Federal Communications Commission.

The worst thing that can happen to a documentary department in a television network is for the ratings race between the three networks to tighten up. When one network is way ahead and another is way behind, the leading network will schedule more documentaries in prime time, confident that the lower ratings in the broadcast's hour will not substantially subtract from the weekly cumulative ratings of the entire network's schedule. The third-place network has nothing to lose either. It is so far behind in the weekly cumulative ratings that the loss of a few points in one hour will not materially affect the whole. It can afford to schedule more documentaries for the prestige, the reviews and the awards. The network in the middle usually plays it conservatively, scheduling just enough documentaries to maintain the franchise but not too many to cost those few rating points that could tip them into the number-three spot.

When the race tightens up, the picture radically alters. Differences in ratings are now calculated in tenths of points. The outcome of each week's cumulative-ratings computations can actually affect the stock market, because buyers pay attention to the regularly published ratings lists of the top-ten shows. For them, the network with more hit shows is a better buy among the broadcast stocks. When one network is only five-tenths of a point behind another, the loss of several points in even one hour can have a bearing on the cumulative ratings for the week. A spirit of caution results. Fewer documentaries are scheduled and those that are added to the broadcast mix are usually slotted into time periods where they will cost the fewest ratings points. Pressure increases to select topics that will attract audiences: subjects like homosexuality, or hedonism in Marin County, California.

Occasionally, a network will make a dramatic statement in support of an important documentary, flying in the face of ratings races and scheduling competition. After the hostages were released from Iran, for instance, ABC preempted its entire three-hour prime time schedule one night to run an investigative report on the secret negotiations that brought about the hostages' release. The network also ran an all-night memorial to FDR on the hundredth anniversary of his birth. NBC has eliminated an evening's programming several times to present three-hour reports on American foreign policy, the American family, and violence. CBS has put an hour a night on the air for five consecutive nights to deal with American defense capabilities.

Those gestures are memorable because they are so rare. By and large, a documentary is tolerated rather than embraced.

"CBS Reports," that network's premiere documentary series, was born in the late fifties because the networks had a problem. The craze on television in those years was the high-prize quiz shows. Unfortunately the integrity of the show producers did not always match the difficulty of the questions. High ratings depended on the viewing public's identifying with one or more of the contestants. Those contestants who captured the audience (and the ratings) were to be kept on; those who failed were to be moved along more quickly. The controlling factor was, of course, the contestant's ability to answer the questions. The producers started to manipulate that aspect, and before long, on the NBC show "Twenty-One," the brilliant young college professor, Charles Van Doren, was caught in a tangle of deceit and lies and prefed answers. When that scandal got out, similar though unproven charges were made against two CBS shows, "The $64,000 Question" and "The $64,000 Challenge."

CBS felt that its reputation was at stake, so the network's highest management decided to devote one hour a month to quality prestige programming. That's how "CBS Reports" was created. Fred Friendly was between assignments at CBS News. The old Murrow–Friendly team was breaking up, producers were leaving and morale was low. The quiz show scandal changed all that. Friendly was called in and told to start producing shows. Work was in progress on one about the world's population problems: overcrowding, food shortages, pressures for birth control versus opposition from the Roman Catholic church. Friendly picked the title "Population Explosion." He changed the focus from a worldwide survey to a concentration on India, where all the problems of overpopulation could be found in one place. The broadcast inserted the phrase "population explosion" into the American vernacular.

"The Population Explosion" took 13 weeks of filming. We used a 35 millimeter Wall camera that weighed about eight hundred pounds including its tripod and other equipment. When he was interviewed in those days and asked to describe what television journalism was all about, Friendly frequently talked about an "eight-hundred-pound pencil." We certainly pushed it around India.

We had been shipping film back to the States as we shot it. Friendly, in New York, would screen the "dailies" and send a cabled list of comments. If he really liked something he would call it "a ten strike!" If he didn't, his cables asked for segments to be redone or for additional material to fill out what in theory had already been finished.

Friendly's cables were directed to what had been our starting point of view: India would be able to handle the problem. By now, on the spot, we knew differently. One night, in response to a cable that reflected Fred's growing loss of confidence in what we were doing half a world away, I sat down and wrote what was later described as "the longest message sent by cable to CBS up to that time." It contained an angry and passionate outline of why the country was going down; why bureaucracy was thwarting all hope; why the people, kept in ignorance and without any traditions for seeking change, were not cooperating and how, in sum, this documentary was going to be a report of failure rather than success. "The fact is, India won't make it and this documentary won't either unless you realize that fact," I wrote. Friendly's answer came back with brilliant terseness. "If your film showed what your cable showed, you would have a ten strike." Friendly had gotten us back on the track.

Although I received credit for writing the script on "The Population Explosion," it really belongs to Friendly. He showed me many of the tricks of combining words and pictures that make both work more effectively. He demonstrated to me the use of scenes for pacing the broadcast. One showed a small boy sitting on the concrete rim of a communal well, playing a shepherd's pipe. The music was not particularly good but the scene was symbolic of hope and of the primitive village life so typical in India. The scene was allowed to play a bit longer with the flute music in the clear and with no narration for a while. The copy began by referring to the boy and his tune. "The sound of a shepherd's flute, drifting across the evening air . . ." helped set a mood and easily led us on to descriptions of life in the Indian village.

★   ★   ★

The first thing you need to produce a documentary is an idea that must include a rich menu of components and have national importance. Because an hour on a television network automatically bestows impact and weight, a small incident can very quickly be blown out of proportion. Deciding whether there is enough material to sustain interest and to be informative for an hour without becoming repetitious is the first task of the executive producer of documentaries.

Take an idea, research it thoroughly, budget its costs, film or tape its elements imaginatively, edit them precisely to a well-written script, check and double-check all the facts for accuracy and for fairness and balance, and then, broadcast it. At each step care must be taken to avoid having the editorial thrust swallowed up by the sheer magnitude of the available air time.

Daily newscasts demand speed of completion and elimination of facts in order to fit the allotted lineup time. Producers who have worked under that regimen often have difficulty in adjusting to the more leisurely pace and looser deadlines in documentaries. After all, sixty minutes once every four months, which is the average production time for a documentary, allows substantially different work habits from a ninety-second piece prepared every day in an average time of six hours. A documentary is not a two-minute spot multiplied by fifteen to fill a half-hour. Much more is required to conceive and execute a "doc."

To begin with, research funds are the "cheapest money" we have. It is well worth spending a few thousand dollars to find out that there is not enough substance in an idea if it prevents a $235,000 fruitless venture from getting under way. Research is directed toward finding out what we *know* we can get to tell a story; what we *hope* we can get to tell a story; and what we will *not* get when we try to tell a story.

Researchers, correspondents and producers of documentaries become experts in the subject being examined. More interviews are conducted off camera than are ever filmed or taped. The information gathering is extensive and widespread. It shouldn't faze budget controllers one bit to discover that producers have flown all over the world to "preinterview" experts and to survey potential filming locales. It is still less expensive to spend money on research than to blow it on a project that is aborted with crews already in the field.

With the research material in hand, it is a good practice to insist on a "position paper"—a written presentation of all the facts, of all the plans for illustrating them, and of the conclusion that the preliminary digging suggested. "Position paper" writing is serious business. It should determine the "go/no-go" decision. One of the best jobs turned in during my tenure as V.P. in charge of documentaries was done in 1973 by Pam Hill, then a producer of documentaries and, by 1978, my successor as vice president and executive producer. Her position paper was seventeen pages long and began: "There is a forceful and disturbing hour program to be done on the subject of fire hazard and consumer safety. It is a program about the failure of government, and industry, to protect the consumer from 'unreasonable risk' of death or serious injury by fire. It is a program about the people who suffer and die because of that failure."

In the first paragraph, Hill had outlined the intent of her proposal. For the next ten pages, she defined the three areas she expected to examine: "I want to outline the regulatory situation in each of the three areas," she wrote, "so that you are aware of both the government agencies and industry interests under examination." There were details presented as the paper continued. First, fire hazard and consumer product safety (". . . there are no government standards for the new hazards"); second, building safety was to be investigated ("Most fire deaths occur in the home, at night . . ."); and third, there was the question of transportation safety ("One third of all fire deaths occur in automobiles. . . .").

Hill's position paper now moved on to describe both methodology and material available to illustrate the subjects. Each "act" would be framed in terms of case histories ". . . drawing on stock footage, survivors' accounts as well as on what we shoot." Sketching out sections of the broadcast or "acts," Hill contemplated the inclusion of ". . . a montage of victims, sharp emotional counterpoint voices, experts' warnings that went ignored." In some places, research and field interviews had already triggered entire sequences in Hill's mind.

Hill's eagerness to get the project under way was tempered by professional concerns for accuracy, fairness and balance. That attitude represents an important defense against slipshod research and half-baked opinions substituted for fact. Her paper, despite its thoroughness, cautioned that more research was needed, not only for facts but for fairness and balance. "Because of the range of jurisdictions involved, and the technicality of some of these issues, we have not been able to complete all the research we feel must be done . . . if we are going to do shows like this, with all of their potential for attracting attention and controversy, it is imperative that they be absolutely accurate and fair." Hill concluded: "I have not had time to locate case histories, or contact the various industry spokesmen who will be included. It is my own judgment that the show needs additional time."

On the basis of that "position paper," we decided to go ahead, but we added an additional month before production was to start in order to complete the advance research and contact work.

The position paper shows how a broadcast will build upon itself and will add, in each section or "act," to the audience's store of knowledge so that the eventual conclusion is understandable in the context of what has gone before. As in the case of short reports done for the nightly newscasts, the final summary has to draw together facts that have been presented within the broadcast. There must be no new information tossed in at the end.

The "topic sentence," an integral part of the position paper, becomes the principal device that assists in the final writing and editing of the broadcast. Some people believe documentaries can be "made" in the editing room. If enough pictures are shot, enough interviews conducted, a producer can sit with an editor over his Steenbeck film-editing table or his CMX computer tape-editing keyboard and put the show together. Thus the attention that needs to be paid in the field to picture sequences, or to obtaining answers to particular questions asked of specially selected interviewees is ignored. I firmly resist this approach.

The "topic sentence" narrows and defines the documentary's purpose, what the broadcast is about. It is written literally to be delivered on air by the correspondent at the opening of the program. It has to be clear and understandable, with no qualifying phrases. Its purpose is to stake out the turf to be examined. Typically it contains the phrase, "In the next hour, we will examine . . ." With that kind of sharp definition there should be no doubt about what is to come. If a critic suggests that the broadcast is lacking because it has not dealt with some tangential aspect, we can go back to the topic sentence, which has carefully defined what we intended.

In Pam Hill's "Close-Up" on "Fire," the topic sentence in the position paper read: "This is a program about the failure of government and industry to protect you from unreasonable risk . . . the unreasonable risk of death or injury by fire. And it is a program about all of those who suffer and die as a result of that failure."

In the end documentaries have to be brought down to time. Editing from the first rough assemblage, which may run more than two hours, to an hour and fifteen minutes is not particularly difficult, nor is it too hard to get to an hour. It is the final cut—sixty minutes to forty-seven minutes—that is the mean business. (The extra minutes go to commercials, visual transitions to commercials, and credits.) Producers moan and wring their hands as the "bone" and "muscle" is cut away. "There is no fat left," is the cry heard in the last stages of production. "Can't we get more air time for this?" The choices are always hard ones. Dramatic film sequences are vying against relevant interview segments. Here again the topic sentence—often Xeroxed and taped to the cutting room walls—provides an invaluable guide. Does a sequence more closely support the topic sentence's guidelines? If it does, its survival is more likely. If it doesn't, the cut is reasonable.

Producers often get so involved with their programs that they cannot make the final cuts. After hours of agonizing discussions I might ask, "Do you want to perform the surgery or shall I?" It isn't unusual for the producer to respond, "You do it; I don't see where any more can come out."

Fred Friendly used to listen to his "CBS Reports" producers insist that the cuts he proposed would destroy the piece. He would ask which deletions would result in a resignation. "Usually they would list four or five segments," Fred told me, "making it perfectly clear that if these went out of the show, a resignation would be on my desk." That was fine. Now he knew where else to look to find what had to go to bring it in on time.

Friendly used to meet producers in the halls at CBS and ask, "Let me see your best twenty minutes." It was a good way to gauge how a project was going. If the "best twenty minutes" evoked his emotional response or was unusually good visually, Friendly could be confident that the broadcast would live up to expectations. It was better to have his detached assessment early in the production so that shortcomings he perceived could be remedied before the rough cuts were completed and presented to him for review.

An executive producer of documentaries must help producers by knowing when to step into the production and when to keep out. In a documentary, it is the producer who directs the cameras and devises pictorial sequences to make editorial points. Though it is shaped in cooperation with the correspondent or narrator and the film or tape editors, the broadcast's substance is largely in the producer's hands.

An executive producer should be able to supply suggestions for ways to solve problems of clarity or visualization within the framework set down by the producer. It's like a Masters chess competition. Bobby Fischer had memorized a million moves from which he could choose to counter his opponent. A good supervisor has memorized a lot of television "moves" and combinations of effects, words and editing techniques that the more junior staff member has yet to learn. The primary "move," however, is to stay within the producer's concept rather than automatically pushing it aside.

Keeping the executive producer out of the production process until the very end usually results in more trouble than bringing him or her in early. It seems to me that if there is a problem, the more time I have to study it and help fix it, the less serious it will be in the end. There's plenty that can be done the month before the air date. There's less that can be done ten days before and even less five days before the program is scheduled for broadcast. Usually what is needed is a small adjustment here and there to make a point clearer. On a few occasions, however, I have to say, "I don't follow what you are trying to tell me." The producer has had the chance in the rough cut to demonstrate whatever approach he or she has selected, and it has missed the mark. On those occasions, and with reluctance, an executive producer's responsibility is to step in and impose a structure.

Whenever I go into a cutting room to screen a rough cut, I get antsy when a producer greets me with long speeches about what I should look for or about what I shouldn't expect to see. The viewer does not get the prebroadcast explanation. All the audience knows is what is transmitted. The producer cannot trot alongside the picture on the TV set whispering clarifications.

"Signposting" is the shorthand we use for inserting whatever clarification is needed in the script to help the audience absorb complex information. These insertions are usually summary points; they collect information already presented on the broadcast and put it into a paragraph. They remind us of what we know before we go on to something new. It's an arrow at a crossroads.

We are now all educated to accept many images at once, but hearing the same voice narrating for an hour can be boring. We devised a sort of verbal fanfare: An announcer's voice is substituted for the narrator's. "DOCUMENT!" He would begin, reading the text of some evidence that emphasized an editorial point, usually refuting a statement made on camera by an apologist. Hearing a different voice lends emphasis.

The format I devised for ABC "Close-Up" documentaries always had a confrontation interview near the conclusion. The buildup of information leaves the audience eager to meet the responsible person. These interviews were deliberately provocative; they assumed that, by now, our correspondent knew as much about the subject as the man or woman behind the desk. Our correspondents would be drilled not only on their questions but on the likely responses. If we could anticipate the answer to the first question, we could keep on with tough follow-up questions.

Mike Wallace is probably the best-known "confrontation" interviewer on television. He is a relentless questioner, and he does a lot of homework before he goes into action. Asked to describe "the Mike Wallace technique for doing an interview," Wallace responds quickly; "Do as much research as you can. And when I say research, I mean read everything you can about an individual. As I read, I'll write down questions. Maybe a hundred or a hundred and fifty questions . . . all on the famous Nixon legal pad. I use six, eight, ten [questions] at the tops, depending on where the interviewee takes the conversation. If you have studied your subject and the subject of the interview thoroughly enough, you are going to be ready to go right with him or her."

On the air Wallace uses a whimsical smile or a wrinkled forehead to express doubt if not incredulity. He acknowledges that his "body English" plays an important part in his questioning. "When you interview someone, in order to make him or her feel that the interview is the sole object of your attention, you listen as though you are fascinated. Frequently, you *are* fascinated and they like that and because you can use your body to convey that you're paying very close attention . . . it makes them a more cooperative witness." Wallace does not believe he uses his eyes as tools to convey feelings. He thinks that it's a question of concentration and it is concentration that is conveyed whenever Wallace's picture—taken simultaneously by a second camera—is shown leaning forward toward his subject.

"It's an old story," he says, "so many interviewers don't listen. They're thinking about the clock. They're thinking about the next question, they're not really paying attention, they're blanking out."

Wallace is recognized as an aggressive and sometimes hostile interviewer. As a result, some of his subjects have insisted that they be permitted to simultaneously record or videotape their interviews. The purpose, they claim, is to have their own record of what was said to guard against improper editing by Wallace and his staff. In at least one case, that separate recording procedure resulted in an embarrassing aftermath.

A story Wallace covered in March 1981 dealt with the San Diego Federal Savings and Loan Company policies, which allegedly defrauded low-income people, particularly blacks and Hispanics, who unwittingly put up their homes as collateral for loans. While his own CBS crew was taking a break, Wallace continued talking with someone in the room who wondered aloud why people sign such contracts without first reading them. Wallace replied that they found these contracts hard to comprehend especially over "their watermelon and tacos."

Wallace did not realize that the camera crew employed by the Savings and Loan Company was still recording. Wallace later explained that he had meant his remarks to be jocular and was trying to elicit "some hint of feeling toward the minority community" from the subject of his interview. That is a questionable technique for an interviewer who is supposed to be dispassionate. It is almost entrapment.

Wallace compounded the problem when he called the bank, insisting that they had violated the ground rules under which they could simultaneously tape the interview. In his view, what he said while the CBS cameras were turned off was to be considered "off the record." He suggested that the bank make their tapes "conform" to those held by CBS. In other words, the bank should erase those portions that contained his offensive remarks. After he hung up, Wallace thought over what he had proposed in the light of Watergate and its scandalous tape erasures. He called back to make it clear that he did not want the tapes altered after all.

Mike Wallace made his early reputation in broadcast journalism as one of the first correspondents to report thoroughly and fairly on the Black Panthers, Malcolm X, and the civil rights movement's struggles for recognition. He took a lot of heat for being ahead of the pack at that time because his reports were sympathetic toward blacks. It is ironic that now he may not be remembered for them. Some younger black leaders with short memories have accused Wallace of gross insensitivity and arrogance. The episode demonstrates that even the superstars of our business sometimes need an extra measure of caution.

Barbara Walters is another of television's great interviewers. She manages to ask the questions that are on the minds of everyone. She is not afraid of probing and putting the indelicate subject before her guest. She has one device I call "word association." She tells her guest that she intends to give a list of names, one name at a time. All she wants, she says, is a brief one-sentence response in reaction to each name. She starts by presenting less controversial names. What she is really doing is lulling her subject into complacency with apparently easy and comfortable questions before zinging in with the unexpected one, which usually gets the unprepared and more candid reply.

Here is how she handled Richard Nixon during the presidential campaign of 1980.

WALTERS: I'd like to . . . to ask you about some people and ask your quick assessment of them. What comes into your mind as I say the names. . . . Jimmy Carter.

NIXON: Very intelligent. Hard worker. Very decent. Excellent campaigner. And, unfortunately, a tragedy for him, a tragedy for the country, a . . . an ineffective President.

WALTERS: Ronald Reagan.

NIXON: Intelligent. Strong. Much younger than his years would indicate . . . and his appearance. Vigorous. And . . . in spite of the media to a certain extent, some of it painting him as being a lightweight and a kook, a very reasonable, responsible man.

WALTERS: You have no unfortunately's to say about him; you have nothing on the debit side about him.

NIXON: No, he hasn't been President yet.

WALTERS: George Bush.

NIXON: Very attractive candidate. Admire the way that he's
. . . hung in there after the shellacking he took in New
Hampshire and then Illinois. He isn't going to make it, but
nobody should try to push him out. And once Reagan is
nominated, as he will be, at the convention, Bush will be a
good Party man and support him.

WALTERS: John Anderson.

NIXON: Very intelligent. Suffers a little from what some people attribute to Jimmy Carter of . . . the arrogance of moral
superiority. That would be his weakness. He . . . he will start
fast. He will end up with less votes, I think, than George
Wallace got. And will probably hurt each candidate about the
same . . . percentage-wise, but will probably hurt Carter
more because he's going to hurt him in the big states, by
taking away the liberals.

WALTERS: Richard Nixon.

NIXON: I've never judged myself, but since you've asked about
politics, perhaps I can tell you about that. I retired from politics six years ago. But while I've retired from politics, I
haven't retired from life. And perhaps I can best characterize
myself by saying that while recalling one of the most moving
speeches I ever heard, and I think you may have heard it too,
in the Congress of the United States, when Douglas Mac-
Arthur was fired by Harry Truman. And he closed the speech
by saying, "Old soldiers never die; they just fade away." And
I would paraphrase that, and this applies to me, that . . . "old
politicians usually die, but they never fade away." I intend to
continue to speak out on occasions when I think it will serve
a useful purpose in foreign policy. I do not intend to participate in politics in any way. My political career is over and so
we'll now go to other questions.

WALTERS: I realize that I left one . . .

NIXON: (Over) You can ask political questions if you want
. . . it's your show.

WALTERS: (Over) That's all right. I realize I left one name out
and that is Edward Kennedy.

NIXON: Suffers from comparison with both his brothers and
particularly with Jack Kennedy. He's . . . I think his greatest
weakness is . . . is not Chappaquiddick, although that of
course has hurt him. But his greatest weakness, curiously

enough, is where Jack Kennedy was strong, and I should know—television. Jack Kennedy had a cool personality on television. And Teddy Kennedy, who is, some people tell me, better looking than Jack . . . was, who comes over quite well when he's speaking to a rally, comes through very hot and rasping on television. I think that is one of the things that makes him weaker.

If being quoted in newspaper columns after an interview is any measure of its effectiveness, Walters' encounter with Nixon was a success. His comments were widely noted for days after the broadcast.

Why do people agree to be interviewed? Wallace sometimes wonders why people sit still for him. "They respect the fact that they are going to have an audience of forty to fifty million people; they think that they are going to get an opportunity to get their point of view across in front of the American public, and unless they have something desperate to hide, there's really no reason not to come on the air. Still," Wallace concludes, "I am frankly surprised sometimes, that people will come on as rapidly as they do."

Self-esteem and pride, overconfidence and ego are partial answers. So is fascination with the medium. Time and again, we have gotten a crew and a correspondent into someone's office only after much negotiation. Yet once they get there, it is hard for them to get out. I've experienced the situation so often: "Please, Mr. Jones, we only want fifteen minutes of your time. We will set up our cameras in another office and you can come in, sit down, answer our questions, and I pledge to you that we'll be out of your way in fifteen minutes."

"Okay, okay, okay, but only fifteen minutes."

We live up to our word, setting up the gear in another room, setting all the lights, standing by nervously waiting on Mr. Big. He comes in, and after fifteen minutes, having asked the key questions, we are prepared to release him. It is hard to count the number of times that a perplexed look has passed across Mr. Big's face. "You're through already, boys? I don't mind. Take

your time." That is when we really get down to business with
more hard questions.

Accuracy is absolutely necessary in fashioning documentaries. It
is equal to fairness and balance. We created a devil's advocacy
system. A staff member who has nothing to do with the documentary is assigned to go through the script line by line, raising
questions about any statement or statistic that seems unexplained, out of context or unclear.

In the case of a "Close-Up" about government regulatory
agencies, for example, correspondent Sam Donaldson had included a "horror story" by a trucker about the Interstate Com-
merce Commission's activities. The story sounded real enough,
so Donaldson had accepted it as true, but the devil's advocate
asked for proof. When it was checked out, it was found to have
been made up. If it had slipped through it could have called all
the reporting into question.

There were some hot arguments when the devil's advocate
asked why an adjective had been put in to describe something as
"very" dangerous. How was the use of that word justified? A
small check mark appeared next to every line of every script
before the broadcast could go on the air. The program was also
reviewed by our attorneys. Thanks to the system of checks we
had in place, not one suit was lodged that stood up in court.

The ABC News "Close-Up" investigative documentaries
provided a base within the news division that we used in 1974
to develop another way of presenting information in the hour
form. Several years earlier, I had produced a special report about
drugs in the army in Vietnam entitled "Heroes and Heroin."
We had been granted permission to film inside a Cabinet meeting in the White House while the President and his Secretaries
were discussing and then actually making the decision to buy
the entire poppy crop of Turkey in order to block its importa-
tion into the United States. That inside look at President Nixon
in action was so unusual that it spawned the concept for what
became the "Action Biography" series.

Television biographies were not new, but they had depended

largely on pictures of the individual coming and going in public. Our concept was to go behind the scenes to spend time with the person as she or he worked, addressing problems, taking action, dealing with substance. We would conduct hours of interviews on audio tape. Specific references were then extracted from the tape and edited to run with pictures. The result was a summary of the subject's youth and of the influences that were at work within him as he confronted decision making as an adult. Egypt's President Sadat recalled ties to the village in which he had been born; the frustrations that grew from his experience as a poverty-stricken farmer's son; and the shock of watching fellow villagers being paraded to the gallows by the British. By the time the "Action Biography" reached Sadat working as Egypt's President, the viewer understood why he was a dedicated patriot, fiercely defending his land and encouraging revolutionary change in his country. "Action Biography" had a successful run for a season and won several awards, which is what the prestige-hungry network needed.

The long-form also gets a network out from under special-interest-group pressure and sometimes impresses the Federal Communications Commission in Washington, D.C. In 1974, "Americans All," a miniseries, actually accomplished both those tasks effectively by presenting interesting, entertaining pieces dealing with the contributions of members of minority groups to American life. The FCC was then chaired by Dr. Benjamin Hooks, a black leader who was very interested in reporting about minorities in the U.S. In the mid-seventies, many of the movies on TV were Hollywood productions made for theaters, and they ran "short" from five to eight minutes. "Americans All" filled the gap neatly, scoring points with minority advocacy groups and the important Dr. Hooks.

"60 Minutes" is the daddy of television newsmagazines and it owes its phenomenal success to at least two factors. The first is Don Hewitt, the series' executive producer. He has managed to find a way to make four grown men speak with his voice and to share his interests in the world. He directs his stellar correspondents like a ringmaster. Combining each of their efforts into one

broadcast each Sunday night is only one of Hewitt's responsibilities. It is he who says "yes" or "no" to story proposals, and
it is he who makes sure that each piece is finely crafted. Hewitt's
"bank" of stories with different moods and subjects enables him
to "stage" a show each week that holds the audience and brings
them back again.

It was Don Hewitt's belief that not all television reportage
should be crammed into the shorter "Evening News" pieces,
nor should they require documentary treatment. He proposed a
broadcast in which three or four stories need only run as long as
their substance warranted. The result is usually a more tightly
constructed and edited presentation.

Backed by Bill Leonard, the series went on the air in 1968 and
struggled along for quite a while, failing to attract the more than
30 percent share of audience that prime-time television then
required as a platform of success.

It wasn't until "60 Minutes" moved to Sunday night that it
became a hit broadcast, the number-one-rated broadcast in the
nation week after week. Sunday is a very important part of the
success of "60 Minutes." That is the day that newspapers are
thicker, filled with magazine sections and reviews of the news
of the week. Sunday is the day all the interview programs are
on the air. Leaders "Meet the Press," "Face the Nation," discuss
"This Week with David Brinkley." The day's tone is one of
reflection and contemplation. People go to church, meet the
family, walk in the park and talk. "60 Minutes" is Sunday-go-
to-meetin' absolution. The viewer can sit back and admit, "I
haven't read a book all week. I haven't listened to the radio
news. I did not keep up with the papers, but if I watch '60
Minutes,' can I not say that I am informed?"

"60 Minutes' " success led to imitation. At ABC, "20/20"
(for perfect vision) was created and scheduled in prime time on
Thursdays at 10:00 P.M., Eastern time. "Thank God, tomorrow
is Friday!" is the audience mood when we start each broadcast.
Unquestionably that affects content. "20/20" viewers, far from
seeking "Sunday-go-to-meetin' absolution," are more likely to
be keyed up for entertainment. "Okay," they might say, "inform us, but you had better entertain us too!"

Each week, the "mix" of "20/20" stories takes into consideration the reality of prime time television competition. It is a form of intellectual "triage" designed to hold the audience's hand from clicking the dial and turning away to watch another provocative clinch in the bedroom at "Knots Landing."

"20/20" 's rationale for selecting stories is based on the theory that one-third of the broadcast should be devoted to a pop culture piece. It deals with music, movies, new books, style, humor and personalities. These pieces are designed to keep the audience tuned in so they will stay for the serious journalism of investigative reports, economic essays, geopolitical backgrounders and pieces about crime, pollution, energy and military hardware. The "20/20" ratings show that, generally, almost 30 percent of the viewing public tunes in each week. That means that they watch the weightier two-thirds. It is a trade-off that is worth making.

"20/20" presentation techniques are a further extension of lessons learned in evening news and documentary production. The twelve-minute length provides some area for maneuver. Stories can be constructed: They are similar to the single segments or "acts" of a documentary. They should contain dramatic elements; have a story flow; demonstrate some surprises; pay off with a smile or a tear or a star singing a musical signature. Each piece is like a miniplay.

Alongside the "mix" of stories on "20/20," we assume that most of the people we are reaching have "zero knowledge and zero interest" in the subjects we intend to cover. More than likely, many people who tune into "20/20" do not want to work to understand what we are talking about. They prefer to have things explicitly presented. We want to get viewers involved in what is coming up. We want to build up their store of information to a plateau so that the report that follows will be understood in a context of the week's news or in the light of some topical development.

As an example of how "zero knowledge and zero interest" is handled, the following is the text of host Hugh Downs's introduction to a "20/20" report by correspondent Dave Marash. It was broadcast on the first anniversary of the successful revolution that overthrew the government of Nicaragua in July 1979.

	HUGH INTRO DAVE
Video: DOWNS ON CAMERA	Up front tonight. What happens after a revolution? It's been one
Video: COMBAT PIX	year since the fighting in Nicaragua ended. What is the
Video: MAP OF CENTRAL AMERICA SHOWING NICARAGUA	U.S. doing to ensure that the new Nicaragua turns out to be democratic instead of totalitarian? It's not a very big
Video: GEOGRAPHY	country, Nicaragua . . . just under three million people . . . smack in the middle of Central America. It's a land of lakes and smoking volcanoes . . . and
Video: PICTURES OF PEOPLE	plantations. The people are a mixture of Indians and Spaniards, from the early days of Spanish conquest . . . and blacks, from the era of slavery.
Video: CHURCHES	It's a Roman Catholic country. Now . . . the Cubans are there and the Russians are coming. But where is the U.S. in
Video: DOWNS ON CAMERA	Nicaragua's future? Here, with a special report on the revolution in Nicaragua is Dave Marash. . . .

A quick dissection of that page of script copy will demonstrate the way information is transmitted to achieve our goal. The first line asks the question designed to engage the viewer's interest and attention. Do you know "What happens after a revolution?" It's bound to be intriguing, conjuring up all sorts of images of battle or patriotism or anarchy. Pick any of those thoughts, and we've got you hooked.

The next line imparts some information about the most recent and successful revolt. "It's been one year since the fighting in Nicaragua ended." So what?

There has to be something that will relate this story to the basic concerns of the television viewer. He or she must care enough about the subject to want to stay tuned. The simplest way is to tie it to American interests. "What is the U.S. doing to ensure that the new Nicaragua turns out to be democratic instead of totalitarian?"

We can now assume that viewer interest is sufficiently piqued to stay with us for some of the background.

More knowledge. "It's not a very big country . . . just under three million people . . . smack in the middle of Central America."

That phrase, along with a map shown on the screen, reinforces the relationship of the country to the United States. Central America is just south of our borders; Cuban interests and other potentially dangerous forces are at work there. An understanding of that locale in terms of American national security makes it all the more important for the distracted viewer to pay attention to what is about to come up. More interest, more knowledge.

Some of the geography and demographics of the country of Nicaragua can now be inserted and, after all, there are pretty pictures of enchanting people and places to be shown. "It's a land of lakes and smoking volcanoes . . . and plantations. The people are a mixture of Indians and Spaniards, from the early days of Spanish conquest . . . and blacks, from the era of slavery. It's a Roman Catholic country."

By now, the viewer has been brought from "zero interest and zero knowledge" to a position of knowing a little bit of why Nicaragua is important and why he or she should "invest" more time to find out even more.

Finally, to ram home the involvement of basic American interests that presumably affect every citizen to some degree, the last two sentences of Downs's preamble lead into the report from the scene. "Now . . . the Cubans are there and the Russians are coming. But where is the U.S. in Nicaragua's future?"

That analysis of Downs's copy provides some idea of the thinking that goes into the words the audience hears on the air. The pictures that went along with the words reinforced them, providing images that showed what Downs was talking about. The entire effort was designed to inform, educate and, of course, to hold the viewer.

Documentaries and magazine pieces have amazing impact. Perhaps because the viewer is "investing" so much time in staying tuned to those kinds of programs, with their combination of pictures and sounds, that the response tends to be more emotional, even partisan. Once involved, the viewer is more easily stirred to anger or to "doing something." Because of the need to cover so much in so little time, there's a tendency on the daily news broadcasts merely to skim a subject. "The world has ended," goes the mock news promo. "Film at 11:00!" Documentaries and magazine pieces do more than that. They are often investigative; they usually make editorial statements. They should leave the audience with a sense that if something is wrong, then something more than watching "film at 11:00" can be done about it. There is a tacit plea by us for audience involvement and follow-up action in each of those broadcasts.

There has always been a feeling about television news that it is a one-way street. We pump material out into the homes of viewers who presumably accept it as gospel truth. There are, to be sure, letters and phone calls that come in, usually in direct ratio to the anger stirred up by some report we have presented. Supporters of our efforts rarely are moved to write. Getting viewers engaged in some kind of dialogue with us and "closing the loop" with the viewers by communicating more actively with them and by getting them to "talk back" to our broadcasts is a long-sought goal.

Talking back is now technically possible, but two-way capability to vote or to be polled or to order from a television catalogue is still awaiting the future development of cable TV.

In TV's earlier days, nothing existed to jog a viewer into any kind of engagement with the set. Then Fred Friendly, while president of CBS News, got a speeding ticket while driving. His failure to drive safely resulted in an order that he take a driver's education refresher course. He decided that if he had to go back to class, the rest of the United States ought to do the same. The result was the "National Driver's Test," which posed a series of illustrated questions to the audience, challenging people to compare their answers and scores with those of a scientifically selected sample of Americans who statistically represented the driving population in general. By engaging viewers' interest in the test, we took a giant step forward toward beginning some kind of a "conversation" with them.

We were reaching out to people in a new way and getting feedback. As a result of the third "test" broadcast, the "National Health Test," I received a viewer letter demonstrating our power to inform. On the "National Health Test," we decided that at least one question had to deal with eyesight. Given the fact that no two television sets in the United States will receive an image exactly in the same way, the eye test we devised had to be crude. It was simply "Cover your left eye and look at the letter 'E' we are projecting. Now cover your right eye and look at the letter. If you perceive any significant difference, we suggest you consult your doctor." The procedure was so simple that we even considered dropping it as meaningless, but time was available so we kept the question in.

"Dear Mr. Westin," a letter read, "I took your test and discovered that my vision was badly blurred in one eye when I covered the other. I saw my doctor and he found a tumor. They have operated, and I will be all right. Thank you for saving my life."

The ability to connect with another human being through our medium had been dramatically demonstrated. I have received two other letters like that one in the course of my television career. One came as a result of Pam Hill's "Fire" documentary. A viewer sought out my name as the series' executive producer and wrote that he had conducted an experiment after seeing the broadcast. The documentary had exposed uncoated polyurethane wallboard as a fire hazard even though it had been sold as fire retardant. The viewer had taken his penknife and sliced out a small sliver on the wallboard in his home. He then took the piece and, as we had shown in the program, held it horizontally while touching a match to it. The sliver practically exploded. It was the uncoated polyurethane. His letter explained that he had quickly replaced all the material in his house, which, he felt, had been a virtual fire trap. He concluded with thanks, saying that as far as he was concerned, the broadcast had probably saved his life and those of his family. No manner of awards or critically favorable reviews can ever compare with that kind of satisfaction.

The viewer letter that resulted in one of the most significant experiences I have had as a broadcaster was one I received in the early sixties after a report by George Herman on the "CBS Morning News." Herman had done a piece that lasted seventy-five seconds. It was a story based on a report from the Food and Drug Administration about newly discovered side effects from a drug that was widely prescribed for a heart condition. Research had turned up the fact that the drug, if taken by someone who also ate cheese, could produce poisons in the human system; poisons powerful enough to cause paralysis and even death. The FDA was warning cheese lovers who might also have a heart condition to beware.

About a week after we broadcast the story, I received the letter. The viewer had taken the trouble to find out that I was the producer of the broadcast, the individual who decided its content. He explained that he had seen the program and had been horrified to learn that he fit the description: a cheese lover with a heart condition who was taking the drug.

"Dear Mr. Westin," he concluded, "you have saved my life!" That incident exemplifies our responsibility as broadcasters. If we had saved a man's life with seventy-five seconds of information, imagine what is involved in all the hours of programming that we do. It was a lesson never to be disregarded.

6
What Sells Is Good
LOCAL NEWS

What is a television network? How does it relate to its affiliated local stations across the country?

Imagine an oval loop consisting of a combination of coaxial cables, telephone lines, microwave relay towers, and, in some places, huge parabolic "dishes" that can pick out signals from satellites in space. A television picture and its audio can be inserted into that oval so that it will travel all the way around the loop. Tied to it by cables or by microwave links are the local television stations located all over the United States. They tap the signals being fed around the oval, amplify them, and then rebroadcast them through their own transmitting towers to television sets in their market area. That's all a television network is: a transmission loop being tapped by local stations.

The network stretches from coast to coast and has spurs that run north and south along both coasts and down the center of the nation. Such a system carries television programming supplied by one of the three major television companies to their more than six hundred affiliated stations. ABC has 207 affiliates, CBS has 196 and NBC has 213. There are other smaller links, such as sports networks, that transmit special programs, and there are mini networks designed primarily to transmit entertainment shows on an occasional basis. Some use satellites to send signals, eliminating land connections entirely. Not all local stations are affiliated with the three networks. These are known as "independents," but for the purposes of this explanation we will omit them.

Each of the local affiliated stations signs an agreement with the network guaranteeing that it will "carry" programming that the network "feeds" down that electronic loop. By calculating how big the audience will rate in each affiliate's market, the networks determine the price of commercials sold to sponsors. Ratings are a measurement of audience size, and they are arrived at by standard statistical research methods that presume that a small, carefully chosen, representative sample of people can duplicate the attitudes of the entire viewing public. There are endless arguments about ratings and whether fifteen hundred selected viewers can or should be allowed to determine what is to succeed or to fail. Nevertheless, ratings are currently the only game in town; like it or not, everyone studies them.

Advertisers certainly pay attention to ratings, regardless of whether they are national companies buying time at the network level or local sponsors like the branch bank or the supermarket or the automobile dealer on Main Street. Advertisers buy air time on the basis of "cost per thousand" (CPM): How much does it cost to reach a thousand viewers? The higher the rating a show receives, the more money the network or station can charge and the more money a sponsor is willing to pay. The lower the rating, the less money the sponsor will pay and the less money the network or station expects to charge. Since both networks and local stations are in business to make a profit, a program with a lower rating, bringing in less revenue, will be canceled. Its replacement will, it is hoped, get a higher rating and higher commercial rates.

Not all the commercials you see on your television screen are network commercials. The networks only feed their programs at certain times of the day. For example, there is "prime time," which runs from 8:00 to 11:00 P.M. in the East, 7:00 to 10:00 P.M. in the Midwest, and 8:00 to 11:00 P.M. on the West Coast. There is early morning "fringe" time dominated by the "Today" show, "Good Morning America" and the "CBS Morning News." There is late-night programming after the 11:00 P.M. local news, such as ABC's "Nightline" and reruns of situation comedies and police shows; NBC's Johnny Carson on the "Tonight" show and CBS's "Late Movie." There are blocks of children's shows on Saturday and Sunday and the religious and interview programs on Sunday morning. On weekdays, there are blocks of soap operas and game shows. Most of the other time—mid-morning, mid-afternoon until 6:00 or 6:30, the 7:30 to 8:00 P.M. half-hour, and Sunday early mornings—is reserved for local stations to fill with their own programs.

This is known as "station time," or "local time," and it is in these periods that the stations sell their *own* commercials. Local stations also sell commercials in certain network shows like "Good Morning America" and "Today," which are specifically designed to provide them with a minute or ninety-second break. Some local ads also appear in the middle of long sporting events or the two-hour movies. Finally, local commercials are also inserted in station breaks between the network's programs. Those are called "adjacencies" because they are adjacent to the network shows.

A local affiliate retains 100 percent of the revenue generated by commercials run in "station time" and during "adjacencies." The networks' sale of commercials to national sponsors for network shows also brings some revenue to the affiliated station, but the network retains a substantial portion of that income before paying compensation to the affiliate for carrying the show. The amount of "comp" money a station gets is relatively small potatoes. After all, if there are two hundred affiliates, what can each one's share be of the $150,000 a minute the network has collected? After paying for the production of the program and the costs of transmitting it, there isn't much left to be shared among the stations. The networks have a complicated formula for paying the stations and some compensation can be as low as a few hundred dollars.

At times, stations have pulled out of affiliate agreements with one network, transferring to another because it provided stronger performance in the ratings. The station affiliated with a network whose programs usually rate in the top ten can collect a lot more money from the adjacencies than a station that finds itself trying to sell commercial spots in a station break following a flop. The swing can be thousands of dollars between the top-rated show and the third-rated show in the same time period. Imagine what a local sponsor might be willing to pay for an adjacency in or around the Super Bowl. The astronomical size of the Super Bowl audience measured by the advertisers' CPM rule of thumb can bring in thousands of additional dollars to a station. The competing broadcaster without that kind of an audience might get a couple of hundred dollars. He might even have to give the time away by running a public service announcement for the Red Cross or some local charity.

Bill Turner is typical of the men and women who run the better local television stations. His operation at KCAU-TV in Sioux City, Iowa, is affiliated with the ABC television network. Usually the ratings fortunes of the network directly affect the ratings of the local stations that take and broadcast the network's programs. If the network is number one in the ratings, the affiliate is probably very strong in the market; if the network is number three, the local station also finds its standing sagging. Turner found to his delight that he could buck that trend in the days when ABC was dismally in third place against CBS and NBC. KCAU-TV News was so widely watched in his market, and the station's reputation was so high among the people who lived in Sioux City, that his overall station ratings remained high all night even though ABC's prime time entertainment programming was generally considered dreadful. KCAU-TV was actually doing better on average than the rest of the stations affiliated with ABC because the viewers stuck with it regardless of whether the programs were poor.

It's Turner's opinion that the strength of his news operation developed viewer loyalty and that had a lot to do with the ratings miracle he was pulling off. It was the search for higher ratings and more revenue rather than desire for "image" that led most stations to the discovery that news programs run in "station time" could provide advertising revenues. Sometime in the early seventies the light bulb went on over the collective heads of station executives. That was the beginning of the "News Explosion."

Once it was understood that more viewers of local news meant higher ratings and higher revenues, it became obvious that news broadcasts had to be better produced. They were no longer to be done on a shoestring. In the early days of television, stations often regarded their own news operations as necessary but expensive image builders. They were not expected to be profit centers. Once they were discovered to have money-making potential, money was allocated to improve the quality of the presentation and hire top-notch people to run the operation.

News directors of local stations recognized they had a problem in filling hour-long newscasts. When they were working in cities that did not generate a lot of "conventional" news each day, directors redefined "news": the content was to be expanded. It wasn't done all at once; there was not a consensus among the producers and broadcasters around the country. Slowly, and observing each other's products, learning what worked in one market and what did not, sharing experiences, they began to develop a form of presentation that suited the narrower areas served by individual stations. "Local news" started to take on a texture of its own—one distinctively different from network programming.

"What sells is good" is operative at too many stations. There's no doubt that "police blotter" journalism attracts and holds viewers. A visitor from Mars watching local television news would have to believe that every city in America is burning down and that the light of the flames combined with the red and amber flashers of ambulances and police cars provides the primary illumination for rescue squads to find the victims of endless automobile accidents or muggings or murders. Why cover such stories? First of all, they are graphic. Second, they are easy to present. There's not much editorial judgment or reportorial skill required in covering a fire. Point the camera at the flames and smoke, interview the fire chief and one of the usually distraught survivors and the piece cuts like butter. I have a term for it—"How do you feel?" journalism—coined many years ago after watching a local reporter's coverage of a tragic Christmas Eve fire. It had wiped out an entire family except for the father who was away at the time. He stood there looking at the wreckage, which contained a gift-wrapped bicycle. The reporter jammed his microphone forward: "Well, sir, how do you feel?" The man hit him.

Certainly coverage of local disasters merits air time, but there seems to be little judgment about the importance of one story over another as long as the pictures are good. A spectacular one-alarm fire with a lot of flame may get more air time than a smoldering lumberyard blaze which, though less dramatic, could mean the loss of a dozen jobs. Air time will be spent on fires and crashes half a world away because of their picture value. Left out, as a result, will be the local school board's debate over library budgets because pictures are nonexistent and because it takes too much time to dig out the facts and explain the more intricate maneuvering.

It's not necessarily the reporter's fault. A local reporter has to produce four or five stories a day. There's hardly time to get to the scene, shoot the pictures, slap down a voice track and race off to the next incident. Like bad money that drives out good, the easy availability of crashes, casualties and corpses fills up the air time, driving out any serious effort to cover politics, economics, education and labor news even *within* the station's own area. Unless there is a major strike or the collapse of a financial institution whose impact on the local viewing public cannot be ignored, that kind of story is usually played well down in a broadcast, if it is covered at all. "What sells is good," and what sells is the sensational stuff of the police blotter.

During special ratings weeks—the so-called "sweeps" when every television market in the country is "swept" by Nielsen to determine how each station is faring against competing stations in the same market—there is even more hype. Oversensationalized series are inserted in the nightly newscasts, dealing with such subjects as sex, prostitution, pornography, child abuse, divorce, alcoholism and drug addiction. The sweeps are important because stations are establishing their ratings positions for the next several months. Commercial rates are set on the basis of those ratings "books," and time salesmen are either saddled with them or propelled into the marketplace to achieve higher revenues for their stations. Every effort is made to pump up the ratings with "hot" subjects on the newscasts.

These abominations grew out of "happy talk news," a phenomenon that nearly destroyed serious news broadcasting. In its worst manifestations, "happy talk" in the seventies meant that news writers were spending more time planning snappy repartee and joke lines than journalistic content. Every story required a punch line; prurience and double-entendre were part of the act. Audiences loved it. In Oklahoma, a weatherman talked nightly to a dog hand puppet. "You don't seem to like the idea," the producer said, observing my expression. "It works in this market. People even send in jokes for the dog to tell. They love it so we keep it in." Elsewhere, there were snowball fights between the anchorman and the weatherman, and a guitar-strumming sportscaster. The weatherman was cast as court jester, the sportscaster as campus "jock." Stations competing for viewers against a "happy talk" format lost ratings when they tried to remain straight. One by one they succumbed and joined the laugh-in brigade. It was the Dark Ages of local TV news.

The granddaddy of "happy talk news" was "Eyewitness News" at WABC-TV in New York. The concept, developed by news director Al Primo and station manager Ken McQueen, was based on their notion that news presentations should be "humanized." Anchors and reporters were to get more "involved" in their stories and were to "care" about what they were talking about. Unfortunately, the concept quickly started to substitute show for substance. As the anchors of "Eyewitness News," Roger Grimsby and Bill Beutel are credited with bringing the Primo and McQueen formula to life. Grimsby appeared actively to encourage salacious banter and sexual overtones. It was all part of the production device that formed the heart of the "Eyewitness" style, with its emphasis on newscasters "relating" to one another in a friendly, "familial" atmosphere on the set. Grimsby enjoyed talking about "horizontal enrichment," his euphemism for sexual intercourse. To him, that kind of story was the "frosting on the cake." "If it ever became the cake itself," he insists, "if it ever became a substitute for substance, we'd have been in real trouble."

But what really made the broadcast's reputation, Grimsby feels, was his on-air fights with sportscaster Howard Cosell and gossip columnist Rona Barrett. Grimsby once accused Barrett of turning "broadcasting into two words." Grimsby said the ratings began to climb as viewers said to one another, "You wouldn't believe what I saw on Channel Seven last night."

In a mea culpa delivered years later, Beutel admits that appeals to prurience became common. "We loved stories about homosexuals," he recalled, "and we did bathroom jokes, gently told. It went too far. We were playing games, and for three years, we did whatever was recommended or considered necessary to become preeminent in the market." Grimsby agrees. "The bottom line is numbers," he said, "and I share the view of an old station manager I once worked for. He said, 'I've never heard of a good sustaining (unsponsored) program, and I have never heard of a bad commercial broadcast.' " What sells is good!

"Hype" also extends to portable camera equipment and transmission gear. There's hardly a station in the U.S. that does not now feature some sort of live report on its early evening newscast. Names like "Actioncam" or "Insta-News" abound, painted on the side of vans that have been set up as mobile transmission centers. Some stations use the equipment for nightly rush hour traffic reports, feeding back reports of congestion or accidents. Some stations have put the camera in "eye in the sky" helicopters, which rove over the city spotting bottlenecks on the highways around town.

Yet news does not break according to a station's desires. "Live reports" can become cheap currency indeed, if they have no substance. It is a case of letting the machine run the reporter. It is almost impossible for a story requiring live coverage to occur every night precisely when the local news is on the air. Still, night after night, men and women stand in front of live cameras and try to justify their existence. One station was reduced to showing up at a scheduled fund-raising dinner dance just to be able to say their Insta-Cam was at a live event.

Since most station managers came up through the ranks of sales or advertising departments, they are unfamiliar with news presentation. In the early seventies, there were not too many trained broadcast journalists available to produce the expanding TV news programs. Faced with an arena that is sometimes frightening in its complexity and volatility, station managers turned at first toward familiar faces to staff their newsroom. Sales managers, advertising directors and publicity directors were frequently tapped to head the newly expanding news departments of major stations. Their lack of experience showed. Somebody had to know how to run the darned thing. Somebody did. The television news consultant.

In the beginning, consultants were often experienced in conducting polls to determine what and whom viewers wanted to see on TV broadcasts. Some came from the ranks of the network audience-research departments. Before long, as demand for their services increased, consulting companies employed former news directors or producers and offered their advice in the services provided to client stations.

The procedures vary only slightly. First, there generally is a survey of the station's broadcast area to determine the strengths and weaknesses of the news presentations. On-the-scene visits by the consultants follow, and from those come specific recommendations about whom to hire or fire as on-air personnel, whom to hire as producers and how to create a "look" and pace for the broadcast.

Though some consultants actually knew more about the gathering of news and its presentation than the newly promoted news directors they worked with in the seventies, there is no doubt that some brought in heavy show business gimmickry, corrupting the news broadcasts into entertainment "shows." More emphasis was placed on presentation than on content. "Personality" and "eye contact" were crucial in determining how well a news reporter fulfilled assignments—perhaps even more important than the substance of his or her report. Marvin Barrett, writing in *Moments of Truth,* called consultants "Trojan horses," carrying with them the elements for destruction of broadcast journalism and its requirements for accuracy and dispassionate presentation.

Among the most influential of the television news consultants is Frank N. Magid, who numbers more than 100 stations among his clients. He is the best of the group, and though he is frequently attacked by critics of the consultancy system, he does know quite a bit about journalistic standards. Even so, his profile of what he calls "The Ideal Newscaster" contains as many personality characteristics as journalistic skills. After extensive polling of viewer preferences around the country, Magid sums up: "In essence, viewers appreciate a newscaster who is a complete professional, comfortable in his job and business-like without being cold, formal or impersonal."

Along with Magid's guidelines, many stations employ "Q

Ratings" to determine how well their newscasters are faring with the viewers. The "Q Rating" is a copyrighted, nationally syndicated system devised by Marketing Evaluations, Inc. The company started rating television programs in 1960 and two years later set up a sister service that measures the popularity of television performers, including reporters and anchors. Advertising agencies subscribe to this survey, which is taken twice a year by asking a national sample of one thousand families who they know and who they like. Every test-family member above the age of six is sent a questionnaire and asked to fill it out. Local stations can also contract for a "Q" run on their on-the-air personalities, reporters and anchors. In those cases, about four hundred news viewers are questioned by mail or by telephone. Viewers are asked to rate a personality as "favorite," "very good," "good," "fair," and "poor." In a theoretical example:

> 100 people are questioned and 10 say X is "favorite"
> 5 say X is "very good"
> 5 say X is "good"
> 2 say X is "fair"
> 3 say X is "poor"

25 have responded with an opinion, which means that 25 out of 100 people questioned, or 25 percent of the sample, recognize the person. His Familiarity Rating is 25. The other part of the "Performer Q" has to do with the viewer's regard for the personality. Again, take the theoretical example used above. Ten viewers out of the 25 who knew X said he was their favorite. Divide 25 into 10, and the number is .40. A .40 rating means that though few people have seen him, a good percentage of those that have like X very much. He has a very high potential and the recommendation would be "Keep him and promote him." "Performer Q" is thus a measure of current standing and potential. Look at another example:

> 100 people are questioned and 10 say Y is "favorite"
> 25 say Y is "very good"
> 25 say Y is "good"
> 12 say Y is "fair"
> 13 say Y is "poor"

85 have responded with an opinion, which means that 85 out of 100 people questioned, or 85 percent of the sample, know the person. Her Familiarity Rating is 85. But this time, the Personality Q is different. Ten people named Y as "favorite." Divide that by the 85 Familiarity Rating and the "Performer Q" rating is .11. Interpreting that data means the subject of this test is well known but has low popularity. Perhaps Y is wearing out or has done something to destroy her image or credibility. At any rate, the advice would be "Start looking for a replacement." Steve Lovett of Marketing Evaluations, Inc., does not claim to be the arbiter of who should be hired and fired by station managers. "If the information is provided," he says, "it can tip the fence sitter. If the viewing public does not find one personality appealing and does like another, that kind of information has to be useful in making choices."

In the pseudo-science of selecting news personnel, station managers have reached far afield to make judgments. A company called ERA, Entertainment Response Analysts, has a device that tests the galvanic skin responses (GSR) of viewers to reporters and anchors. The system is based on the physiological phenomenon that people emit electric impulses from the surface of their skin if they are moved positively or negatively by something they see.

The system was used in Dallas where a newsman named Bob Brown was working. He had been moved up to anchor a news broadcast because management liked his folksy and low-key style and because he had demonstrated considerable reporting skill from the field. Four weeks after he got the job, ERA moved into town at the request of the station's executives and began to run tests. "They got some people off the streets in shopping centers," Brown recalls. "They were wired up to machines and shown a reel of videotape on which several anchors were seen doing the news. I didn't test well, and within two weeks, I was off the show." (Ironically, the GSR test was shelved by ERA—not because they did not believe it was effective nor because they couldn't interpret the results. It was put aside because of the bad press the technique received. It became too controversial to continue to publicize.)

Although responsible television news consultants cautioned

their clients about requirements to be accurate, fair and balanced, they also dealt with "presentation." Reporter "involvement" in stories was part of the advice liberally handed out.
They urged that newsmen and women be seen on camera at the
scene of the events they were covering. Responding to that kind
of suggestion, some reporters went to extremes. One in Florida
actually donned Hare Krishna robes and shaved his head to present a report on that religious group; another made a point of
wearing a firefighter's rubber coat and boots every time he
showed up at a fire.

A reporter's "bridgework" has become a test of competence.
The term does not refer to one's dentures but rather to the style
employed in an on-camera appearance "bridging" from one aspect of a story to another. A "walking bridge," in which a
reporter walks into the picture while talking into the camera and
then keeps on walking and talking, leading the viewer from one
scene to another behind him, is regarded by some as more effective than the simple "stand-upper," in which the reporter stands
stock-still while delivering the "bridge copy." Unfortunately,
"bridgework," with all its movement, may distract the audience, losing the thread of the story. Sometimes the goal of reporter involvement (acting?) fails to edify (entertain?) the
viewer.

"Stunting" is another gimmick that local news presentations
frequently use. If the network's prime-time entertainment
schedule includes a drama about a subject like child abuse, for
example, its highly charged on-air promotional announcements
will most likely have raised viewers' awareness of the subject.
The "stunt" occurs when a local news program hastily prepares
a report on the same subject to run on the same night as the
drama in order to capitalize on the high audience sensitivity.
Never mind if the "news" report contains little or no substance.
Show over substance unfortunately counts when what sells is
good.

The same preference manifested itself in the consultants' concern for "pace." No one would argue that a well-produced and
energetic broadcast has more chance of retaining the viewer's
interest than a dull and plodding one. However, consultants
often emphasized pace at the expense of content. They provided

suggested guidelines about lengths of reports. Those that had pictures could run longer; those that were picture poor were to be cut short or eliminated. The phrase "story count" was introduced to newsrooms, and comparisons of the quality of competing newscasts were made on the basis of how many stories were included rather than on how well they were reported.

Consultants also offered definite recommendations about which reporters were doing a good job and which should be replaced. Frank Magid's reports frequently recommended specific replacements, and his company, Frank N. Magid Associates, Inc., runs a television school for reporters employed by client stations. Often a Magid student will be recommended to a client station as a replacement for someone Magid believes is not performing well. Magid denies that he ever engineers a switch from a sitting anchor or working reporter to one he represents. It is true, however, that Magid has been known to suggest that a client station try to recruit an anchor from another city, particularly if that anchor is at a station that competes with a Magid client station. Moving the tough competition out of town helps the distant Magid client and conceivably helps the acquiring station.

Sherlee Barish is the premier mover of news personalities, reporters, anchors, sportscasters and weather forecasters. Her advertisements claim: "She knows the talent business better than anyone in the business." The quote is from a *Wall Street Journal* article. The copy under her smiling photograph says, "She's Sherlee Barish and television news people are her specialty."

Ms. Barish became one of the most important catalysts in the television news business in the late seventies and early eighties. She screens over one thousand videotape auditions a year and shuttles the tapes from station to station. Station managers call her frequently. Barish is known to find holes; she also creates them by moving a newscaster or reporter she represents and replacing him or her with another she represents.

Barish has earned her reputation as the best "talent headhunter" over a number of years of working at the periphery of the television news business. In that time, she has watched trends come and go. She can tell what's "in" or "out" by the kinds of requests she gets from station managers. She recalls that what was at first desired was "a big sexy stud with youth, charisma and credibility . . . a gorgeous twenty-five-year-old with ten years experience." Times change. By the 1980s, the "sexy stud" has been replaced by the "mature" anchor. Part of the reason may be found in demographics. There are more older Americans than ever before, and older people relate better to older reporters. Also some of the young men and women have turned into mature newscasters who have gained respect in the viewer's mind.

Barish is certain that many of her clients are worthy of that respect. They have journalistic credentials and are able to work under the time pressures and accuracy requirements that news-gathering imposes. She also regards some of them as "spoiled rotten" children who go out and cover stories but then "want to be kissed on the forehead and told how wonderful they are." There is no doubt that Sherlee Barish understands the funda-mental facts of television life. It is a competitive business where a loss of a ratings point on a local news program can be worth between $200,000 and $1 million a year. Each on-the-air "tal-ent" is constantly being evaluated either as a coming personality who will build ratings or as a fading flower who might have to be cut off before any more points are lost.

Television news offers a nomadic existence. A broadcast career usually begins with an "entry-level" job at a small station and leads to an assignment as a street reporter. Those accomplish-ments are stored in a résumé and a reel of videotape. The tape is generally circulated to larger stations as a job application. Open a copy of *Broadcasting* magazine, which is the basic source for news of the industry. Turn the pages to Situations Wanted ad-vertisements. Many stress the applicants' search for "greater visibility" or "growth." Then turn to the weekly Fates and Fortunes pages. The dozen or so little squibs printed there each week demonstrate the movement around the country of news-men and women who have found new berths at different sta-tions. Mr. X has "moved from WNEP-TV in Scranton, Pa., to KOVR-TV in Stockton, Calif."; Mr. Y joins "WNAC-TV Boston from KTEW (TV) Tulsa, Okla."

The motivation for moving around the country is only occasionally because the work is more challenging somewhere else; selling oneself into a bigger market means bigger paychecks. It is rare that a station will pay more than a known salary range for its market's size. In the smallest markets in 1980, salaries for anchors or the "star" reporter ranged from $17,000 to $19,000 a year. They rose rapidly to the $35,000 range in the stations ranked between eleventh and fiftieth in size. In the ten largest markets, they could soar from an average of $87,000 to more than half a million dollars a year. Atlanta pays $75,000 to $100,000; Phoenix pays $45,000 to $75,000, and Fort Wayne averages $35,000 to $45,000. With that kind of money involved, the hunt for greenback pastures is constant and so is the movement among proven on-air talent. Raiding is expected. In one instance, two stations in Albuquerque, New Mexico, were competing for the same anchorman. They engaged in a bidding war, finally upping the ante $40,000 a year over the original contract offers.

This upward or lateral mobility has frequently resulted in reporters and anchors knowing nothing about the place they are reporting on each night. Covering a city or a metropolitan area should require some knowledge of neighborhoods, tension points between competing ethnic or racial groups, the recent history of the place and who is scratching who's back at City Hall. Viewers may count themselves lucky if the place names are pronounced correctly. Nothing can alienate an audience faster than a newscaster's continued mispronunciation of well-known local names. A constant trip-up for an out-of-towner in New York City is Houston Street. It is not sounded like the Texas city but, in its own peculiar way, "Houseton." It took a gaffe like that to start a newly introduced anchor on his way back to Boston.

A different sort of problem confronted another itinerant anchor, Larry Kane. A fast-talking hotshot, he was moved from Philadelphia to New York. A massive advertising campaign was launched to promote his arrival. The print ads and on-the-air promotion heralded the fact that Kane was originally from New York (he *had* been born there, little more than that) and that he intended to visit every neighborhood in the city. The come-on was so hyped that New York's cynical press was sharpening its knives for him. Kane helped them along by deciding to keep living in a suburb of Philadelphia while commuting each day to New York in a limousine. If people are concerned about the ability of a newcomer to anchor a local nightly newscast, the idea of a *commuting* newcomer proved too much for the New York television audience.

Marvin Kitman, a columnist whose sharp wit often pricks the side of self-important TV performers with the force of a bayonet, wrote that Kane ought to be given the "man of the year" award by the New Jersey highway authorities because he was spending so much money in turnpike tolls, driving to and from Philadelphia. He finally returned to a Philadelphia station, working where he lived, and, incidentally, able to do a better job because he knew the territory.

The on-air personality should also know and understand the responsibilities that go with his or her job. Too often, at the local news level, that is not the case. The fundamental point is that the broadcast isn't one person's, or one station's. The airwaves are the property of the people of the United States, who give access to them to broadcasters in the expectation that they will be used fairly, accurately and responsibly. As Harry Reasoner puts it, the broadcaster is "the last S.O.B. who can say 'I won't say it!' " When the control is removed, or is not exercised because of inexperience, laziness or poor judgment, the worst can and does happen.

There have been cases of misuse of the television airwaves, but few as irresponsible, in my view, as an incident that occurred in Boston on April Fools' Day, 1980. Viewers of WNAC-TV heard anchorman John Henning introduce a "report" by a reporter, Jim Harrison, that purported to cover the "eruption" of the 635-foot "Great Blue Hill" in suburban Milton, Massachusetts. Shots of Great Blue Hill were shown and, superimposed, pictures of the then-erupting volcano at Mount St. Helens. There were statements by President Jimmy Carter and Massachusetts Governor Edward King, presumed to be expressing concern about a natural disaster. At the end of the report, the reporter, Jim Harrison, held up a sign that said "April Fool." After all, people in and around Boston and Milton would know that Great Blue Hill couldn't possibly burst forth as if it were a volcano.

Really? Milton's police lieutenant, David MacDonald, said, "We had people crying" on the telephone, asking anxiously if the story was true and inquiring about loved ones. That night, on the 11:00 P.M. news, anchorman Henning read an apology. The next day, the executive producer of the broadcast, Homer "Skip" Cilley, was fired by the station, which found itself under investigation by the Federal Communications Commission. The FCC ultimately decided against any action to punish the station.

Local stations say they look for experience and credibility. Local anchors are defensive about a perception that they are merely pretty faces. Roger Grimsby and Bill Beutel have impressive biographies and they place great emphasis on the stories they have covered, the awards they have won, and their news-gathering assignments. Despite his preeminent role as a television news "star" in the New York metropolitan area, Grimsby's 1980 biography goes into great detail about trips overseas to cover international events. Bill Beutel's write-up concentrates on his international news credentials: "Beutel's deep knowledge of international as well as national affairs has given wide scope to his 'Eyewitness Reports.' "

Network newsmen and women are frequently critical of anchors and reporters at local stations. Charles Kuralt, who has had several runs at anchoring in the course of his CBS News career, is best known for his "On the Road" series, which appears on the "CBS Evening News" and requires him to travel constantly. A newsman in a strange town will buy the local newspaper and turn on the local TV news. Kuralt expressed his dismay at what he had been seeing on local TV. He recounted his primary observation: It was "Hair. Hair neatly parted, hair abundant, and every hair in place." He was biting. "I can't remember much that came out beneath that hair. I don't think much did. I remember the style but not the substance. And I fear the reason may be there wasn't much substance there."

Walter Cronkite hit the same theme in an off-the-cuff speech to the CBS affiliates in May 1976. He attacked the hiring of local newscasters solely for looks and ability to perform. Cronkite believed this trend was symptomatic. "Just as it is no good to put out a superior product if you can't sell it, it is far worse to peddle an inferior product solely through the razzle-dazzle of a promotion campaign. And aren't we guilty of that when we put the emphasis on performers rather than content?" Cronkite has repeatedly come back to this theme, criticizing what he calls "pretty-boy newsreaders."

John Chancellor has written of his "hope that the next generation of anchor people will be drawn from the men and women who have been floor reporters, field reporters, foreign correspondents. There is just no substitute for riding the press bus, doing the shoe-leather reporting, writing under the deadlines, working overseas." Chancellor finds that these criteria operate at the networks. He's not so sure about local operations. "I worry sometimes that the demands for poise and personality on the air will come to outweigh the basic requirements of journalism. . . ."

There is probably no issue of greater contention between network news and local news than that of greater that of the competence of reporters. Local newscasters believe their network colleagues are too often stuffed shirts, "aging giants" (emphasis on *aging*) who are "transmitting from atop Mount Olympus."

Some local news executives and reporters concede that the network view of local news may be true about some markets. Stations in smaller communities have neither the money nor the prestige to attract the caliber of newscaster drawn to the big cities.

There are 212 TV markets in the United States, and the viewing populations of the ten largest in 1981 were:

1.	New York	6,398,000
2.	Los Angeles	4,050,700
3.	Chicago	2,849,700
4.	Philadelphia	2,399,300
5.	San Francisco	1,883,600
6.	Boston	1,807,200
7.	Detroit	1,600,100
8.	Washington, D.C.	1,397,600
9.	Cleveland	1,348,900
10.	Dallas–Ft. Worth	1,175,100

That means that millions of Americans get their news and information from stations in the "smaller markets." The smallest market, in Miles City, Glendive, Montana, reaches 9,700 viewers, and the bottom ten cover 176,100 people. If statistics hold, two-thirds of those individuals get all or most of their news from television.

The alternative source should be newspapers, but in smaller cities newspapers are often marginal. Reader–viewers there are getting an even higher percentage of their news and information from television compared with reader–viewers in larger cities with better papers.

Even if it is correct that the quality of local reporters and anchors is adequate everywhere but in the "smaller markets," a substantial number of Americans hear the news from the lips of men or women Cronkite has called "pompadoured, pampered announcers," who often do not know the locality, who come from "500 or 1,000 or 2,000 miles away," who were chosen because they had already achieved good ratings. After all, "What sells is good."

Audience appeal grows out of a number of considerations, and some have nothing to do with journalism. A blatant case of playing to the audience occurred when station executives at WABC-TV decided to play the "Three 'I' " game. Politicians in New York often try to balance their election tickets by picking an *I*talian, an *I*rishman, and a Jew (*I*sraelite) to appeal to the major ethnic groups. WABC-TV's "Eyewitness News" decided they could use an Italian; they hired Rose Ann Scamardella, who had no news experience. Her previous job was as an unsalaried New York City commissioner, looking into discrimination against minorities. Nonetheless, she was unquestionably an Italian-American from Brooklyn. First, she was given assignments as a street reporter, and then she was moved into an anchor role. To her credit, Scamardella recognized that her experience was limited, and she moved to correct her inadequacies. She worked hard in an on-the-job training program. As a former colleague put it: "To a certain degree she was successful. You cover enough fires and eventually you learn what to look for and what questions to ask."

Scamardella's success in attracting a segment of the audience lay behind another move at ABC-TV. Now it was decided that a blond WASP was required to balance the team. Joan Lunden was hired. Her credentials as a journalist were as unimpressive as Scamardella's. She had been a weather reporter and had run a charm school in Sacramento, California. She too moved up to an anchor chair, where she was quickly spotted by executives from the network's entertainment division. Eventually she left local news to become cohostess of "Good Morning America" with David Hartman.

I served for a while as a news consultant for a group of TV stations to help improve their level of coverage. My interest was not whether the anchorman smiled or had wavy hair or whether he wore the channel number on his blazer. My concern was how well the station's news programming was doing the job it was supposed to be doing: providing the latest information thoroughly and accurately.

Before I went to the local station to meet the news staff, I spent some time in town watching all the local programs. Invariably I felt cheated by at least one of the stations. Sometimes I recognized the "cheat" because a competing station provided more details or more stories, other times because the local evening newspaper had clearer and more focused coverage. The result was the "A. Westin Cheat Factor." My theory states that the station that "cheats" its audience most has the lowest ratings in town. It doesn't necessarily follow that the station with the lowest "cheat factor" will have the highest ratings.

How can a station overcome and eliminate a high "cheat factor"? Television newsrooms get most of their information from a few standard sources. There are scheduled events like a mayor's news conference or a preplanned opening of a supermarket or an exhibition at the library. There are breaking stories whose importance is usually first discerned when the local fire or police radio breaks in with that dramatic call for assistance in the numerical jargon so popular in TV police shows. There are stories that develop through the enterprise of reporters at the station or at the local newspapers. The wire services, the Associated Press and United Press International, are also sources for stories, but few of those address local issues. A development in Washington or at the state capital turns up first on the wires.

And there's one little-known news service provided by all three networks. They all run news syndication services that feed their local affiliated stations with short news clips that otherwise would not be seen. Sports, indeed, is a big segment of this syndicated material, but ABC's Daily Electronic Feed (DEF), NBC's NPS—News Program Service—and CBS's Syndicated News pump hours of news-tape spots down the line every day. Local stations are able to present their congressman as he reacts to breaking news stories, and they can share the reportage of another station and broaden their sweep.

The problem is that local stations, with their smaller staffs and their younger and less-experienced personnel, tend to limit their thinking and cover the local news in an unimaginative way. This lack of imagination means that significant aspects of stories are left uncovered. Every angle of a story deserves some attention, and the more angles the reporting staff discovers, the better the coverage. Take a mayor's news conference. There's probably no regular City Hall reporter. Whoever got the assignment that day will merely tape the conference and cut up the material, interspersing connective narration between the mayor's words. In fact, the conference ought to be the beginning, not the end of the day's work. If the mayor talked about hospital costs, that should be a peg for a report on hospital admissions procedures; if he or she has spoken about crime in the streets, it is time to ask the police for permission to ride on a patrol. Such stories can be done quickly too, for broadcast that same evening. That kind of enterprise will provide a fuller menu for the viewers and the "cheat factor" will decline. When a staff does things predictably, with no hustle, the coverage is awful and the competition is handed the ratings on a silver platter. Worse, the viewer is not properly served.

As a consultant, I visited many local stations around the country, large and small. One of them was WANE-TV in Fort Wayne, Indiana. I addressed the local news staff, engaging them in a journalistic game that is an important learning tool. "Imagine," I said, "on pain of being fired, that you had to find a local angle to whatever story appears next on the Associated Press

news ticker. No exceptions or excuses! Find a local angle worthy of coverage in the next story on that wire service machine."
The story that showed up next in the Fort Wayne newsroom
was about a major truck crash in Kansas City. There were
groans all around and mutterings about the impossibility of the
assignment. "Come on, no excuses," I insisted. "Give me a
local angle to that story."

One reporter suggested that perhaps the driver of the truck
was from Fort Wayne. Another suggested that the truck may
have been en route to Fort Wayne or heading away from Fort
Wayne. All agreed that those ideas were too weak to merit
coverage in Fort Wayne. Before long, connections were being
made between the truck crash in Kansas City and truck transportation statistics in Fort Wayne; between the crash and inspec-
tion provisions in Fort Wayne for handling driver qualifications;
and, finally, one reporter suggested that it might be time to
examine the state of the superhighway that courses through Fort
Wayne and whether the local police were equipped to respond
properly to emergencies and major disasters.

That was an idea that had enough merit to warrant assignment
for that night's newscast. "Now go suggest it to the assignment
editor," I said. "He'll probably reject it because there are other
more important stories breaking around town today. But don't
be discouraged, keep the stories coming at him." The point is
that the assignment editor, even while rejecting the suggestion,
had at least been offered an option. No editor can possibly think
of all the stories or all the angles. If the staff keeps pushing them
in front of him or her, eventually there will be one that works.
An editor cannot say "yes" to a story that is not proposed. Even
saying "no" represents a choice, and he or she can keep an eye
on it as a potential contribution toward enriching the broadcast
and diminishing the "cheat factor."

The teaching experience in the Fort Wayne newsroom paid
off handsomely by week's end. On Friday, UPI carried a story
from Washington, D.C., about an Air Force test of bacteriological warfare techniques. The exercise had used planes to drop
aerosol mists over American cities to test wind and coverage
patterns and to simulate what would happen if bacteriological
material was spread over communities from the air. Using the

lessons learned from our exercise earlier in the week, one woman reporter called the Pentagon and asked if any of those tests had been conducted in or near Fort Wayne. She received a call back from an Air Force information officer who confirmed that Fort Wayne had indeed been involved, and that one of the drops had occurred in or near the city's airport. She scored a substantial beat that night over the other stations and the local newspaper.

There is now a pool of talented and experienced people working at local TV stations. They handle personally more parts of the news-gathering job every day than most network employees. They supervise coverage and production, run cameras, edit tape. That "hands-on" experience cannot as easily be acquired at the network level. Despite the criticisms, the people who do the work at these stations are learning their craft, and the experience is invaluable. Most local stations were broadcasting weekly special series long before NBC started its nightly "Segment Three" and ABC began "Special Assignment." The men and women who handled that form of segment production at the local level formed the corps of those who stepped in to do the job when network news adopted the same form.

There is greater demand for writing skills in local news operations than there is at a network. Correspondents at the networks write all their own copy and network anchors write most of theirs. At the local station, with its one-hour news broadcasts to be filled every night, the staff has to write far more of the material that gets on the air. At a station, everyone takes a turn as assignment editor, gaining experience in how to cover a story and how to run news-gathering operations with limited resources. With those kinds of experiences listed on résumés, the networks fill more and more openings for production staffs from the outside, with versatile people who have demonstrated their skills at local news. One can move ahead by starting with the network, but local experience certainly helps on the way up.

Television stations recognize that they have become the farm system for the networks. The smaller stations know that their personnel will move on. There is a trade-off. They can pay only modest salaries, but they do offer talented and ambitious people the chance to learn on the job.

Local station managers and news directors have one complaint that is heard more often than any other. They want the network to bring news content closer to home. Each year, managers and owners of all of a network's affiliated stations meet and network news executives get a chance to listen. Inevitably, the local people ask for livelier content on the network's newscast. They are a constant pressure group, lobbying for more "pop." Almost without fail, they criticize the choice of stories because they are not domestically oriented.

"Here comes the nightly piece from Israel," was one comment I heard in a Kansas City newsroom as the local staff sat around watching the network's feed come down the line. "There has to be something happening west of the Mississippi," was the sarcastic response to one more Washington hearing. "Integrity doesn't mean you can't give us some real-life excitement involving everyday people. My daughter is just as interested in Elton John as she is in the Ayatollah Khomeini. Give us both," was the plea of an important figure in the galaxy of ABC affiliated stations. At the better stations, local people believe they are in closer touch with the concerns of their audiences and that they are providing more information in ways that meet those concerns.

The most recent trend at local stations is the creation of the fast-paced interview programs, which are replacing late-afternoon movies and game shows. The "Live at Five" concept, developed at WNBC-TV in New York, brings in the hottest personality in town or the latest author or the hero firefighter from last night's blaze. It is breezy, vapid and superficial, but since no guest is on the air more than five minutes, there's no time to get bored or feel cheated and tune out. What's good sells, and if imitation is any measure of a concept's success, the "Live at Five" idea is a smash hit. It has rapidly spread from station to station across the country.

In a sense, it is true that local news is where the action is. Local news is picture oriented, and, further, it goes for the sensational angle. Local news does more consumer investigations about products sold down the street in the neighborhood supermarket. It carries more reports on movies, hit records and community theater groups, which means that there is more reporting on the arts than on the networks. Local news is more like the Sunday magazine insert or the daily tabloid than a newspaper of record.

There are some positive signs. The pendulum of "happy talk news" has swung back. There is still excess, but a balance is achieved at many stations. Anchors and reporters are less frequently required to fill comedic roles. They are regarded as human beings who can have legitimate reactions to the stories they are reporting or to the stories they introduce. A smile, a somber shake of the head in disbelief, even an occasional comment is now acceptable. An anchor or a reporter now can show that he or she is at least as interested in the story as the viewer is expected to be.

As the networks revamp their evening newscasts in the wake of Cronkite's departure from CBS, and with the debut of NBC's Mudd–Brokaw anchor team, their planning reflects some of local news's influences. There is a broadened table of contents; reporters are more involved in the stories they cover. There are more graphic displays, a brisker pace, a more relaxed on-air demeanor. (Dan Rather even shows up on camera wearing a sweater.)

God forbid that network newscasts would ever become "happy talk" shows. But as network news programs are thought through for new time periods, it is certain that even more of the techniques that were developed in local stations will be adapted. It will be a time for caution. What sells is not necessarily good. TV news is always in danger of being reduced to entertainment. If it is, if show business techniques are allowed to distort information rather than to help convey it, then, as Edward R. Murrow warned, television will merely be a box with a lot of lights and wires.

7
All in a Loose-Leaf Notebook
RULES, REGULATIONS, POLICIES

"Congress shall make no law respecting an establishment of religion; or prohibiting the free exercise thereof; or abridging the freedom of speech, or of the press; or the right of the people peaceably to assemble, and to petition the government for a redress of grievances."

—The First Amendment to the Constitution of the United States

Broadcast journalism has many of the protections of the First Amendment, but there are also government regulations that apply specifically to broadcasters. The Federal Communications Commission was created by Congress in 1934, and through the years, the FCC has issued a number of rules. These have been challenged in Federal courts and argued before the United States Supreme Court. Since the Court has upheld them, they have the force of law. They affect broadcast journalists in ways that they don't affect newspaper reporters and editors.

The rationale for regulations that restrict the absolute First Amendment protection for broadcasters goes something like this: Anyone with desire, money and skill can set up a newspaper. Acquire a printing press and newsprint and you're in business as a newspaper publisher. But not anyone with desire, money and skill can set up a television station. One can buy the equivalent of the printing press, that is, the broadcast equipment, but access to the airwaves, which are the equivalent of the newsprint, is limited by technical considerations. Since only a limited number of channels are available, the principle of regulating them has been established and upheld. The FCC has ruled that the limited number of broadcasters—unlike the *un*limited number of publishers—must (1) obey rules concerning fairness and balance; (2) provide equal air time for political candidates; and (3) allot time for responses to personal attacks that are delivered on the air.

Those three categories are known as the Fairness Doctrine; the Equal Time Provision, or Section 315; and the Personal Attack Rule. One must understand all three to understand how careful broadcasters have to be.

The Fairness Doctrine, the most important rule, evolved almost from the beginning of broadcasting. In 1929 the then Federal Radio Commission became concerned that station owners were using the airwaves to promote their own ideas while excluding those of others in the community. When a particularly offending station came before the FRC, the commission took the occasion to issue a ruling that stated, "In so far as a program consists of discussion of public questions, public interest requires ample play for the free and fair competition of opposing views. The Commission believes that this principle applies to all discussions of issues of importance to the public."

Through several more cases and rulings, the FCC, which succeeded the FRC, kept on paying attention to the question of protecting fair and balanced coverage on the air. In 1949, in a Report on Editorializing by Broadcast Licensees, the commission finally put down in writing a definition of the Fairness Doctrine. It directed broadcast licensees to "operate in the public interest," and then it went on to require that they "devote a reasonable amount of time to the coverage of controversial issues of public importance" and that when they undertook that kind of programming that it be done "fairly by affording a reasonable opportunity for contrasting viewpoints to be voiced on these issues."

What does that official language mean? It requires the station licensees to devote air time to covering at least some of the issues facing the communities they are licensed to serve. The FCC says the broadcasters must do the job by presenting "representative and contrasting points of view" in their overall programming. No such legal requirement affects newspaper publishers or editors, who can be as one-sided as they choose and ignore whatever they please.*

The Fairness Doctrine leaves it to the broadcaster to determine what issues to cover and who should be chosen to present the "representative and contrasting views." (The dumbest jackass in town always presents your side; the smartest and most articulate Handsome Harry is picked to handle the opposition.) The broadcaster can also decide when to present the arguments: within the same program, another day on the same program or, indeed, at another time altogether. If a broadcaster's overall coverage of an issue is fair and balanced, then even if one broadcast is deemed to be one-sided, no violation of the Fairness Doctrine has occurred. Also there is no requirement under the Fairness Doctrine for equal time. People who write to demand equal time to reply to what they regard as an unfair broadcast have not done their homework about the basic requirements that define fairness and balance.

Despite all the professional care and expertise that reporters bring to bear on their work, they are human beings with potentially strong feelings about the subjects they are assigned to cover. Reporters try to remain dispassionate and neutral when they select the pictures and write their scripts. Editors and producers read those scripts and view the completed tape or film spots before they are broadcast. The purpose is to check for accuracy but also to be sure "hot" adjectives or "cheap shots" are edited out. Still, there are inevitably occasions when personal prejudices slip through on a daily news broadcast, usually under the deadline pressure of getting the story on the air.

To counter that and to try to maintain fairness and balance, I had a "7-day rule" at ABC for the "Evening News" broadcast when it was under my command. It was a form of self-policing through the professional judgments of the program's senior staff. After we presented a report on a controversial issue, if any

---

* In 1968 a publisher banned the name of Robert Kennedy from his paper during his state's presidential primary campaign; another publisher decreed no coverage of local power company operations, and one I heard of insisted that no pictures of antiwar demonstrations were ever to run in his daily.

of the senior staff felt that one side had been treated unfairly, or that the powerful combination of picture, sound and narration had resulted in distortion, we would redo the story within seven broadcast days. Actually the counterbalancing story was transmitted within two days. The "7-day rule" was a recognition of our immense responsibility.

It also seemed to me that as long as producers and correspondents and assignment editors at headquarters in New York were being "briefed" each morning by the same newspapers and radio reports, we were all likely to begin the working day by assessing the relative importance of stories according to an agenda already set down by the *New York Times,* the *Washington Post* and the "CBS World News Roundup." Those are powerful influences that greet each of us every morning. I became concerned that they represented an East Coast, socially activist view of events that could affect our outlook. I thought it important to distinguish between those stories that supported the thesis that sweeping changes or reforms would be required to handle contemporary problems and those that supported the status quo. Both views merited coverage during the weeks or months an issue remained "hot." It did not matter to me which stories were assigned as long as both approaches to current events were equally reported.

In social issues, filled with emotion, one side is usually advocating change while the other is defending the status quo. Too often for my taste, the advocates of change were given the first opportunity in a report to present their ideas. It was an unconscious display of bias on the part of correspondents and producers who frequently agreed with those suggesting new or different approaches to current problems. The correspondents would put the dramatic pictures suggesting change up front, establishing a mood for the remainder of the piece. The "other side"—those resisting change—would generally find itself having to defend, react and answer. The rebuttal frequently failed to achieve enough emotional or factual punch to overcome the initial advantage. The reports would be unbalanced.

To handle the problem, we consciously set out to do stories with what I called "reverse perspective." An example: The issue of legalizing abortion was hot in the early seventies. It was being debated in many state legislatures and covered endlessly. In time, a virtual formula developed for constructing stories about the debate in state after state. The spots would begin with pictures of unwanted babies, and the narration would make the point that these children exist in their sorry condition because of antiquated abortion laws that forced pregnant women to have children they did not want and could not afford. The alternative opening in this formula showed a silhouetted woman telling how she nearly died after an illegal abortion at the hands of a "butcher" or some back-alley crone. With the case for legalized abortion powerfully presented, an opponent of abortion would be given a chance to make the prolife side of the case, usually without dramatic pictures, inserted merely as a "talking head." The correspondent would then provide a closing summary, balancing the two cases and indicating how the debate stood in the particular state he or she was in.

To "reverse the perspective," a correspondent covering one state's debate was told to begin with dramatic pictures of a human fetus. The narration was to start by presenting the anti-abortionists' position that the fetus was a human being killed by an abortion. That was buttressed by the appearance of an anti-abortion spokesman setting forth the rest of the arguments against legalization of abortion. Then the other side was heard. The proabortion positions were presented by qualified advocates. "Reverse perspective" broke the formula deliberately, giving the "anti's" a chance to go first, making the "pro's" respond for a change. It does not matter what my view on the issue is or what the correspondent feels is the better argument. What is essential is that we broadcast a fair presentation, and "reverse perspective," when applied, is a way to ensure that the continuing coverage of a debate is balanced.

Certainly there are stories that do not merit a "reverse perspective" effort. Criminals, rapists and muggers have no cause to advocate. There is no debate in covering that aspect of the social issue of crime. Though their views would be included in civil rights reports, it would be hard to find any justification for racists or outright segregationists to merit a reverse perspective on a story about equality for minorities. Fair and balanced reporting is achieved merely by including their views somewhere in a piece.

The *Wall Street Journal,* learning of the "7-day rule" and "reverse perspective," commented approvingly in an editorial page note: "Obviously two very different stories can emanate from the same event, depending on the perspective which is used." In a sense, that is incorrect. It was the *same* story. We were merely taking steps to ensure that the impact of television coverage on the "Evening News" did not change it into two different ones.

In June 1969, the Supreme Court handed down a decision in a case dealing with the Fairness Doctrine as it applied to a specific individual or, in the Court's words, "to an identified person or group." It was a case involving the Red Lion Broadcasting Corporation, which owned and operated WGLB, an AM and FM station in Pennsylvania. Here's what happened under Fairness Doctrine requirements: Red Lion Broadcasting was presenting a prerecorded episode of the "Christian Crusade" over WGLB. The Reverend Billy James Hargis, an Oklahoma evangelist who dealt with public issues, was on the air attacking Fred J. Cook as "a professional mudslinger" while also accusing him of dishonesty and of falsifying stories. Cook had written a book critical of Senator Barry Goldwater, and Hargis believed it was part of a left-wing conspiracy that had defeated Goldwater's bid for the presidency in 1964. It was coverage of a controversial issue of public importance. That part was all right, but it was the nature of Hargis' attack on Cook that crossed the line. He had railed against Cook's "honesty, character or like personal quality" when he accused him of faking stories. Cook petitioned the FCC, demanding a right to reply. The FCC agreed with him, and, as a result, it issued a new set of regulations—the Personal Attack Rule—as a corollary to the Fairness Doctrine. The Supreme Court heard Red Lion's challenge to that ruling and upheld the FCC in a decision that has come to be known as "Red Lion."

The Personal Attack Rule does not prohibit personal attacks on the air, but it does require that a station that broadcasts an attack take certain steps within one week following the broadcast.

First, the person or group attacked has to be notified of the date, time and title of the program on which the attack occurred. Second, a tape or script of the attack must be sent to the person or group that was attacked. If there's no script or tape, a summary will do. Finally, the person attacked must be offered a "reasonable opportunity" to reply over the station or network. Again, these regulations affect only broadcasting. They do not apply to print.

The Red Lion decision does not apply to attacks made on foreign groups or foreign public figures. It would not apply, for example, in the case of a broadcast in 1980 entitled "Death of a Princess," which purported to be a "docu-drama" about the execution of a Saudi Arabian princess and her lover. The Personal Attack Rule does not apply to attacks made during newscasts, news interviews and on-the-spot coverage of news events. It does not apply to commentary or analysis when it is included in those forms of programming.

The right to respond on the air under the Personal Attack Rule has nothing to do with the truth of the reply nor with the accuracy of the attack. The attack may be based on 100 percent documented fact, but as long as it occurred during a discussion of a controversial issue of public importance and as long as it dealt with the integrity, honesty or like personal quality of the persons who were attacked, the rule is triggered.

The Personal Attack Rule is not a license to steal air time from broadcasters. There are some important questions that have to be answered before one can start typing a rebuttal. First, was the statement really an attack on honesty, character or integrity, or was it just an unfavorable reference to the person or group? Painful though they may be, unflattering references are not personal attacks; so, no response time. Second, was an identified person or group actually attacked or was it an idea or philosophy put forward by that person or group? An attack on an idea carries no right for response. Third, did the attack take place during a discussion of a *controversial* issue of public importance? That's a critical adjective: controversial. For example, an attack on a corrupt judge does not qualify. There is nothing controversial about corruption in government—it is unquestionably a bad thing so the issue does not qualify. Similarly, attacking an arsonist does not give him the right to respond. Arson is uncontroversially wrong.

In 1972, the *Miami Herald* ran two editorials during an election campaign endorsing one candidate for state senator. In the course of that endorsement, the editorials were openly critical of one of the candidates, Pat Tornillo, Jr. Tornillo sued, claiming he had a statutory right to have answering letters printed. A lower court in Florida ruled that Tornillo had no right to demand space, which is the newspaper's equivalent of air time. On appeal, however, the Florida Supreme Court overturned the lower court. Citing the Red Lion case, it extended to print, for the first time, the right of response required of broadcasters. The *Miami Herald* was ordered to print Tornillo's letters "in the interest of full and fair discussion." Then the U.S. Supreme Court heard the case and unanimously reversed the Florida court. Chief Justice Burger's opinion said that what goes into a newspaper, whether fair or unfair, constitutes the exercise of editorial judgment, and government cannot interfere in that. In short, the First Amendment protected the *Miami Herald* from any mandated requirement impinging on its right to print what it wanted, when it wanted and for however much space it wanted.

Once again, broadcasters do not have that liberty. Section 315 of the Federal Communications Act takes care of that. This is the "equal time" provision. "Equal time" refers *only* to political campaigns and to *bona fide* candidates. It does not apply to companies or individuals who are seeking the right of reply. Section 315 is a major problem for broadcasters because it opens them up to demands for air time from every minor candidate no matter how insignificant his candidacy for the office in question. That's why presidential debates are next to impossible to arrange. The 1960 debates between Kennedy and Nixon got a special congressional waiver of Section 315 so that all other presidential candidates including a pig farmer in Secaucus, New Jersey, did not have to get equal time. The presidential debates in 1976 between Carter and Ford and again in 1980 between Carter and Reagan and between Reagan and Anderson were made possible because they were arranged by the League of Women Voters. The networks were merely providing "on the spot coverage of a *bona fide* news event," which is one of the exemptions from Section 315.

Coverage of legitimate news events is exempt, as are the nightly newscasts and other regularly scheduled news interview broadcasts such as "Face the Nation" and "Meet the Press." Otherwise, every time the President appeared on the evening news during a presidential campaign, it would provide some minor candidate with the right to demand equal time. The minor candidates do get some coverage but nowhere near what the principals get. Once more, newspapers do not operate in this governmental environment.

Many stations are parts of television station "groups." Only five VHF television stations and two UHF stations can be held by one ownership, and there are many group owners in the United States. Most have a central office in New York or Los Angeles, and their interests are watched over at the station by a general manager who is responsible to the home office for his or her station's financial bottom line.

Although television stations have licenses that last for five years, they are subject to periodic renewal, and at renewal time, they can be challenged by people who feel the station is not doing a good job. Since there's lots of money to be made by owning and running a TV station, challenges have cropped up by "outs" who want to get "in" and demand that the FCC take away a station's license. Lawyers representing a station's interests are quite frequently based at the home office of the group. They are not part of the community, and they do not share the immediate concerns of the station's average viewer. Their job, simply put, is to keep the station out of trouble and avoid challenges to the license. Challenges are costly to meet. Often hundreds of thousands of dollars need to be spent to defend against them. A troublesome report on a news broadcast can stir up viewers and lead them at renewal time to try to find ways to cause the station's management to lose the license. Lawyers worry about that.

A story about fat content in a supermarket's meat counter is an unfortunate example of this kind of concern. A television consumer affairs reporter uncovered the fact that too much fat was being included in a product being sold as prime hamburger meat. The reporter had taken meat samples and tested them at a reputable laboratory. He was prepared to give time, place, date and names. The local station's news director suggested that, to anticipate legal questions—but not to kill the piece—the attorneys in the home office read the script. That was done and the lawyer reacted by suggesting some "minor alterations." Eliminate the name of the market, don't identify it as a fat content problem and just suggest that consumers ought to be more careful when they buy. The story was gutted. The news director told the reporter to ignore the advice and the story was run. The lawyer, of course, had simply been doing his job, as he saw it.

Too often, attorneys drop behind legal jargon to dissuade reporters from going with information they have discovered. The fact is, there are very few things reporters must avoid. The tragedy from the broadcast journalist's point of view is that very few know how far they really can go without running afoul of FCC regulations and broadcast law. There's an entire series of cases that should be known to everyone to clear up this area of broadcast journalism.

I've found some network lawyers helpful in getting the story on the air, rather than keeping it off. Sam Antar, vice-president and general attorney for ABC News, takes the position that the report ought to be broadcast. All he asks us to provide in advance is sufficient proof that, if sued, he will have the weapons to meet and beat the suit. His questions always go to that point. "Tell me how you can prove that allegation," he'll say, "and I'll defend it all the way." Capricious lawsuits are filed all the time against network news divisions. By and large, the attitude is to take the suit but be prepared to defend against the charge before we broadcast, not after we broadcast.

Pictorial, on-the-spot coverage of riots, civil disturbances and demonstrations was not anticipated when network coverage standards were first formulated. As the civil rights movement, with its sit-ins and marches, boiled up in the sixties, and as antiwar parades began to dominate the news in the seventies, guidelines were created based on the experiences news personnel were gathering in the field. "News should be telecast in such a manner as to avoid panic and unnecessary alarm," news department memoranda read, calling for extra care to keep stories in perspective so that "a scuffle doesn't become a riot in reporting" or that "a whole city is aflame just because someone has started a bonfire." Facts rather than supposition are the paramount requirement. Sources for reliable information are suggested. Civil rights leaders, merchants and residents in the area of a disturbance who were not directly affected by it are among those to be approached for a fuller picture of what really happened. Neither the police nor the street leaders should be a correspondent's sole source for accurate reporting of causes, issues or casualties.

As civil disturbances became a way of political life in the U.S. in the sixties, television was accused of heightening tense situations merely by being present. Critics claimed that cameras, lights and microphones caused relatively passive bystanders to "put on a show." Dedicated and street-trained demonstrators seized on minor occurrences to publicize their views before the cameras. On-the-spot judgments about the cause and effect of television's presence on disturbances were generally left to the field team. They were urged in network policy guides to use unmarked cars to bring personnel and equipment to the scene. Vans and station wagons with the network logo displayed on the side or with flashing and rotating red "gumball" lights were to be avoided because they drew attention. Cameras were to be set up as inconspicuously as possible, and long-range sound pickups with newly developed "shotgun" microphones were preferred to wading into the crowds. Lights always attract attention, drawing crowds and heightening the "performance" quotient of the rowdier elements at any demonstration. Crews were instructed to turn them off if it appeared that they were worsening the situation. CBS News's guidance was most explicit: "If, in your judgment, your presence is clearly inspiring, continuing or intensifying a dangerous or potentially dangerous disturbance, cap your cameras and conceal your microphones regardless of what other news organizations may do."

No executive happily sends his colleagues into danger, but it is one of the requirements of television news coverage that the event be witnessed on the scene by cameras and correspondents. The instructions for all networks are filled with warnings: "It is your responsibility carefully to gauge the likelihood of bodily injury and then to elect which of the following alternatives seem appropriate: i) continue your coverage or ii) move to a less exposed position which will still permit coverage or iii) leave the scene."

To what extent should field crews cooperate with police during a disturbance? All reporters and crews have credentials issued by police and fire departments that give them access to events in front of police lines—and once there, news staffs are supposed to obey all police instructions without question. On the other hand, if some orders seem designed to suppress or manage news coverage, field teams are told to protest and to notify senior executives of the news department, presumably so they can take appropriate legal action to protect access to the news.

Finally, there is universal concern over staging or having some action repeated for the benefit of the camera. FCC rules specifically bar the "creation" of events. They stem from an incident in Chicago in which a producer for WBBM-TV, assigned to do a report about marijuana, helped to arrange a party and supply the cigarettes. He then filmed the gathering as "typical." As a result of the "WBBM Pot Party Case," what is shown on the air in news programs must really have happened the way it appears on the air or the narration must explain what was created for the cameras.

Local stations and networks are quick to discipline staff members who cross the line, because of the damage to the credibility of the entire news organization. A case in point: A field producer turned in a story about policemen's wives and their anxieties about the safety of their husbands while on radio car patrol.

In one scene, the producer filmed a police car dodging through traffic apparently in pursuit of an escaping criminal. Police wives had told researchers that they felt their husbands faced the greatest life-threatening danger in those siren-screaming incidents. The TV news report was built around just such a high-speed chase. The fact was, however, that it had been staged, and if the chase was a setup, the audience could legitimately ask what else was a fictional re-creation.

There are ways to use re-creations to illustrate important points in a news story. They are perfectly okay if the audience is told clearly that some sort of staging has been involved. "The Seattle Police Department demonstrated just how dangerous a chase can be. . . ." would have done the job but when the report went on the air, there was no such qualification in the narration. Production devices must never be allowed to distort the viewer's understanding of a story's real elements. In the case of the police story, the producer was ordered suspended for thirty days without pay.

Staging is impermissible. Equally bad is reenactment.

Instructions are unmistakably clear: If an element of a story is missed, asking for a repeat performance is absolutely forbidden. Events are to be covered exactly as they happen with no repetition. No suggestions or requests to the participants are to be made. In fact, casual conversation with demonstrators or the police is discouraged. Anything that could influence the participants either to do something or to refrain from doing something is prohibited.

Although guidelines rarely get into the specific language to be used in reporting stories, the standards set for riot coverage do make some suggestions about "hot" words. Reportage must be somber and unemotional and phrases such as "angry mob" and "police brutality" are to be avoided. The word "riot" is also warned against unless it is clearly justified. Dispassionate vocabulary is generally used in tense situations. When the Three Mile Island nuclear accident occurred in 1978, ABC News personnel received instructions not to use adjectives that quantified danger or risk. There was enough official confusion at Three Mile Island without us adding to it by reporting that conditions were "extremely" dangerous or that officials were "highly" uncertain about the degree of radiation leakage.

There is always the unforeseen. In 1977, a sect of Hanafi Muslims seized hostages all over Washington, D.C. Led by a man whose family had been killed by another sect of Muslims, the Hanafis demanded, among other things, that the jailed mur-

derers be brought from prison to the Hanafi leader for his judgment; that the murderer of radical black leader Malcolm X also
be brought forward from prison for Hanafi judgment, and that
a movie about the life of Mohammed be removed from theaters
because it was blasphemous. As the hostage drama took shape
at various locations in Washington, live cameras focused on the
buildings where the Hanafis were holding out. Max Robinson,
then an anchorman on a local television station, figured promi-
nently in the negotiations to free the hostages. He received
phone calls while on the air from the Hanafi leader. Demands
and threats to kill some of the hostages were broadcast unedited
on live television and radio. It was not immediately clear
whether that action helped the situation—defusing the passions
of the hostage-takers by giving them the publicity they craved
—or whether the live coverage merely inflamed them to greater
bravura threats. In the end, ambassadors of several Moslem nations entered the negotiations, and the hostages were freed and
the Hanafis arrested.

In the aftermath, news executives realized that they needed
guidelines for coverage of terrorist and hostage situations. To
cover or not to cover and, if coverage is allowed, how much is
permissible remain incompletely resolved questions. Officials in
the Reagan administration have publicly called upon television
not to cover hostage situations, believing that the terrorists de-
pend on the publicity that TV provides and amplifies. No television coverage would make the act of hostage-taking futile, the
argument goes, and fewer incidents would occur if access to TV
were denied. There is equal concern that coverage spreads the
idea of hostage-taking. Like street demonstrators who "perform" for cameras, terrorist acts that get publicity encourage
other, more passive groups to try something spectacular.

Walter Cronkite spoke about the question before an audience
that included Secretary of State Alexander Haig. Haig had earlier urged noncoverage as a policy. Cronkite responded by pos-
ing the news department's dilemma. If one story is suppressed
for an apparently good reason, viewers might well wonder what
other stories are also being held back. "What else are they keeping from us?" is a question Cronkite raised. Another question
that is a corollary of the first is "Who determined that the rea-

sons to suppress the first story were good; who will make the determination, and on what grounds, the next time?" The overriding concern of news executives is for the "public's right to know." The debate continues with the balance tipped correctly toward regular coverage on newscasts with extreme sensitivity to the potential dangers involved.

The basic tools for print reporters are the pencil and notebook. That is where their observations, their quotations and their discoveries are recorded. The basic tools for television reporters are the camera and its videotape or film. The use of those tools is subject to carefully conceived and strictly enforced guidelines.

For years, print reporters had an advantage. They could slip unnoticed into a location to cover a story; indeed, they could even pocket their pencils and pads, making notes after leaving the scene. The very size of a television camera and its need for special lighting made that kind of unobtrusive coverage impossible for the broadcast journalist who wanted to remain undercover while investigating a story. Technology once again rose to meet editorial needs and cameras have now grown smaller and no longer need special lights. In fact, some of the gear nowadays is no larger than the print reporter's stenographer's pad.

A hidden camera's recording of a crime being committed or planned has far more impact as evidence than a written description in a newspaper. Abscam certainly demonstrated that. Though TV reporters still have problems getting cameras and microphones into position to tape an event, they no longer have to hang back. Investigative reporting on TV is the newest area to develop. Once again, there are special restrictions that apply only to TV. In many states, laws of privacy apply to protect individuals from having their voices recorded or pictures taken without their consent. Since investigative reporting on TV is relatively new, policies in force at the beginning of the eighties in the era of film and videotape may well have to be drastically revised as new technology makes laser recording of pictures and sound possible at incredibly long distances.

If the gathering of news material is subject to control, its use after it is gathered is also handled under guidelines. Interviews are almost always edited down. The "cutaway" of the correspondent apparently listening has already been discussed. The "reverse question" is another device used in the editing process. Sometimes, on major interviews, two cameras will roll simultaneously. One generally gets a "single" shot of the interviewee. The other varies its pictures, showing the correspondent alone or in a "two-shot" with the guest. When the interview is edited, the pictures of the correspondent asking a question on one camera are spliced into the finished sequence. Most of the time, however, only one camera is used in interview situations. It varies its shot from a "single" of the guest to an "over the shoulder" shot showing the back of the correspondent in the foreground with the guest in the background. On those occasions, in order to get a picture of the correspondent, the camera's position is literally reversed; that is, it is moved behind the guest's chair, putting *his* back in the foreground and showing the correspondent in the background. This action is taken after the interview is completed and the correspondent actually asks the questions all over again while facing the camera himself. Sometimes the correspondent repeats the questions after listening to an audio tape made during the interview. In my view, that is the preferred way to do the job, the way to be accurate and to recapture the tone and context of the original question. Unfortunately, some correspondents try to remember what they asked by using notes or simply their memories. It is better to have the guest stay around while the "reverses" are shot, but many times they are recorded after the guest has left, with the camera shooting a close-up of the reporter. The potential for error is great if extreme care is not taken to use precisely the same words and inflection.

News departments' guidelines mandate that editing with "reverse questions" must be done in such a manner as to "reflect accurately the spirit, tone and intent of the interview." As far as the reverse questions are concerned, they are to be used only if, after comparison with the originals, their use does not distort the tone or content of the interview as it was initially conducted. The "reverse" is not supposed to be used to sharpen up a poorly phrased question asked in the first place.

As a direct result of documentaries in which answers to one question were spliced in as if they had been answers to an entirely different question, very specific rules were issued at CBS. ABC's guidelines on the subject are the most detailed even though the misediting did not occur there. "In editing interviews," ABC News decreed, "questions *and* answers may be presented in a sequence which differs from the sequence in which such questions and answers were recorded provided that in so doing, the spirit of the interview is unchanged." That rule enables a producer to take question *and* answer sequences from the beginning of an interview, for example, and use them at the end of a documentary because they refer more specifically to subject matter being handled at the end of the broadcast. What is not permitted is separating questions *from* answers. A producer can not take question seven in an interview and put answer ten with it. Worse still would be to take answer seven and tack it onto question ten because it seemed to make the point better.

Television journalists, like their print colleagues, are barred from serving two masters. Membership in or service to the CIA or the FBI is cause for dismissal if it is uncovered. There have been instances where broadcast journalists have been unmasked and asked to resign. There have been more unfounded allegations than fact in stories that broadcasters have actually been spies. The obvious fact is that if any member of the journalism fraternity is suspected of working as an undercover agent for a government agency, it calls into question the credentials of all newsmen and women. There is already suspicion in many parts of the world that American news personnel are tools of Washington. If a case against a correspondent or field team were ever proved, it would endanger all the journalists working to gather information.

The networks keep their standards and rules in loose-leaf notebooks. This is not an accidental practice, because rules are constantly being changed and updated to accommodate new situations. The loose-leaf binders are certain to click open and shut many times in the years ahead as television continues to grow as America's dominant news-gathering medium.

8
Never Say "Never"
THE FUTURE

Up to now, my observations in this book have been based on the actual experience of producing, reporting, editing, being an executive. Journalists deal in facts and try to keep speculation to a minimum. Having said all that, there is room for some educated guesses about the future of information and news programming on American TV.

We're in for a lot of changes in television news. It is probable that what we will be watching by the end of the decade will be considerably different from what is on the air in 1982. News and information programming may be the only exclusive service provided by the networks on free, noncable television. All the sports and most situation comedies, police shows, the movies and other familiar prime-time fare may have shifted to pay television or to syndicated distribution by then.

That is not a will-o'-the-wisp prediction. It is based on trends that became visible and started accelerating after 1976. In 1968, less than 5 percent of American homes had been wired for cable. By April 1982, 23,219,200 homes were hooked up, representing about 29 percent of the country. It is conventional wisdom that cable television will be a viable commercial entity, capable of

selling advertising and of being supported by it, when 30 percent of the nation becomes wired. The cable industry claimed in
1981 that 250,000 subscribers are signing up each month and the
critical level will be reached by 1982. Certainly it won't be much
later than that because cities like Boston, Chicago, Cleveland,
Detroit, suburban Washington, D.C., and the populous bor-
oughs of Brooklyn and Queens in New York City are about to
get service. By 1990, according to a report by Doyle Dane Bern-
bach, Inc., 60 percent of the country could be wired for cable.
The number of subscribers to pay-television services offered by
cable is increasing dramatically too. It went up fifteen-fold in
the five-year period from 1976 to 1981. Some of the cable systems being installed throughout the United States provide as
many as sixty separate channels. Boston, for example, contains
fifty-two channels; Columbus, Ohio, has sixty. Systems are on
the drawing boards that will contain more than one hundred.

In 1968, cable television, pay television and independent television stations began cutting into network shares of the national
TV audience, reducing them over the years by nine points, three
points in 1981 alone. One study predicts that the networks'
overall share of audience will continue to decline even more
dramatically in the next ten years, dropping to 71 percent by
1985 and bottoming out around 59 percent in 1990.

At first, cable systems were separate companies, not connected to one another and designed simply to improve television
reception. It was too expensive to hook up another national
network for the cable companies because of the fees for interconnection charged by AT&T. Space technology changed all
that when satellites started going up rapidly. Now every cable
system has a "dish" and can take "downleg" signals that carry
programming from a distant source. Satellite interconnection is
what made possible the first serious venture into cable news.

The Cable News Network (CNN) was the first attempt at
all-news television. It is an imitation of what local and network
news programs do each day, but it is continuous. Although the
networks and local stations may spend more money and provide
wider coverage, CNN's advantage is that its output is always
there. The idea of a continuous source of information on televi-

sion is a good one, but the problem is CNN's inability to match the portability of all-news radio. A person wanting to *hear* the news can have it whenever and *wherever* he or she is because portable radios are so small. All-news television requires one to be in front of a TV set that is wired for cable. Once that restriction on mobility exists, then the question becomes "Why not wait for the network news to come on?"

The commercial networks have already begun to work on that problem because there is a potential for additional revenue despite apparent competition between what they are already putting on the air and what they might put on cable. One alternative to CNN's approach is a joint ABC News–Westinghouse Broadcasting operation, scheduled to begin in June of 1982. Westinghouse pioneered a successful all-news radio formula by offering an eighteen-minute segment of news and headlines that rolls over regularly. "Give us eighteen minutes and we'll give you the world!" is the slogan. The ABC News–Westinghouse venture on cable proposes to do that for television. It's conceived as a supplement rather than a replacement for the news already being presented on commercial TV. A viewer who wants to get caught up on headlines can do so by simply tuning in for eighteen minutes. At no time will many people be watching an individual eighteen-minute segment, but the reasoning is that cumulatively enough people will watch so that advertisers will soon add their commercials and thus give the system financial viability. News pictures will be supplied to the venture by ABC News and twenty-four other commercial stations geographically distributed across the United States. Undoubtedly there will be as much aggressive coverage of news and information between the various cable services as there already is between the network news departments. If an audience exists and can be captured, it won't matter if it is only viewing cable.

As more of America becomes "wired" for cable reception, "narrowcasting"—catering to special information interests—will supplement "broadcasting." Research has already shown that 40 percent of the households in the United States do about 63 percent of the viewing, and four out of ten men do 70 percent of the viewing. That's a fairly standard finding: About one-third of the public consumes about two-thirds of any product. That means there are a great many television sets in American homes that hardly ever get tuned in unless there is something their owners really want to see. That "narrow" audience will find its needs satisfied more on cable in the years ahead. There will be special programs about science, the arts, economics, personal growth, business management, foreign language courses and much more. Broadcast journalists, already skilled in presenting brief information about a variety of subjects, will be in the vanguard of those tapped to provide services at greater length. They can be counted on for in-depth analyses, discussions, continuous coverage of congressional hearings, major public speeches and illustrated lectures on a broad spectrum of current affairs.

It is ironic how close cable's prospectus is to the original concept for public television. Cable, like PTV, has plenty of air time and a national distribution system with lots of channels to provide lots of choices. When those cable channels come along and when they get commercial support, they may be the ultimate undoing of public television, which couldn't deliver on its promises. What went wrong?

Money! It's the key to understanding public television. The great expectations for PTV as a system of alternative programming never could be realized without money. The problem is that money hardly ever comes in sufficient amounts, and that could mean that PTV will ultimately fail.

When Fred Friendly left CBS News in 1966, he joined the Ford Foundation, advising its president, McGeorge Bundy, on broadcasting matters. They wanted to make public television an important force, sometimes competing with commercial television but more often filling in the blanks with forms of programming that commercial television did not have the time or financial inclination to supply. (The Carnegie Commission issued a report in 1966 on its view of ETV, "educational TV." Among its recommendations was one to change the name of the system from ETV to PTV—public television.)

By and large, in 1967 public television consisted of some

dramas, some musical performances, a few documentaries, a lot
of discussion programs among experts and a substantial amount
of in-school instruction. Shows were "bicycled" around on film
or videotape. The bigger stations would show an episode of a
dramatic series or a documentary and then pack the film or tape
off by mail or United Parcel Service to another station. That
one, in turn, would show the program and then move it onward
to another. The ability to show the same program simultaneously across the nation was technically possible, of course,
since the same microwave towers and coaxial cables that the
commercial networks used were also available to educational
television. The problem for ETV was twofold: First, there
wasn't enough money to rent the network lines, and second,
most of the stations preferred to remain independent, unhooked
from each other and from any central programming source that
might demand specific air time in exchange for providing a
program.

Local station managements jealously guarded their preroga-
tives to schedule whatever program they wanted, when they
wanted. There was fear that some centrally produced programs
might be offensive to the local communities. If a viewer was
offended, a pocketbook might be shut when appeals for contributions were made. There was plenty of evidence to support
that concern. In a documentary about banking practices, a list
of congressmen who owned bank stocks or other financial interests in banks was shown on the screen. Congressional appropriations for educational television were being debated and some
of the legislators named on the broadcast did not like the exposure. Educational television station managers made it clear to
the producers that they felt their economic lifeblood had been
jeopardized.

In another case, NET, National Educational Television, the
prime supplier of PTV programs, based in New York, had
produced a consumer report about gasoline additives. In that
year, the Shell Oil Company had been advertising heavily a
super additive named Platformate. That element, according to
Shell, gave better gas mileage and helped an engine run cleaner.
The NET report said that Platformate was simply Shell's name

for an ingredient found in many gasolines, and the cost of advertising it was being passed along to the consumer, raising the
price at the pump. According to a story circulated by ETV
station managers as a warning to one another, a Shell Oil whole-
saler in a Midwest state called up his local ETV station the
morning after the broadcast to inform the management that it
could forget his annual contribution of several thousand dollars.
The dealer did not believe he should have to support programs
that were critical of his product. Since his contribution was a
measurable percentage of the station's operating budget, the station's management was understandably upset. It was even more
reluctant to clear air time for any future broadcast that came
close to ruffling a contributor's feathers.

Because so much depends on the contributor, PTV trims its
sails to the most conservative viewpoint of what ought to be on
the air. Most PTV/ETV stations are governed by boards of
directors representing the more "substantial" elements in the
community, who constitute a good source of revenue and fund
raising. The board members tend to be conservative, middle-
class, middle-aged, and white; in some states, they are political
appointees or university officials. They are not the adventure-
some kids, the blacks, or the political radicals. They are not
likely to be tolerant of nonconformists. In my years in public
television, we were often faced with complaints from station
managers who were reacting to instructions from their boards
of directors. At the same time, there would be telephone calls
or letters from young staff members at those PTV/ETV stations
or from students in the university communities served by the
stations in favor of our programming. The worst censorship
was never imposed by Washington or government agencies, but
by overcautious station managers reacting to what they believed
was the consensus of their boards of directors.

One of the myths of public television's potential was built on
the expectation that it would be free from sponsor interference.
The flip side of that analysis implies that commercial television
news broadcasts, documentaries and investigations are dominated by what advertisers want the public to know. Sponsors
are supposed to "dictate" the subject matter of programs; they

supposedly "huddle" with top news management and demand editorial cuts or control. At the network level, nothing is further from the truth. The reason is simple. Television is a seller's market. Every broadcast can be sold at some price. With that economic club in hand, a commercial broadcaster can politely tell a complaining advertiser to withdraw sponsorship if the subject matter is offensive. If Coke wants to pull out, Pepsi is right behind, waiting to buy the air time being vacated. It's an oversimplification, of course, but not much of one. Contrasted to that position, PTV *depends* on the good will of people and corporate contributions.

Offense there means withdrawal of cold cash and there may not be another good Samaritan standing in line to fill in the gaps. In the entire time I have been producing network television news broadcasts, including documentaries, magazine shows and the nightly news, I have never been told what to put in or what to leave out by a sponsor. I just left holes in the program for the insertion of commercials for products I frequently did not know about. In the two years I was in public television, I received countless warnings from station managers about the material we proposed to use.

In one case, the warnings dealt with so-called "anticommercials," mildly humorous one-minute presentations done up to look and sound like commercials for aspirin (they are all alike); no smoking (it is injurious to your health); and antacid tablets (generic products like baking soda will probably do as well). This was before antismoking commercials appeared on commercial television as regular fare. Word of our plans reached the advertising agency of one of the manufacturers of a better-known brand of aspirin. An official of that agency called an East Coast ETV station and threatened to withdraw a special grant if the station did not bring pressure on our organization to stop production of the anticommercial.

When the manufacturer heard about the threat, high executives called with assurances that no threat was intended. A public scandal was avoided, but the story illustrates the precarious position ETV constantly finds itself in. The tale does not have a happy ending in any case. The furor aroused skittish stations and the ETV Board of Affiliates eventually forced us to drop the idea by threatening not to carry the broadcasts.

In commercial television there *is* a ground rule. The name of the game is: Make the network look good by doing good programs, getting good ratings, and thereby making the profits go up. One program's success, one division's success, within a network, means the entire network benefits. If the entertainment division has a "hit" with high ratings and the network's revenues go up from sale of commercials in those shows, the news division benefits in a very practical way by having its requests for more funds honored. The same is true when the news division finds that its evening newscast is rising in the ratings or garnering critical acclaim. The evening news starts every night's broadcast schedule. If it is high in the ratings, it serves as a strong lead-in to the rest of the evening's programming. Awards won by documentaries reflect well on the rest of the network's image. There is a genuine feeling of pride in the success of the "sister" units within a commercial network. But it frequently is not so in public television, where the success of one station or one regional network makes it easier for that unit to get a new grant or larger production contribution next time around. Since there are limited resources available to PTV from corporations, foundations and public funds, one station's getting a larger share of the financial pie means that the slices are smaller for everyone else.

There is jealousy and envy and a lack of unity in PTV, and that disarray, particularly at a time in which it is being challenged by cable television, could, I fear, undo it. Cable television with its hundreds of channels and its platform of financial stability provided by subscribers can and probably will satisfy the special desires of viewers. But all need not be lost for PTV. Variety has always been a significant part of America's life style. Television supplies a good deal of it these days. Without a viable public television system, diversity could simply become a function of dollars.

Cable requires payment for service. A home has to be wired; a tuner has to be rented and installed. Maintenance of the system demands money, which automatically makes it an elitist facility, available only to those who can and will pay. No rent is paid for the use of the airwaves. Now if PTV dies, people who have been able to afford a television set will have to find additional money in their monthly budgets to get the services that up to now have been free.

Even with all its shortcomings, PTV, in its formative years as educational television, supplied some part of the variety we all crave. Arts, performance, exposure to literature and science were in the package that television transmitted. Perhaps before cable erodes the audience that has voluntarily contributed money and support for PTV, PTV will find a renewed purpose: one that is more sharply defined, concentrating again only on fundamental services that provide alternative programming, education and public affairs coverage in depth. PTV lost that direction when it began to present old Hollywood movies and tennis matches instead of shows that more directly addressed the special needs of its viewers.

With a narrower mandate, PTV might become even more attractive to corporations and foundations who would underwrite programming with no strings: a sort of "blind trust" with long-term unrestricted grants. Another alternative: Corporations or foundations could subsidize the installation of cable in the homes of those who otherwise could not afford to pay. In either case, the public's acquisition of information, knowledge and exposure to culture and variety through the tube should continue to grow.

What about commercial television news? What will the networks be doing in the years ahead?

Network news definitely will not disappear. If anything, newscasts will grow more important in the schedules. The only programming that cannot serve audience needs by being taped on a home videocassette player for delayed viewing is the news. Commercial television may well find that news and information broadcasts will be among its major weapons in facing challenges posed by cable and the burgeoning alternative sources of viewing, such as cassettes and videodiscs.

Viewers crave information more than ever. When the Iran hostage crisis began in November 1979, ABC News began a series of programs entitled "America Held Hostage" at 11:30 P.M. Predictions were freely made that audience interest would quickly wane. Johnny Carson and the late movies were expected to drown the news specials in their ratings. It didn't happen. Americans knew they could go to bed each night brought up to the minute on crisis developments. The audience grew substantially, finally matching Carson, rating point for rating point. The special reports about Iran were converted into a regular series, "Nightline," covering all aspects of the news.

The ratings remained competitive even after the hostage crisis was over. In fact, they were so good that they presented ABC with an "audience flow" problem. Viewers who stayed up for news analysis on "Nightline" were not interested in remaining tuned in even later for repeats of "Loveboat" and "Fantasy Island." They turned off their sets. Ratings after "Nightline" fell sharply, costing the network and local stations revenue from the now less-valuable commercials they tried to sell in the reruns. By spring of 1982, the news division was told to develop yet another information program to follow "Nightline" with content that would be compatible with it. Theoretically, news viewers would stay awake for more information, and the ratings and commercial sales could be restored to their former levels.

News department executives know they can continue to move into other parts of television schedules and other forms of programming. Consequently, there will be more network news broadcasts on the air, and those already on the air will expand. The ABC News late-late-night program, for example, will be seen initially between midnight and 1:00 A.M. and will be built primarily around an audience-participation concept. Another ABC News effort will go on the air at 6:00 A.M. CBS News scheduled an early morning news broadcast that will air between 2:00 and 6:30 A.M. CBS News President Van Gordon Sauter predicts his organization's efforts will make "more efficient use of material that . . . is already . . . gathered throughout the day. It will be a farm school" that will enable CBS to develop new talent in a more relaxed broadcast. NBC News intends to

present a similar venture called "Overnight" to be seen from
1:30 to 2:30 A.M. The president of NBC News, Reuven Frank,
expects his broadcast to "provide an important service by reporting the news of the day and looking ahead to the events of
the coming morning." Executives of all three networks expressed confidence that there will be enough people awake during those morning hours to make their operations commercially
viable.

There is another competitive reason behind the move toward
late-late-night programming of news: the real threat posed by
Cable News Network President Ted Turner, who offered to
supply his cable programs to television stations already affiliated
with one of the networks. If affiliates were to accept the offer
and run CNN materials in the overnight time block, it was
feared they might be tempted to accept other CNN programming, perhaps instead of the networks' own newscasts at the
dinner hour. Turner made it clear that network affiliates could
carry his product under extremely favorable commercial sales
arrangements. As a result, the networks accelerated their plans
for late-late-night programming to counter the Turner threat on
the overnight, before it became too serious to deal with during
other times of day.

Though the commercial networks and public television find
cable news threatening, its growth may help eliminate some of
the FCC regulations that have been found burdensome by
broadcasters. The original rationale for the Fairness Doctrine
grew out of technical limitations on access to the airwaves. Fairness and balance, it was felt, needed to be mandated to ensure
that all points of view would be heard on the small number of
channels that technology provided. Cable, with its hundreds of
channels and hours of available time, has made it possible for
any point of view to be heard at almost any length at almost any
time. Viewers could have access to any opinions. Fair treatment
of every issue would result not from any mandated balancing
act but rather from the fact that every point of view was being
put on the air someplace, sometime.

That flexibility, combined with the Reagan Administration's
policy of deregulating American business, including broadcast-

ing, may lead to an end of the Fairness Doctrine. Certainly the broadcast industry has been lobbying in Congress for its roll-back, and the FCC, using Reagan Administration guidelines, has become quite supportive. With that kind of backing, changes are likely to occur.

The safest prediction that can be made is that all three networks will put plans for an hour-long evening newscast on the back burner. They have been working on formats for quite some time, but the major stumbling block is the opposition of their affiliated stations, which do not want to yield another half-hour (and the revenue from commercials in that air time) to the network for *its* programming. Some affiliates also argue that *they* are better able to serve the viewers in their own market areas with broadcasts produced locally rather than with broadcasts produced in network newsrooms half a continent away.

Group W Television commissioned a study by the Roper Organization to find out if viewers wanted an hour network newscast at the dinner hour. Not surprisingly, Group W, which owns five local television stations affiliated with networks, was happy to report that the people surveyed preferred the network newscast to remain at its traditional half-hour length by a margin of better than two to one. According to Group W, half the audience said it would switch away to entertainment shows offered on other local stations if the network news were expanded to an hour.

Ever since 1975, the half-hour from 7:30 to 8:00 P.M. Eastern time—that is, the thirty minutes immediately preceding prime time—has been reserved by the Federal Communications Commission for the local stations to program for themselves. It was called "Access Time"; the stations were to have "access" to it exclusively in order to do all the programs about their communities that dreamers about TV's potential had always contemplated. It didn't work out that way. Local stations found that producing half-hour programs taxed their resources. They did not have the staffs, the camera crews, the editors and, in some cases, the subject matter to fill the time themselves. Producing programs is an expensive business, and the profitability is very low. Local sponsors could not or would not pay enough for commercials in locally produced efforts to make the bottom line look good.

What was less expensive for stations were syndicated programs, produced in Hollywood or New York, looking very slick and at a price that was easily affordable. There were animal and wildlife series on the serious side and quiz shows and "Gong Show" amateur contests on the bizarre side. There were also reruns of situation comedies and police shows that had already been seen on the networks. "Access time," instead of becoming community programming time, looked like a lot more of the same. The irony is that local stations actually "preempted" the syndicated shows on the few occasions they did manage to produce a locally important information program. It was, once more, a question of profits, and since the cost of buying a syndicated rerun or a game show was relatively low and the ratings were pretty high, they were substantial.

Then a change began that became apparent in the late seventies and early eighties. Game shows lost their appeal. The audience was tired of amateur hours, and the animal travelogues had been overexposed. Reruns of top-rated network comedies or detective stories were being sold at such exorbitant prices that many local stations could not afford them. Local sponsors could not or would not pay the freight even for the slickly produced shows. What was about to happen was a repeat of some of the factors that caused the news explosion of the seventies. Station managers found that news programming and informational broadcasts were attracting audiences and the cost of doing those kinds of programs had become relatively low compared to the cost of the syndicated reruns.

As television magazine broadcasts such as "60 Minutes" and "20/20" grew in popularity, a number of frank copies appeared, produced by groups of stations who banded together to pool their resources. A new "news explosion" was about to happen —this time, in the "access time." The networks launched a challenge to the FCC's ruling that had prevented them from providing programs for that time period, arguing that the concept had failed and should be replaced. They were ready to reenter the period with news programming, but the opposition of affiliated stations to an hour-long network newscast did not soften. CBS had been the most optimistic, but it abandoned plans in April 1982. NBC had given up earlier, and ABC never made a formal proposal to its affiliates.

What could happen someday is a broadcast format that would accommodate local stations' desires to participate in the profits from the commercials on the network broadcast, and their insistence on the opportunity to insert locally produced and oriented content. These are not merely mechanical questions. What will probably emerge is an hour-long program structured with "windows," or cutaway periods, into which local newsmen and women can put stories. The more successful formats will make the local material and the network material mesh closely. Visualize a Venetian blind that, when closed, presents a unified facade of information. Some of the "slats" will be network supplied, some will be locally produced. There will need to be careful editorial coordination between the network newsrooms and local newsrooms across the country, but it could be done.

Economic news in Washington might be followed by a local angle covered in Kansas City and inserted in the "window" by the Kansas City newscasters. Other cities would insert similar stories from their own market areas in the same "window." Interrelating national and local aspects of the same stories will provide viewers in each community with a total picture—national or international from the network, local and regional from the station in town. If it happens, whatever emerges, television news will have expanded once again, and, as before, the reason will be the confluence of financial considerations and editorial capabilities.

It is the same cycle that has, after all, been responsible for all the major advances in broadcast journalism. There's no reason to doubt that it won't happen again and again and again in the future.

9
Closing
Announcement
CHALLENGES
AND RESPONSIBILITIES

Americans take television news for granted. If we live in a global village, TV news is the open window on the scene. But precisely because TV news offers so much, it is the cause of a fundamental shortcoming. For most of those who watch it for their news and information, the habits of a lifetime of viewing have left them unlikely to seek out other sources like newspapers, magazines or books. It is possible to postulate that viewers' criticisms of TV news are due in some measure to the realization that they, as viewers, have cheated themselves by relying so heavily on television. People do not read as much as they should, and they are dependent on the crutch of television, which has rendered them passive.

There is no doubt that television news is the lazy person's way of keeping informed. Sit back, turn on the set and we do the rest. It's fairly painless and requires no work on the viewer's part. What a shame! Television news can be little more than a "daily dose" of news and information. TV news never claimed to represent what an informed citizen needs to know. Reading a newspaper (beyond the first two paragraphs, please) might be considered useful. Reading a magazine once a week for the analysis it provides is essential. But too many viewers do nothing more, preferring instead to complain that television news fails in roles it never set out to fill.

Our mail is generally negative. Complaints significantly outweigh the compliments. Phrases like "unwarranted verbal attack," "shallow and glib," "racism, conscious or unconscious," "unfairness for focusing upon isolated negative experiences" and "superficial and manipulative" are just a few of the hot comments that letters contain. In addition to individual expressions of anger, resentment or paranoia, special interest groups often organize write-in campaigns, sometimes even before a program has been broadcast. Many letters are obviously copied from a form: The words are the same, the postmarks are the same. Organized campaigns are quickly spotted, and though they are not ignored, they receive less attention.

Some mail is simply irrational. Harry Reasoner got a fierce letter from a viewer berating him for just about everything he had said on the air over an extended period of time. There was absolutely nothing she found right about Harry. "Dear Madam," he replied, "Why do you watch?" He signed it "Sincerely yours."

A veterinarian in Florida went on at length in a letter to me about various breeds of dogs, observing that some were raised to hunt, some to point and others just to be lap pets. He was making the point that because I am Jewish, my "breed" did not prepare me to run a nightly broadcast on a network. (I have been singled out by "Thunderbolt," a white supremacy publication that circulates throughout the nation, as the "JEW Avram Westin" who ought to be removed from his job.) Stealing a line from the late Senator Stephen Young of Ohio, I replied: "Dear Doctor. Some lunatic has gotten hold of your stationery and is sending out idiotic letters over your signature. I just thought I'd let you know." I never heard from him again.

After a heavy run of news that results in news bulletins and interruptions of regular programming, there are always calls from viewers demanding an end to the extended coverage. Soap opera devotees are especially vehement. Phone calls jam the switchboards if any scene, let alone *the* critical scene, of a day-time serial is burst in upon by a news bulletin. Even word of Iran's release of the hostages was resented by some viewers, who complained about "overcoverage" of their return. "How much longer are you going to hang on to them?" one viewer wrote. "Their reception was blown out of proportion." Some in the audience complained that they could not see their friends and relatives marching in President Reagan's Inaugural Day Parade because the networks kept cutting away from Washington to report hostage-release developments.

There is plenty of evidence that, despite our best efforts, we miss connections with viewers who see and hear things through a filter of personal prejudice or political commitment. Morley Safer, the coanchor of "60 Minutes," did a report on Liberia telling his viewers that many young Liberian men went to the United States and then returned home *from abroad* to marry. A few days later, Safer learned how badly he had been misunderstood when angry mail started coming in from feminists. The mail charged Safer had insulted all women by saying that Liberian men went to the United States and then returned *with a broad* to marry.

The fact is, however, that there are thoughtful letters mixed in with the screwy. Thoughtful letters get thoughtful replies. Criticism that is well reasoned does have an effect. If warranted, apologies and corrections do result. Screaming rhetoric is flatly disregarded but we do listen to everything else.

Another important barometer of TV news performance is comments by newspaper and magazine critics. One of the most provocative and thoughtful is Michael J. Arlen, who writes in *The New Yorker* magazine. One of his observations requires a particular response. Arlen wrote that "the tendency of network news to fragment and trivialize events . . . has become virtually automatic."

If fragmenting means boiling it down to fit a twenty-two-minute-and-thirty-second nightly newscast, then Arlen is correct. But many people also skim their newspapers, reading two paragraphs or hitting the headlines or the little box on page one that gives a series of one-sentence summaries of the stories contained inside. They engage in fragmentation themselves.

As for "trivializing" events, TV news broadcasts *do* pay attention to human interest angles in order to emphasize the impact of important stories. Television news broadcasts *do* present vignette pictures of people, places and things. Television news broadcasts *do* concentrate on brevity in reportage. So do newspapers, which, of course, also give the reader an opportunity to read beyond the first two paragraphs, if they want to. Television news only has time to put its equivalent of two paragraphs on the air, and, as a result, it can only deal with impressions. It does not have the capacity to provide material that a person can study. There is no printed record. John McWhethy, a correspondent who left the fast track at *U.S. News & World Report* to join the "new class" of television correspondents, thinks that what television does is "leave a certain emotional aftertaste in your mouth. You will not understand, after you've seen a three-minute spot, what the specifics of the story were. After you've watched a thirty-minute broadcast, you may not know what the hell has gone by, but there *are* a couple of things left in your mouth that you're tasting, and you'll remember that for a long, long time."

Television newscasts go by so fast that it is often the impression of what has been said that counts more than the actual words that were spoken. David Horwitz, a senior producer at CBS News and later at ABC News, is convinced "viewers leave the set with impressions rather than facts." He suggests, for example, that the presidency of Richard Nixon was ended by impressions. "We put him on the air looking a bit more guilty every day," Horwitz explained. "His words were quoted in the newspapers, to be sure, but the way Nixon said them could not ever be captured in their columns. Watergate was not understood in detail, but people understood something *was* being hidden. Nixon simply hung himself."

Impressions, words, pictures, graphics, music, sound effects, ideas: They are all part of television news. Journalism, at first, was just words. Then it became words and some drawings and then it was words and photography; then the picture started to move. Video and words, words and video. For the past thirty years, from 1950 to 1980, the barrier between journalism and television's technology has been diminishing each year.

Making current events understandable on television has always been the primary task. In recent years, making current events *interesting* on television has become the new challenge. *Time* magazine, covering Walter Cronkite's departure, said the "battleground of post-Cronkite television news . . . may become . . . whether pictures or content will dominate coverage." *Time*'s writers were working, of course, from their own print orientation. Ironically, the very page on which this comment was made included five pictures, taking up at least one-third of the available space. Why is it a question of content *or* pictures? Does "protecting the integrity" of the news mean that its presentation has to be dull? Critics of TV news always seem to assert that attempts to make news presentation more interesting with visuals automatically diminishes the credibility of the reporting.

There is nothing wrong with using pictures to convey the idea to help the word. One has to start with an idea and with words but then the pictures can enhance the thought. Larding in pictures or graphics for the sake of keeping something moving on the screen is as ineffective and confusing as putting on a "talking head" simply because it is a "purer" form of presentation. It is not, as *Time* would have it, a matter of content versus pictures; it is the improved combination of content *and* pictures (which, after all, are content too) that will make television news even more effective in the post-Cronkite era.

TV news—both network and local—will expand in the future, and with more air time, more programs and more money to spend, the business will have to safeguard against abusing its power even more than before. It should not be dismissed as an easy task, but it will not be an impossible one if command is given only to trained broadcast journalists who are sensitive to the responsibilities that go with the power to influence the lives of the American viewing public.

Most of us in decision-making positions have had experiences that sharpened that awareness. For me, it was an incident that occurred in Iran in 1972 during President Nixon's trip to the Soviet Union, Iran and Poland. It made me aware of the arrogance of power.

The press corps accompanying the presidential party had been divided into two contingents for the flight from Minsk in the USSR to Teheran in Iran. I was on the first plane, which was to land about forty-five minutes ahead of the President's plane, Air Force One. I needed to get downtown to check on coverage plans with Peter Jennings, who was already in town, but I also wanted to be at the airport for the President's arrival. It would require some fast traveling into town and back. Ron Ziegler, Nixon's press secretary, heard about my dilemma and ordered a White House limousine. We sped off down a cleared highway behind an escort of motorcycle police. The car hardly stopped before I bailed out of it, saw Jennings, found out that he had everything under control, piled into the limo again and raced back to the airport in plenty of time. It was an intoxicating experience and was the prelude to a lesson that was to be learned two days later.

The next stop was Warsaw. Again, the advance party took off, but this time we were in Poland four hours ahead of the President. The Poles met us with a bus. In contrast to Iran, it was stop and go. No roads were cleared. We were part of the regular traffic flow. Though there was plenty of time, hours instead of minutes, my annoyance grew. Didn't they realize how important we were? At each traffic light, my irritation increased. After all, this was *the* network presidential party stuck behind a truck full of freight. By the time we reached downtown Warsaw—still with hours to spare before the President was due —I was furious and intolerant of our hosts. Nothing they could do was good enough. Criticism of everything came easily. Later I realized how distorted one's views can become when unchallenged privilege is suddenly extended. The story of the Warsaw bus ride is one that I have told many times since 1972 to junior staff people who are being given chances to command small units for the first time. What they do—what we all do—is a responsibility and not a right. Just because the privileges and opportunity of command are given and available, they must not be allowed to distort reality. It is difficult to retain dispassionate judgment while speeding along in a White House limousine. The test is to regain equilibrium quickly enough to put everything back in perspective while riding in an ordinary bus.

Being an executive producer for TV news programs of any

length ipso facto makes one a "gatekeeper." At the gate, one lets some stories through, holds others back. It is one of the most important positions in America.

I remember standing at a cocktail party in Moscow in 1962. Khrushchev was the boss, and he had just revealed in a secret speech that Joseph Stalin was really not a nice man at all. The speech had been delivered secretly to government leaders in Russia and had been obtained through channels operated by the CIA. It had been a shock for the loyal members of the Communist party of the Soviet Union to find out that Stalin was not the "man of steel" but a ruthless killer who had almost lost the war to the Nazis by his inept planning, purges and paranoia.

Khrushchev had opened the gate just a little bit to serve his own purpose and to launch the campaign of "de-Stalinization" we heard so much about.

I was mumbling through my pidgin Russian at the cocktail party to the then official government spokesman of the Soviet Union, pointing out that the secret speech was bound to have an effect on the average Russian citizen now that it had become public knowledge through the efforts of the Voice of America. The VOA was making certain that everyone in the USSR heard about it.

The spokesman acknowledged that it would have an effect. "Why didn't you make it public," I asked, "instead of letting it leak back?"

His explanation was a perfect one for an official government gatekeeper. "You Americans allow yourselves too much noise," he said. "We like things much quieter. We need not shout as much to be heard with our message. We make just enough noise to be heard and listened to."

"Just enough noise to be heard and listened to" is a nice euphemism for government censorship and control. Keep things quiet, the Russian was saying, and the public will get to know what we want it to know. In the United States, all the FCC licenses and the Fairness Doctrine and the Equal Time Provision of Section 315 that are "imposed" on television news, all our self-imposed "7-day rules" and "reverse perspectives"—none of it even remotely adds up to the government's manipulation in other countries of the public's right to know.

There are shortcomings in the way we do things on American television news broadcasts. The individuals who decide what you see and hear on television and radio newscasts are probably more powerful than newspaper editors and book publishers these days because of that (troublesome) fact that 64 percent of the population of the United States gets all or most of its information from TV news broadcasts.

The gatekeepers, however, are American citizens just like their viewers. They share the same concerns, face the same cost-of-living index, worry about the same rise in street crime, the same medical bills, the same nuclear threats, OPEC oil embargoes and winter storms. They root in the same World Series and Super Bowls. They are not bureaucrats, answerable to political authorities or an authorized party dogma. They are not faced with censors' blue pencils, which, if opposed, could result in loss of their jobs. They are, in fact, the strong adversaries of any attempts to limit or stifle the flow of information, opinions, facts and news.

Television news—broadcast journalism—has come of age. John Crosby, the television reviewer columnist for the *New York Herald Tribune* (a newspaper put out of business partially because of TV news) once described a young CBS news producer as "a boy wonder." Like that long-ago child of TV news, TV news itself has grown older, wiser and better. From "boy wonder" it has become a "youthful veteran." And if the past is prologue, then some other child of TV news will soon pick up this story. He or she will go out to cover the news in more places than ever before, using better and more sophisticated equipment and filling up even more air time than ever before. The excitement and the challenges and the responsibilities will grow and, as they have been until now, they will be met.

Index

JAN 3 1983